Digital Divides

The New Challenges and
Opportunities of e-Inclusion

D1482534

PUBLIC ADMINISTRATION AND PUBLIC POLICY
A Comprehensive Publication Program

EDITOR-IN-CHIEF

DAVID H. ROSENBLOOM
Distinguished Professor of Public Administration
American University, Washington, DC

Founding Editor

JACK RABIN

RECENTLY PUBLISHED BOOKS

Living Legends and Full Agency: Implications of Repealing the Combat Exclusion Policy, G.L.A. Harris

Politics of Preference: India, United States, and South Africa, Krishna K. Tummala

Crisis and Emergency Management: Theory and Practice, Second Edition, Ali Farazmand

Labor Relations in the Public Sector, Fifth Edition, Richard C. Kearney and Patrice M. Mareschal

Democracy and Public Administration in Pakistan, Amna Imam and Eazaz A. Dar

The Economic Viability of Micropolitan America, Gerald L. Gordon

Personnel Management in Government: Politics and Process, Seventh Edition, Katherine C. Naff, Norma M. Riccucci, and Siegrun Fox Freyss

Public Administration in South Asia: India, Bangladesh, and Pakistan, edited by Meghna Sabharwal and Evan M. Berman

Making Multilevel Public Management Work: Stories of Success and Failure from Europe and North America, edited by Denita Cepiku, David K. Jesuit, and Ian Roberge

Public Administration in Africa: Performance and Challenges, edited by Shikha Vyas-Doorgapersad, Lukamba-Muhiya. Tshombe, and Ernest Peprah Ababio

Public Administration in Post-Communist Countries: Former Soviet Union, Central and Eastern Europe, and Mongolia, Saltanat Liebert, Stephen E. Condrey, and Dmitry Goncharov

Hazardous Materials Compliance for Public Research Organizations: A Case Study, Second Edition, Nicolas A. Valcik

Logics of Legitimacy: Three Traditions of Public Administration Praxis, Margaret Stout

The Politics–Administration Dichotomy: Toward a Constitutional Perspective, Second Edition, Patrick Overeem

Available Electronically
Public ADMINISTRATION*netBASE*
http://www.crcnetbase.com/page/public_administration_ebooks

Digital Divides

The New Challenges and Opportunities of e-Inclusion

Edited by Kim Andreasson

CRC Press
Taylor & Francis Group
Boca Raton   London   New York

CRC Press is an imprint of the
Taylor & Francis Group, an **informa** business

CRC Press
Taylor & Francis Group
6000 Broken Sound Parkway NW, Suite 300
Boca Raton, FL 33487-2742

© 2015 by Taylor & Francis Group, LLC
CRC Press is an imprint of Taylor & Francis Group, an Informa business

Printed on acid-free paper
Version Date: 20140919

International Standard Book Number-13: 978-1-4822-1659-2 (Hardback)

Library of Congress Cataloging-in-Publication Data

Digital divides : the new challenges and opportunities of e-inclusion / editor, Kim J. Andreasson.
       pages cm
Includes bibliographical references and index.
ISBN 978-1-4822-1659-2
    1. Information technology--Economic aspects. 2. Information technology
Government policy. I. Andreasson, Kim J., editor.

HC79.I55D54 2014
303.48'33--dc23   2014030598

Visit the Taylor & Francis Web site at
http://www.taylorandfrancis.com

and the CRC Press Web site at
http://www.crcpress.com

To my friend, Trâm, and my grandmother, Vera.

Contents

Foreword

Access to Information and Communication Technologies (ICTs) is more critical than ever as countries are increasingly seizing the opportunities of a digital society. It is estimated that every 10-percent rise in access to broadband leads to a 1.38-percent growth in gross domestic product (GDP) for developing countries, according to a World Bank study.

Tremendous progress also has been made in closing the digital access gap. By the end of 2013, an estimated 2.7 billion people use the Internet and there are 2 billion mobile broadband subscriptions, which corresponds to a global penetration rate of almost 40 and 30 percent, respectively. Fixed- and mobile-broadband prices also are falling, making ICTs more affordable.

Mobile devices are particularly promising in bridging access gaps. In 2013, mobile cellular telephone subscriptions stood at an estimated 96.2 (per 100 inhabitants) globally and about half of the world's population is covered by 3G networks, potentially offering an opportunity for mobile Internet connectivity.

Despite this progress, some 4.4 billion people remain offline. This is particularly concerning as those without access fall farther behind in an increasingly digital society. For instance, those who are online can benefit from ever improved e-government, e-commerce, e-health, e-education, and other e-programs while those without access are excluded from such opportunities, leaving the full potential of a digital society unfulfilled.

In order to meet the United Nations Millennium Development Goals (MDGs), the International Telecommunication Union (ITU) and the United Nations Educational, Scientific, and Cultural Organization (UNESCO) established the Broadband Commission for Digital Development in May 2010. The Broadband Commission embraces a multistakeholder approach in which the private sector plays a key role in promoting implementation of broadband. Yet, global progress remains patchy, in particular in rural areas and in regard to greater speeds that can benefit a range of areas, such as e-health and e-education programs, that often require faster connections.

By 2015, the Broadband Commission aims to make every country have a policy for universal broadband while making broadband affordable. Specific targets also include household connectivity of 40 percent in developing countries and reaching a global Internet user penetration rate of 60 percent.

However, in the process of enhancing access and improving speeds, new divides have emerged. They include the gender divide. In 2013, ITU estimated that there were 200 million more men than women online. As a result, the Broadband Commission endorsed a fifth policy target, calling for gender equality to broadband accessibility by 2020.

In the process of replacing the MDGs, which expire in 2015, with the post-2015 Sustainable Development Goals (SDGs), it's increasingly important that females have equitable access to ICTs. Looking forward, our position in the post-2015 debate also is to recognize ICTs as a cross-cutting enabler for all three pillars of sustainable development: economic growth, social inclusion, and an environmental balance.

With the global rise of a digital society, realizing the right of all people to access and use ICTs can help achieve the full potential of sustainable development. In this effort, broadband emerges as a basic human right because it is a catalyst for sustainable development across all dimensions.

To achieve this goal requires not only infrastructure but also human capacity building in order for people to take advantage of the services available to them. This necessitates a need for greater affordability of ICTs, enhanced education as well as availability of local—and relevant—content.

I'm pleased to note that these themes are all part of this edited book and I hope the analysis contained within these pages will raise awareness of them and help the public, private, and civil society sectors to come to a mutual understanding of how to best work together toward an inclusive digital society for sustainable development.

Dr. Hamadoun I. Touré
Secretary-General
International Telecommunication Union

Acknowledgments

This edited volume would not have been possible without a number of people and events.

In 2012, Denis McCauley and Jason Sumner, my former colleagues at The Economist Intelligence Unit (EIU), asked me to author a paper on "Smart Policies to Close the Digital Divide: Best Practices from Around the World."

Given that the digital divide is part of the United Nations global e-government survey for which I have been an adviser for some time, I was aware of the developments in this area. However, after interviewing 20 experts around the world, I discovered that few people had documented the shift from "the" digital divide in terms of access for certain population groups to redefining it as "digital divides" and their underpinnings. I decided the time was ripe to capture these efforts in a book.

My initial response was overwhelmingly positive and I'm grateful to those who encouraged me at the beginning and along the way, including Laurel West at the EIU in Hong Kong, who asked me to write another paper on the topic in 2013.

Besides my former colleagues, I'm grateful to my publisher Rich O'Hanley at CRC Press who took a chance on me in 2010 when I proposed my book on *Cybersecurity: Public Sector Threats and Responses*. It turns out to have been a timely topic. I'm equally grateful to Rich for taking on this edited volume with Lara Zoble, who embraced the topic from the outset, and made my life as editor as pleasant as it can be.

I've interviewed some 50 experts—from the private, public, and civil society sectors—around the world regarding their views on digital divides. I'm grateful to all of them for contributing their knowledge on the topic and am pleased that some have joined this book by authoring a chapter. As an editor, I couldn't be happier with the contributors who are participating and can't thank them enough. I am also grateful to Dr. Hamadoun I. Touré, Secretary-General at the International Telecommunication Union, for his support and for taking the time to provide the foreword.

Personally, I'm thankful to my wife, Diane, for giving me the support I needed to edit yet another book, and for providing suggestions on my introduction and conclusion. My parents, Kenth and Gullvi, were helpful as ever in offering their general assistance, which freed up my time to work on this volume.

And, then, there are those to whom I dedicate this volume. My grandmother Vera never had the opportunity to enter the digital society. At 88, she could use it more than ever to schedule appointments and receive reminders, but does not know how. Conversely, my friend Trâm is essentially a digital native who has great knowledge of ICTs, but never seemingly uses them to her advantage in terms of "useful usage," a term to describe the difference between using ICTs generally and for their productive purposes. In 2012, Trâm was a source of encouragement and she reinforced my notion that those without a complete understanding of the digital society will miss out on many opportunities.

We must bridge these gaps to help people seize the benefits of the information society, whether it is in Việt Nam, Sweden, or in between. My hope is that this book can make a contribution toward that aim.

Kim Andreasson
Sài Gòn, Việt Nam
and Varberg, Sweden

Contributors

(*In order of appearance*)

Hamadoun Touré, PhD, secretary-general of the International Telecommunication Union (ITU) since January 2007, was re-elected for a second term at the ITU Plenipotentiary Conference, Guadalajara, Mexico, in October 2010. He served as director of ITU's Telecommunication Development Bureau (BDT) from 1998 to 2006, and has wide professional experience in both the public and private sectors. A national of Mali, Dr. Touré holds a masters degree in electrical engineering from the Technical Institute of Electronics and Telecommunications of Leningrad (LEIS, USSR) and a PhD from the University of Electronics, Telecommunications and Informatics of Moscow (MTUCI, Russia). He is committed to ITU as an innovative, forward-looking organization adapted to meeting the challenges created by the rapidly changing ICT environment, and to continuing to spearhead the Union toward implementing the resolutions of the World Summit on the Information Society (WSIS) and achieving the Millennium Development Goals (MDGs).

Kim Andreasson is managing director of DAKA advisory AB, a Swedish consultancy. He has advised the United Nations since 2003, most recently in preparation for the global 2014 e-government survey, which includes measures of the digital divide. Andreasson has spent more than 10 years in consulting, including as interim associate director and a senior editor at The Economist Group where he co-edited the annual report on the Digital Economy Rankings. He serves on the editorial board of the *Journal of Information Technology and Politics* and is an elected member of the International Institute for Strategic Studies and the Pacific Council on International Policy. Andreasson is a senior fellow at Good Governance International and a John C. Whitehead fellow at the Foreign Policy Association. He is the editor and author of numerous publications, including *Cybersecurity: Public Sector Threats and Responses*, published in December 2011 by CRC Press.

Jeremy Millard is managing director of consultancy Third Millennium Governance, senior research fellow at Brunel University, Middlesex, United Kingdom, and chief policy analyst at the Danish Technological Institute, Taastrup. He advises the United Nations, European Commission, OECD (Organization for Economic Cooperation and Development), World Bank, and many governments and clients around the world on e-government, digital inclusion, social innovation, digital entrepreneurship, and smart cities. He works with clients to develop new business and social development models of change at organizational, spatial, and societal levels. His aim is to get the most out of technology and to ensure that the benefits are widely spread, both bottom up and top down, to maximize smart, sustainable, and inclusive growth providing prosperity and welfare for all through open governance institutions and processes.

Gary Fowlie is an economist and journalist. He was a producer/reporter for the news service of the Canadian Broadcasting Corporation (CBC) for 10 years and a freelance reporter for *The Economist*. Prior to joining the International Telecommunication Union in 2001, Fowlie worked as an account director for the technology practice of the global consulting firm Hill and Knowlton. His clients included global technology leaders such as Microsoft and Cisco. Fowlie was responsible for communications for the UN World Summit on the Information Society (2003 and 2005) and from 2005 until 2009 was the chief of media liaison for the United Nations in New York. He is a graduate of the University of Alberta, University of Alabama, and the London School of Economics. He has been a part-time instructor in the British Columbia Institute of Technology, School of Business since 1993.

Phillippa Biggs is an economist and qualified accountant at the International Telecommunication Union (ITU) since 2005. She holds a natural sciences degree from Cambridge University, an accountancy qualification from the ICAEW, and a master's degree in economics for development from Oxford University, where she won the Oxford University Prize for Best Overall Performance in her master's degree and gained two diplomas in economics and statistics from the United Kingdom's Open University. Prior to joining ITU, Biggs worked for two other UN agencies as an economic affairs officer at UNCTAD and as a consultant with UNIDO in Tanzania and Egypt. She is now an economist, editor, and author of the *World Information Society Report* (www.itu.int/wisr), the *Status of VoIP Worldwide Report*, *Confronting the Crisis* reports (www.itu.int/crisis2009), and *State of Broadband 2012 and 2013* reports. She analyzes developments in broadband, VoIP (Voice over Internet Protocol), and 3G markets around the world.

Johanna Ekua Awotwi is director of Research and ICT Operations of a Ghanaian private NGO, the Centre for e-Governance, based in Accra. She was a research fellow at the Center for Electronic Governance at UNU-IIST in 2010; COO of AQ Solutions Ghana Ltd, a board member of the Women's Initiative for

Self-Empowerment NGO, and Cape Coast ICT Park Company, Ltd. Currently, she is an editorial committee member of the *Ghana Business and Finance Magazine*. She first earned a degree in political science and law from the University of Ghana in 1976, and a graduate certificate in economics from North Carolina Central University, Durham, in 1979.

Yuanfu Jiang is general secretary of the e-Government Consulting Committee at the Chinese Academy of Governance and the branch director of its e-Government Research Centre. He is a member of the advisory committee of China National e-Government Engineering and an advisor for the China national audit informatization engineering. He was the key organizer of the China e-government Forum (CEF) from 2006 to 2010, and serves on the editorial board of the *Journal of e-Government in China*.

Tatiana Ershova, PhD, has considerable practical experience in strategic consulting, developing, and implementing conceptual documents, large-scale programs and projects in the ICT4D (ICT for development) area. She participated in the activities of a number of national and international expert bodies. She has been both a speaker to and an organizer of multiple national and international conferences and workshops. Dr. Ershova also is an author of over 130 publications in Russian and foreign professional journals and mass media; she also has edited and compiled several books and collections of articles. Since 1996, she has been general director at the Institute of the Information Society, and, since 2009, also editor-in-chief of the scientific and analytical *Information Society Journal*. She graduated from the Moscow Institute of Foreign Languages (currently Moscow Linguistic University). In June 2013, she obtained a PhD in economics.

Yuri Hohlov, PhD, has had a career that includes lecturing and research in mathematics, creating and implementing large-scale programs in science and ICT, and strategic consulting. He is a pioneer of the information society agenda in Russia and a world-class expert in ICT4D. He presided over or has been a member of quite a number of relevant national and international professional associations. In 2004, he was elected as a full member of the Russian Engineering Academy. Since 1998, in his capacity as the chairman of the board of directors, Dr. Hohlov has been a permanent leader of the Institute of the Information Society. He graduated from the Mechanics and Mathematics Department of Kazan State University, and earned his PhD in physics and mathematics in 1980. He is an author of over 200 research works published in Russia and abroad.

Sergei Shaposhnik has conducted research in the field of science and technology studies. He was involved in the elaboration and implementation of nationwide and regionwide information society development concepts and programs while heading works related to the information society monitoring. He is an initiator and the coordinator of the development of the Russian Regions' E-Development Index. He graduated from the Moscow Engineering and Physics Institute, Department of Cybernetics. He is now senior research fellow at the Department of Sociology of Science at the S.I. Vavilov Institute for the History of Science and Technology of the Russian Academy of Sciences. He is also head of the Directorate of Information Society Monitoring at the Institute of the Information Society. He is an author of more than 70 research works.

Scott Ewing is a senior research fellow at Swinburne Institute for Social Research at Swinburne University of Technology, Melbourne, Australia. He has more than 20 years of experience as a social researcher, both at Swinburne and in the private sector. He is currently managing the Australian component of the World Internet Project, a global survey of Internet use and nonuse. He has considerable expertise in information policy, the social impact of new technologies, the use of quantitative data, and economic evaluation.

Ellie Rennie is the deputy director of the Swinburne Institute for Social Research at Swinburne University of Technology in Melbourne, Australia. Her research focuses on media policy and community communication, with a current focus on Indigenous broadcasting and broadband in remote Australia. Rennie also is working in partnership with Goolarri Media Enterprises to develop new approaches to online education for Indigenous students living in remote areas through Swinburne University's Indigenous Futures Collaboration project. She has published two books: *Life of SYN: A Story of the Digital Generation* (Monash University Press, 2011) and *Community Media: A Global Introduction* (Rowman & Littlefield, 2006).

Julian Thomas is director of the Swinburne Institute for Social Research and a professor of media and communications at Swinburne University of Technology, Melbourne, Australia. His research interests are in new media, information policy, and the history of communications technologies. Recent publications include *Fashioning Intellectual Property* (Cambridge University Press, 2012), *Amateur Media* (Routledge, 2013), and *The Informal Media Economy* (Polity, forthcoming).

Ellen Johanna Helsper, PhD, is an associate professor in the Media and Communications Department at the London School of Economics and Political Science. She studies the links between digital and social exclusion, mediated interpersonal communication, and quantitative and qualitative methodological developments in media research. Current projects focus on the definition and measurement of digital skills, engagement, and outcomes of use (http://www.oii.ox.ac.uk/research/projects/?id = 112); online marketing to children; opportunities, risks, and harm for European children (www.eukidsonline.net); and national and individual determinants of Internet use (www.worldinternetproject.net). She consults widely for industry, the third sector, and local, national, and regional governments.

Alexander J.A.M. van Deursen is an assistant professor at the Department of Communication of the University of Twente, Enschede, the Netherlands. His research focuses on digital inequality, often with specific attention to digital skills. His recent book, *Digital Skills: Unlocking the Information Society* (Palgrave MacMillan, 2014), uses conceptual analysis and empirical observations to show what digital skills are, how they are distributed, how skill inequalities develop, and how these inequalities can be remedied by designers, educators, policymakers, and different types of Internet users. Currently, van Deursen is collaborating with scholars from the London School of Economics and Oxford University on a project focusing on skills, usage, and Internet outcomes.

Lim Swee Cheang is the director/CEO of the Institute of Systems Science (ISS), National University of Singapore and has been instrumental in leading ISS research, education, and consulting programs since 1998. In 2006, he initiated and set up the Singapore e-Government Leadership Centre in partnership with Infocomm Development Authority of Singapore (IDA) and the Lee Kuan Yew School of Public Policy. Lim recently became a member of the IDA Infocomm Industry Productivity Roadmap Steering Committee as well as the Infocomm Media Masterplan 2025 Working Committee driven by the Ministry of Communications and Information. He was awarded the Singapore Public Service Medal in 2009 and the Long Service Medal in 2010. In 2012, Lim was inducted into the Singapore Computer Society (SCS) Hall of Fame.

Guo Lei, PhD, is a postdoctoral researcher with the Institute of Systems Science, National University of Singapore. She has been actively involved in research, education, and consulting activities of technology-enabled service innovation and user behavior study. She has advised e-government projects, such as value co-creation with government open data, user experience design of government websites, and emerging digital technologies landscape study.

Vikas Kanungo is an expert on the use of SMAC (social, mobile, analytics, and cloud) technologies in the government domain, especially in the areas of m-governance, ICT for development, e-governance, and knowledge management. He has been an advisor to the government of India in formulating the policy on mobile government. He is the founding director of mGovWorld, Global Observatory on Mobile Government, and chairman of The Society for Promotion of e-Governance, India. He also works as senior consultant with the World Bank Group. His recent assignments include overseeing the deployment of mobile- and cloud-based projects in South Asia and the Middle East.

Soobin Yim is a doctoral student in the University of California, Irvine, School of Education in the language, literacy, and technology specialization. She earned her BA in English language and literature from Ewha Woman's University in Seoul,

South Korea, and a master's degree in language and literacy from the Harvard Graduate School of Education. In South Korea, Soobin worked as an English proficiency test developer at Seoul National University, and as an English outreach program coordinator at the U.S. Embassy in Seoul. Her research interests include computer-assisted language learning (CALL), digital literacy and equity, and second language learners' academic vocabulary and writing development.

Melissa Niiya is a doctoral student in the University of California, Irvine, School of Education. She was previously an Americorps VISTA volunteer at the nonprofit Little Tokyo Service Center in Los Angeles where she taught digital literacy and media technology courses to underrepresented minority youth and adults. She also worked with a technical college to develop online learning applications for healthcare education. Her research examines digital literacies, social media activity, and the ecology of student technology use in and out of school.

Mark Warschauer, PhD, is a professor of Education and Informatics at the University of California, Irvine, and associate dean of Irvine's School of Education. He previously taught and conducted research at the University of Hawaii, Moscow Linguistics University, Charles University in Prague, and Waseda University in Japan, and served as educational technology director of a large educational reform project in Egypt. Dr. Warschauer is director of the Digital Learning Lab at UC Irvine, where, together with colleagues and students, he works on a range of research projects related to digital media in education. He is the author or editor of 11 books and more than 150 papers on digital literacy and learning. He also is founding editor of *Language Learning & Technology Journal,* inaugural editor of *AERA Open,* and a fellow of the American Educational Research Association.

Bernardo Sorj, PhD, received his doctorate in sociology at the University of Manchester in 1976 and is currently a visiting professor at the Institute for Advanced Studies, University of São Paulo, Brazil. He was a professor of sociology at the Federal University of Rio de Janeiro and a visiting professor in several universities in Europe, United States, and Latin America. He is the author of more than 100 academic articles and 27 books published in several languages related to the international system, Latin America, and the social impact of new technologies, including *Information Societies and Digital Divides: An Introduction* (Polimetrica, 2008) brazil@digitaldivide.com; *Confronting Inequality in the Information Society* (Unesco, 2003); and Internet and Poverty (UNESCO, 2005).

Denise Vaillant, PhD, is the dean of the Institute of Education, University ORT– Uruguay, and president of the Teaching Profession International Observatory based at the University of Barcelona (OBIPD). She earned her PhD in education at the University of Québec à Montréal, Canada, and her master's in Educational Planning and Management at the University of Geneva, Switzerland. Dr. Vaillant coordinated several teacher education programs in Uruguay and in Latin America and is a university professor of postgraduate studies, consultant to several international organizations, and author of numerous articles and books on the subject of public policies, teacher education, and educational change and innovation.

Helen Milner is chief executive of Tinder Foundation, a United Kingdom social enterprise and staff-owned mutual, which supports people in getting the capabilities they need to reap the benefits of the Web. Her organization and its 5,000 hyperlocal partners have helped 1.2 million people with the foundation's learning platform: www.learnmyway.com. Milner has almost 30 years of experience in working on the Internet, starting in 1985 in the private sector developing online education services for schools in the United Kingdom, Australia, and Japan. She ran the Institute of Public Policy Research (IPPR) and University of Sunderland's "university for industry" pilot program that inspired the creation of learndirect and, subsequently, was a group director leading the learndirect network. In 2012 she was included in the Digital Hall of Fame for the 20 influential Britons in digital. Milner is a commissioner for Social Mobility for Brent Council, and is a member of The House of Commons Speaker's Commission for Digital Democracy.

Paula Uimonen, PhD, is an associate professor in the Department of Social Anthropology at Stockholm University. She has over 17 years of experience in ICT for development (ICT4D) and served as director for the Swedish Program for ICT in Developing Regions (Spider) from 2011 to 2013. Uimonen was one of the first scholars to treat the Internet as a tool for social development (1997) and has worked extensively with ICT4D in multilateral (UNRISD, UNDP, UNHCHR, ITU) and bilateral development cooperation (SDC, Sida), as well as global policy-making (WSIS 2003 and 2005). As a scholar, she is specialized in digital anthropology, with research projects based on ethnographic fieldwork in Southeast Asia and East Africa.

Introduction

Gaps in access and usage have been present since the invention of information and communications technologies (ICT) and, without question, digital divides will always exist. However, the rapid development of the information society, spurred by the growth of the Internet, has now accentuated their importance. Old challenges, such as differences in adoption, remain key hurdles to greater participation in the digital economy. At the same time, new divides also are emerging about as quickly as the development of technology.

This is a challenge to all levels of society—from the international community and individual countries to the public, private, and civil society sectors within them. The 2014 United Nations e-Government Survey also highlights that digital divides are omnipresent and affect developed and developing countries alike.[1]

This book, therefore, defines digital divides broadly as the access, skills, and capacity to take advantage of ICTs in order to reap the full benefits of the information society. Today, digital inclusiveness (e-inclusion) is not only important from a social perspective, but also makes financial sense as countries move toward greater cyber dependency. More than ever, tackling current—and future—digital divides is paramount toward an inclusive society and to reap the economic benefits thereof.

The Benefits of e-Inclusion

Enhancing digital access and usage rates allows countries (and their constituents) to save time, money, and effort while enhancing productivity. For instance, a commonly cited World Bank report on Information and Communication for Development in 2009, noted that low- and middle-income countries could raise economic growth by 1.4 percent for every 10-percent increase in broadband penetration.[2]

More recently, a study by the McKinsey Global Institute, a consultancy research arm, found that the Internet's contribution to GDP (gross domestic product), on average, accounted for 3.4 percent in the G8 countries (Canada, France, Germany, Italy, Japan, Russia, the United Kingdom, and the United States) and South Korea, Sweden, Brazil, China, and India.[3] The gap between the lowest share (in Russia at 0.8 percent) and the highest (in Sweden at 6.3 percent) shows that emerging markets not only need to improve their information society, but that there are great potential opportunities if this is possible. Specifically, among the mature economies, the Internet's contribution to GDP growth between 2004 and 2009 averaged 21 percent while it was only 3 percent in the BRIC (Brazil, Russia, India, China) countries.

Because of the benefits of an information society, governments are encouraging private sector ICT investment and are also moving public sector services online (e-government). In the United Kingdom, service delivery is now "digital by default," which means it is conducted digitally in the first instance, and sometimes only so. Compared with an "offline" interaction, the move to digital will save between £3.30 (British pound sterling) and £12 per transaction, according to a U.K. government study conducted by PwC, a consultancy.[4]

The private sector is similarly keen to move customers to digital channels as evidenced by the rise of online banking and commerce. In fact, companies compete on making their services accessible to a wider audience. In an interview for a report from The Economist Intelligence Unit, Axel Leblois, founder and executive director of the Global Initiative for Inclusive Technologies, an advocacy initiative of the United Nations Global Alliance for ICT and Development, says NTT DoCoMo, a Japanese mobile carrier, actively targets senior citizens through improved accessibility in order to gain market share in an increasingly competitive environment, benefitting consumers, the company itself, as well as society at large.[5]

Digital Divides

As the opportunities of the information society rise, so do the consequences for those who are not able to take advantage of them. This is a global problem as 60 percent of the world's population remain offline, but also a challenge to developed countries.[6] In the United States, where information and services are increasingly digital, one-fifth of the population is not using the Internet.

Access, affordability, and awareness remain fundamental barriers toward e-inclusion. At the same time, connectivity rates continue to improve, in large part thanks to ubiquitous and cheap mobile devices.[7] However, once connected, new questions emerge as to whether people have the ability to take advantage of their access and if they want to. The supply of relevant and useful content is only one aspect as the demand for it is equally crucial. Even in South Korea, the country that leads the world in the supply of online public sector services, according to the most recent UN e-government survey, constituents do not utilize them to a large extent, thereby limiting inclusiveness and public sector efficiency.[8] A report shows that while 73 percent of South Korean citizens are aware of e-government, only 47 percent actually use it.[9]

Using ICTs for their productive purposes—useful usage—remains a challenge. Despite having about 9 in 10 people online, Olli-Pekka Rissanen, a special adviser for public sector ICT to the Ministry of Finance in Finland and chairman of the governing board of the Information Society Development Centre, voiced concern in an interview for a report from The Economist Intelligence Unit regarding the country's usage pattern in which interest in office software often lags more popular social media activities among youth.[10]

Even when Internet adoption and demand for useful services is high, there are new questions regarding web accessibility, speed, and quality. For instance, people with disabilities may face disproportionate challenges in using online services if they are not designed appropriately, while insufficient bandwidth and network capacity to transmit data can limit their usefulness.

Thus, digital divides can be classified into three simple stages: (1) access, in providing ICTs in the first instance; (2) usage, in the ability and interest to use them; and (3) useful usage, from which users can reap the potential benefits of the information society.

A Connected Future

The world has a long history of dealing with social inequalities offline; it is obvious that we face the same challenge online. However, bridging those gaps also will be increasingly important as the two are often conflated. By 2015, the European Commission (EC) reckons that 90 percent of all jobs in Europe will require some level of digital literacy.[11] Although unsurprising as the information society continues to develop rapidly, it also illustrates the challenges of a connected future in which the public, private, and civil society sectors must find ways to work together to meet existing—and emerging—digital divides.

As some gaps are narrowing, such as basic access to mobile phones, which are near saturation level in many countries, others are widening, such as the speed and quality of those devices. Digital divides are a multifaceted global challenge, but also a local problem. The notion that there was "a" digital divide, either between those who have access and those who don't or between developed economies and emerging markets is an understatement of the complexities underpinning the challenges ahead. In essence, countries face the same digital divide challenges, yet prioritize them differently depending on context and local variations. Figure I.1 illustrates a variety of today's digital divides.

The path toward greater e-inclusion must be dealt with at all levels, from the international community to the national and local levels, particularly as countries move up the information society development curve in different ways and at various speeds. Consequently, that is how the book is organized: from global problems (and some potential solutions) to the prospects for greater e-inclusion.

Divide	Description
Access	It starts with access or the lack thereof. Although Internet penetration has increased, it continues to be a key barrier as more people globally remain offline rather than online.
Age	Older people are generally using ICTs to a lesser extent than younger populations, despite the notion that they could benefit from online social and health services.
Bandwidth	International bandwidth and the capacity to transmit and receive information over networks vary greatly between countries, but also within them, limiting potential useful endeavors.
Content	The creation and consumption of local content are important as useful usage can depend on context and language.
Disability	Those with disabilities face additional hurdles to use ICTs, although this can also be turned into a potential e-inclusion opportunity by increasing digital accessibility.
Education	Like social divides, education and literacy rates are fundamental challenges to bridge digital divides.
Gender	There is a small but persistent difference in online usage between men and women.
Immigration	Migrants may not possess the same levels of digital skills as the population in their new country and, if they do, may be subject to content and language divides.
Income	The gap between rich and poor affects affordability of ICTs, but also usage patterns and is as important within countries as much as between them.
Location	Rural and remote areas are often at a disadvantage in terms of speed and quality of services as compared to their urban counterparts.
Measurement	There is a divide in measuring progress between countries, within them, and also in the evaluation of specific development projects.
Mobile	Mobile devices provide opportunities to bridge the access gap, but can also introduce new forms of divides in terms of technology, speed, and usage.
Speed	The gap between basic and broadband access is creating a new divide as speed is important to reap the full benefits of a digital society.
Useful usage	What people do with their access or "useful usage" is a key divide in using ICTs productively according to their abilities.

Note: Intended to be illustrative, not exhaustive.

Figure I.1   A selection of digital divides, from access to useful usage.

Section I: Digital Divide Challenges

The first part of the book illustrates global challenges and provides examples from emerging markets and developed countries alike. Although some cases are context-specific, there are also a number of reoccurring themes surrounding access and usage.

In Chapter 1, The Digital Divide and the Global Post-2015 Development Debate, Jeremy Millard, at Third Millennium Governance, Brunel University, and the Danish Technological Institute, provides a global overview to put digital divides into perspective with a view toward the future. He argues that ICTs have a critical role to play in the proposed Sustainable Development Goals (SDGs), which will replace the Millennium Development Goals (MDGs) after they expire in 2015, but that stark digital divides, both between and within countries, could limit their potential effect.

In Chapter 2, The Digital Broadband and Gender Divides, Gary Fowlie and Phillippa Biggs at the International Telecommunications Union (ITU), show that women lag men in terms of connectivity, in part because of the social barriers they face. Yet, female participation in the information society is both socially and economically beneficial. In 2013, the ITU/UNESCO Broadband Commission for Digital Development also endorsed gender equality in access by 2020 as an advocacy target. To achieve this goal, the authors call for better policies and measurement as well as improved affordability and content.

Johanna Ekua Awotwi at the Centre for e-Governance in Ghana, discusses the country's digital divide challenges, especially for women, and the strategies for bridging them in Chapter 3, Challenging the Digital Divide in a Developing Country: Ghana Case Study. The chapter outlines Ghana's overall information society development before providing an analysis of its ICT environment and usage levels. As in many developing countries, affordability and bandwidth remain key challenges, hence the high use of mobile devices for access.

In Chapter 4, China's Digital Divides and Their Countermeasures, Yuanfu Jian, at the e-Government Research Center at the Chinese Academy of Governance, illustrates the broad range of divides facing a large and populous country. Basing the analysis on three underlying factors—technical, content, and personal—the chapter concludes by providing suggestions for overcoming current deficiencies, including, but not limited to, increasing education and improving public information literacy, cutting telecommunications charges, and enhancing e-government and public service for vulnerable groups.

In Russia, the development of the information society has resulted in new kinds of geographical and social divides, as shown by Tatiana Ershova, Yuri Hohlov, and Sergei Shaposhnik, all at the Institute of the Information Society in Russia. In Chapter 5, Spatial and Social Aspects of the Digital Divide in Russia, the authors compare the extent of the digital divide in Russia with the European Union (EU) before delving deeper into their underlying reasons. Using the Russian Regions e-Readiness Index to highlight domestic challenges, they find that economic premises are a necessary (but not sufficient) condition for purposeful ICT usage.

In Australia, about 86 percent of the population has home access to the Internet. However, as Scott Ewing, Ellie Rennie, and Julian Thomas, all at the Swinburne Institute for Social Research, discuss in Chapter 6 (Broadband Policy and Rural and Cultural Divides in Australia), the access divide may be narrowing, but it is deepening as well. Detailing the history of the country's ambitious National Broadband Network to connect all households to high-speed access, the authors use the example of broadband adoption amongst Australia's Indigenous households to demonstrate cultural challenges to Internet usage.

To conclude the first part, Ellen Johanna Helsper, at the London School of Economics and Political Science, and Alexander J.A.M. Van Deursen, at the University of Twente, move beyond access to look at what people actually do with it in Chapter 7 (Digital Skills in Europe: Research and Policy). Using a broad definition of digital literacy as the sum of access, skills, and engagement, they find that measurement of digital skills is insufficient, evidenced by its lack of inclusion in large-scale European surveys, thereby leading to ineffective policy formulation in this area.

Section II: Digital Inclusion Opportunities

Although there is some overlap in terms of challenges and solutions, the second part focuses on e-inclusion and describes recent efforts to bridge digital divides through a number of initiatives. Yet, the success (or lack thereof) is not always easy to determine and this part concludes with an assessment of evaluation mechanisms and some thoughts concerning future divides.

Singapore consistently ranks among the top countries in the world in numerous ICT reports. Chapter 8 examines the history and current state of the digital divide in the country, in particular, how its public, social, and private sectors help citizens use ICT in relevant ways that improve learning and foster the skills necessary for meaningful participation in a digital economy. In Digital Inclusion: The Singapore Perspective, Lim Swee Cheang and Guo Lei, at the National University of Singapore, illustrate the city–state's experience while highlighting remaining challenges.

In Chapter 9 (Leveraging Mobile Revolution for Turning Digital Divide into Digital Dividend: Examples from India, Bangladesh, and Sri Lanka), Vikas Kanungo, at mGovWorld, The Society for Promotion of e-Governance in India, and a consultant with the World Bank, offers insight into the opportunity to leapfrog traditional infrastructure via mobile devices, particularly phones, which have helped establish a new way to access information. The chapter focuses on how innovative uses of these devices are enabling more inclusive participation and access to service delivery in South Asia, a region that is home to 44 percent of the global poor.

In addition to access, questions linger about whether technology provides an educational benefit. In Chapter 10 (e-Inclusion in Education: Lessons from Five Countries), Soobin Yim, Melissa Niiya, and Mark Warschauer, all at the University of California, Irvine, examine five countries, all of which have implemented some kind of program to provide individual computers to children: Romania, China, Peru, Uruguay, and the United States. Drawing on these examples, the chapter shows which efforts were effective in increasing social inclusion and academic outcomes.

In Chapter 11 (e-Education at the Local Level: Challenges and Pitfalls of Public Policies in Rio de Janeiro), Bernardo Sorj, currently at the Institute for Advanced Studies at the University of São Paulo, and Denise Vaillant, at the Institute of Education, University ORT-Uruguay, discuss the challenges of implementation. The authors use Brazil and Rio de Janeiro, its second-largest city, as a practical example and find that the introduction of computers is simply one element in the e-education chain, and usually the least difficult to put in place, indicating that the move toward a computer-centered environment is going to be a long process.

Nongovernment organizations (NGOs) are often instrumental in improving access rates in a local context. In Chapter 12 (Local + Digital + Scale: A Mass Movement for Digital Inclusion), Helen Milner, at the Tinder Foundation, describes what makes its digital inclusion model different from others because it is both highly targeted and delivered at scale. The chapter shows how the Tinder Foundation has accomplished its goals and provides blueprints for success in the hopes that other organizations around the world can learn from this approach.

In Chapter 13 (Beyond Failure: Rethinking Research and Evaluation in ICT4D), Paula Uimonen, at Stockholm University, argues that ICT for development (ICT4D) continues to be perceived as a risky endeavor with high failure rates, despite the fact that it has a significant effect on development. The chapter investigates the practical complexity of assessment and uses two recent scholarly works in Latin America and East Africa to argue for an alternative evaluation model using a combination of research and practice, which is also exemplified by Spider, one of the world's leading ICT4D centers.

To end the volume, your editor takes a stab at recent trends and upcoming challenges in Chapter 14 (In Conclusion: Tackling Future Digital Divides). The first part of the chapter outlines current obstacles to greater access, usage, and useful usage, such as affordability and data capacity. The second part introduces the cyber dependency matrix to illustrate where countries are in their journey toward an information society and what happens as they reach higher levels. Emerging concerns include a global information divide, courtesy of cyber security and data policies.

References

1. United Nations (2014). E-government survey 2014–E-government for the future we want. Online at http://unpan3.un.org/egovkb/Reports/UN-E-Government-Survey-2014
2. World Bank (2009). Economic impacts of broadband. Online at http://siteresources. worldbank.org/EXTIC4D/Resources/IC4D_Broadband_35_50.pdf

3. McKinsey Global Institute (2011). Internet matters: The Net's sweeping impact on growth, jobs, and prosperity. Online at http://www.mckinsey.com/Insights/MGI/Research/Technology_and_Innovation/Internet_matters

4. PwC (2009). Champion for digital inclusion: The economic case for digital inclusion. Online at www.parliamentandinternet.org.uk/uploads/Final_report.pdf

5. The Economist Intelligence Unit (2013). Redefining the digital divide. Online at http://www.economistinsights.com/analysis/redefining-digital-divide

6. International Telecommunications Union (ITU) (2013). Measuring the information society 2013. Online at http://www.itu.int/en/ITU-D/Statistics/Pages/publications/mis2013.aspx

7. International Telecommunications Union (ITU) (2014). ITU releases 2014 ICT figures. Press release. Online at www.itu.int/net/pressoffice/press_releases/2014/23.aspx#.U4jogSil4WA

8. United Nations (2012). E-government survey 2012–E-government for the people. Online at http://unpan1.un.org/intradoc/groups/public/documents/un/unpan048065.pdf

9. *The Korea Times* (2010). E-government web sites underutilized. February 19. Online at http://www.koreatimes.co.kr/www/news/nation/2010/02/117_61097.html

10. The Economist Intelligence Unit (2012). Smart policies to close the digital divide: Best practices from around the world. Online at http://www.economistinsights.com/analysis/smart-policies-close-digital-divide

11. European Commission (2014). Digital agenda. Online at http://ec.europa.eu/information_society/newsroom/cf/fiche-dae.cfm?action_id=215; European Commission (2012). Neelie Kroes blog post. Online at http://ec.europa.eu/commission_2010-2014/kroes/en/blog/digital-champions

DIGITAL DIVIDE CHALLENGES

Chapter 1

The Digital Divide and the Global Post-2015 Development Debate

Jeremy Millard

Contents

1.1 Introduction and Context

In September 2000, world leaders adopted the United Nations Millennium Declaration, committing their nations to a new global partnership to reduce extreme poverty and setting out a series of targets known as the Millennium Development Goals (MDGs).[1] The eight MDGs (Figure 1.1), which range from halving extreme poverty rates to halting the spread of HIV/AIDS and providing universal primary education, are time-bound to the target date of 2015.

Although impressive gains have already been achieved in some MDGs, such as the reduction of extreme poverty, access to safe drinking water, gender parity in primary schools, and improvement in lives for at least 100 million slum dwellers, targets were only partially met for many goals (Figure 1.2). Serious shortfalls are

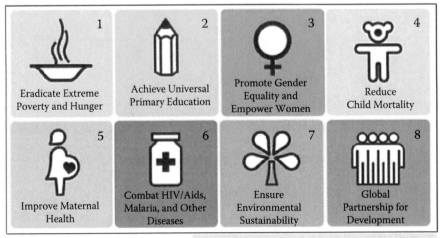

Figure 1.1 2015 MDGs. (From http://www.un.org/millenniumgoals/. With permission.)

expected in targets like access to basic sanitation, deaths from tuberculosis, and maternal mortality. In addition, hunger remains a global challenge, illiteracy still holds back more than 120 million young people, progress on primary school enrollment has slowed, and one in five children under age five in the developing world are still underweight.[2]

As 2015 approaches, the United Nations (UN), in partnership with many other international bodies, institutions, and private and civil actors at all levels, is engaged in wide global consultations on the framework for a post-2015 sustainable development agenda. For example, in order to address the 2015 shortfalls, it is increasingly realized that institutions and governance generally need to be considerably strengthened as the role of the public sector is critical, and this must include changing its forms of cooperation with both private and civil sectors. Moreover, it is accepted that new technologies, such as Information and Communication Technology (ICT), have a critical role to play, and although some important achievements have already been made in using ICT to achieve development impact, stark digital divides, both between more and less developed countries as well as within countries themselves, are having a limited effect on the potential which could be achieved.[3]

The UN High Level Panel report proposed that the post-2015 development goals, which are likely to be termed the Sustainable Development Goals (SDGs) should ensure that everyone ought to have access to modern infrastructure: drinking water, sanitation, roads, transport, and ICT.[5] However, this report and others recognize that a serious barrier to the potential development impacts that ICT and other infrastructures and tools might have is inequality of access and use.[6] This

Target	Base	Latest
Poverty: halve the proportion of people living in extreme poverty	1990 46.7%	2010 22%
Hunger: halve the proportion of hungry people	1990 18.6%	2010–2013 12.0%
Education: ensure all children can complete primary school	1990 82.1%	2012 91.1%
Gender equality: end gender disparities in schools[a]	1990 0.89	2012 0.97
Child mortality: cut under-5 mortality rate (per 1,000 live births) by two thirds	1990 90	2012 50
Maternal mortality: cut maternal mortality rate (per 100,000 live births) by three quarters	1990 380	2013 210
HIV and AIDS: halt and begin to reverse the spread of HIV and AIDS[b]	2001 0.09	2012 0.05
Water: halve the proportion of people without access to safe drinking water	1990 24%	2012 11%
Sanitation: halve the proportion of people without access to basic sanitation	1990 51%	2012 36%

Source: Data from United Nations (2014) "Millennium Development Goals Indicators: world and regional trends—Statistical Annex: Millennium Development Goals, Targets and Indicators, 2014": http://mdgs.un.org/unsd/mdg/Host.aspx?Content=Data/Trends.htm

[a] Gender parity index (ratio of girls to boys)
[b] Incidence of new cases (per 100 people)

Figure 1.2 MDG 2015 status, 2014.

is strongly linked to other aspects of inequality, such as income and education. According to a UN Task Team Report, "We are deeply aware of the hunger, vulnerability, and deprivation that still shape the daily lives of more than a billion people in the world today. At the same time we are struck by the level of inequality in the world, both among and within countries. Of all the goods and services consumed in the world each year, the 1.2 billion people living in extreme poverty only account for 1 percent, while the richest 1 billion people consume 72 percent."[7] Moreover,

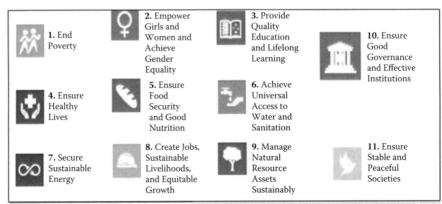

2013 UN High Level Panel's proposed post-2015 MDGs

Figure 1.3 Proposed post-2015 SDGs. (From the United Nations, http://www. un.org/en/development/desa/policy/untaskteam_undf/report.shtml. With permission.)

there is increasing evidence that inequality directly damages economic growth, so that countries with high levels of inequality suffered lower growth than nations that distributed incomes more evenly.[8] Thus, regardless of any social or ethical objections to large and increasing inequality, strong evidence is now available that it also damages the economy and, thereby, prospects for development.

Given this background, the UN's 2013 High Level Report, amongst others, concludes that the post-2015 development agenda needs to be driven by a number of big, transformational shifts, the first of which is to "leave no one behind." It emphasizes that "the new agenda must tackle the causes of poverty, exclusion, and inequality" in the context of a proposed set of 11 post-2015 SDGs (Figure 1.3).

Among the proposed new SDGs, most if not all can be enabled or strongly supported by ICT, for example, good governance and effective institutions underpinned by freedom of speech, civic participation, and anticorruption measures, health, education, jobs, resource management, and, not least, ending poverty. In addition, the High Level Report also states "we also call for a data revolution for sustainable development, with a new international initiative to improve the quality of statistics and information available to citizens. We should actively take advantage of new technology, crowd sourcing, and improved connectivity to empower people with information on the progress towards the targets."[9]

1.2 ICT for Sustainable Development

There is strong and burgeoning evidence of the positive impact of ICT on sustainable development. According to the World Bank, as the leading global institution investing heavily in ICT for development, this technology is no longer a luxury for developing countries.[10] In fact, many ICT innovations are emerging from developing countries. They are creating new ways of communicating, doing business, and delivering services. Through extending access to ICT and encouraging the use of ICT, the World Bank aims to stimulate sustainable economic growth, improve service delivery, and promote good governance and social accountability, according to its infoDev website.[11]

In a 2012 report, the World Bank suggested a number of so-called pillars by which ICT positively impacts development:[12]

- Transform pillar: Making development more open and accountable and improving service delivery, for example, through mobile and social networks and by governments using ICT to transform public service delivery across sectors (health, education, social protection, justice, agriculture, water, energy, and transport) both central and local.
- Innovate pillar: Developing competitive IT-based service industries and fostering ICT innovation across the economy, for example, through government action as well as by incentivizing and providing tools for entrepreneurs.
- Connect pillar: Scaling up affordable access to broadband, given that this is a key driver of national competitiveness and economic growth, supported, for example, through appropriate broadband policies and selective public financing.

Taking specific examples, the World Bank also has demonstrated the real impact of ICT on development, for example, in Africa. The eTransform Africa report shows that ICT innovations are delivering home-grown solutions in Africa, transforming businesses and driving entrepreneurship and economic growth.[13] For example, with some 650 million subscribers, Africa's mobile phone market has eclipsed that of the European Union (EU) or the United States (Figure 1.4).

At the same time as the mobile revolution, in the five years previous to 2010 Internet bandwidth grew 20-fold as hundreds of thousands of kilometers of new cables were laid across the continent to serve an increasing number of its 1 billion citizens. Much of Africa is finally getting high-speed Internet. Two new underwater cables running down the west coast of Africa were inaugurated in 2013, and the expectation is that they will soon have the potential to replicate the success that some of Africa's east coast countries, like Kenya, have already shown in benefitting from higher speed Internet. For example, a study on the use of mobile devices in Kenya found that 25 percent of users could get more work and earn money because they were more "reachable."[14]

According to the eTransform Africa report, easier access via mobile and broadband "is quickly changing lives, driving entrepreneurship fuelled in part by collaborative technology hubs, and delivering innovation and home-grown solutions for Africa." The report focuses on eight key areas: agriculture, climate change, education, financial services, government, health, ICT competitiveness, and trade

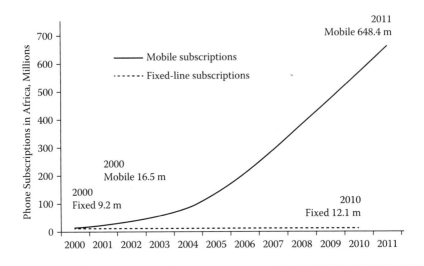

Figure 1.4 Africa's mobile revolution. (From the World Bank, http://www. eTransformAfrica.org)

facilitation and regional integration, and emphasizes the need to build a competitive ICT industry to promote innovation, job creation, and boost the export potential of African companies. The report highlights how countries, such as Kenya and Senegal, are implementing ICT-enabled trade facilitation initiatives and outlines the key role that Africa's regional economic communities can play in supporting greater regional integration for boosting economic growth and reducing costs. Part of this is the flowering of technology hubs across Africa, such as iHub and NaiLab in Kenya, Hive CoLab and AppLab in Uganda, Activspaces in Cameroon, BantaLabs in Senegal, Kinu in Tanzania, or infoDev's mLabs in Kenya and South Africa. These hubs are creating new spaces for collaboration, innovation, training, applications and content development, and for preincubation of African firms. "Africa is rapidly becoming an ICT leader. Innovations that began in Africa, such as dual SIM card mobile phones, or using mobile phones for remittance payments, are now spreading across the continent and beyond," says Tim Kelly, lead ICT policy specialist at the World Bank and an author of the report. "The challenge going forward is to ensure that ICT innovations benefit all Africans, including the poor and vulnerable, and those living in remote areas," he adds.

The World Bank Institute is also supporting the Information and Communication Technologies for governance (ICT4Gov) network dedicated to the idea that increased civic participation can lead to better governance.[15] For example, if citizens can provide feedback to government about service delivery using the increasingly ubiquitous mobile channel, even in places with little infrastructure, and even rate the quality of specific programs, then government will have more information to prioritize services and should be more accountable to citizens. A prominent example of this approach is participatory decision making and budgeting, processes that allow citizens to discuss and vote on how some parts of a government's budget should be used. The archetypal example at Porto Alegre in Brazil is recognized internationally as a groundbreaking initiative at the local level where the state government has engaged over 1 million residents in its multichannel (online and offline) participatory decision making.[16] There are also examples of participatory decision making using mobile technology in Cameroon and in South Kivu in the Democratic Republic of the Congo, a country known more for conflict than innovative governance.[17] In the latter example, communities were given the chance to voice their development needs, and the government has responded. Apparently, tax collection rates in South Kivu have gone up as people have come to believe that their government can actually deliver valuable services, and this may demonstrate one way to increase tax collection in developing countries, where such rates are notably low.

An example outside Africa comes from urban India that uses mobile technology to track how citizens experience water service delivery.[18] It collects and analyzes citizen feedback using innovative mobile applications, thereby providing a "reality check" on service levels from the citizens' standpoint. It gives city managers more granular data at the subcity level (ward/zone) that can facilitate improved monitoring and problem solving, and provides input into project planning processes for service providers. Most importantly, the project provides a suitable platform to engage citizens in performance monitoring processes and encourages them to demand better services. Given the large urban populations living in informal settlements in Indian cities, and the service inequities commonly prevalent in service provision, the project enables explicit tracking of service delivery in slum areas including public facilities, such as public stand posts and community toilets. The project was implemented in two cities of India during 2013 and is now being replicated in 20 more.

One challenge is the constant march of technology innovation and its deployment possibilities, and, although ICT is far from being a panacea and can have negative effects (see below), new possibilities for ICT for development (ICT4D) continue to appear. A number of trends in this area have recently been identified by a group of experts for 2014 and beyond to address the digital divide and maximize beneficial development impacts, according to *The Guardian*:[19]

- **Innovative business models are replacing ad-driven campaigns in emerging markets:** Given the lower incomes of consumers in emerging markets, traditional ad-driven businesses will falter. Creative business models will emerge. Success will require a deep understanding of "base of the pyramid" consumers and nontraditional partnerships will form between the private sector and those working to reach last mile consumers.[20] (David Edelstein, director of the Grameen Foundation Technology Center, Grameen Foundation.)

■ **Improved quality of mobile apps:** There will be an increase in the quality and quantity of mobile applications being developed within Africa, to improve social outcomes. With technology innovation hubs springing up across the continent, technology communities within many African countries are gaining access to state-of-the-art facilities, events, mentorship, and training, making it more likely that they will devise impactful solutions. These hubs also provide the opportunity for collaboration with civil society and each other, which maximizes the chance of success for new projects. (Dr. Loren Treisman, executive, The Indigo Trust.)

■ **The girl effect:** With more mobile phones than people on the planet in 2014, it may seem like there is no new frontier left for the market. However, the most visionary mobile operators will take on the final and most potent growth market of all: the 750 million girls and women around the world who don't have phones, but can afford one designed for them and at the right price. When those girls and women get the power of a phone in their hands, they will use it to change not only their lives, but those of their family, community, and nation. (Maria Eitel, president & CEO, Nike Foundation.)

■ **ICT to improve government accountability:** We are encountering a dramatic increase in the planning and discussion of applications and advocacy for transparency that confronts basic questions of government accountability. Civic ICT project designers are becoming increasingly networked internationally (through communities, such as OpeningParliament.org), and are seeking collaboration around issues of political and state power. Early ICT successes that relied on service delivery and civic mapping are creating an appetite among developers and civil society organizations to confront power through public information, and practitioners are becoming more sophisticated in their approaches to these questions. (John Wonderlich, policy director, Sunlight Foundation.)

■ **Rise of machine-to-machine (M2M) technology:** M2M technology is becoming increasingly important for ICT for development as it reaches critical mass. The biggest benefit will be its ability to address social and economic needs, fundamentally transforming every aspect of society and industry. Enabling complete control over every aspect of the supply chain, it will reduce inefficiencies. At the same time, M2M technology can help with the shift to a more sustainable economy, from reducing food wastage to dramatically curbing energy consumption. It will allow the world to do more with less. (Matthew Key, chief executive, Telefónica Digital.)

■ **Harnessing mobile phone data:** As noted in *The Economist*, "... poverty used to be about scarcity, now it is about targeting and distribution."[21] Given that fact, one of the most impactful trends in technology that will lead to global poverty alleviation will be governments and development partners using data collected from ubiquitous mobile phones to focus their efforts to provide better services to the most vulnerable citizens. We will see improved food security and increased agricultural yields, rural education transformed, disease outbreaks detected, mothers sent vital information, and all of this done by sophisticated systems that take advantage of a basic mobile phone. (Chris Vein, chief innovation officer for global information and communications technology development, World Bank.)

1.3 The Global Digital Divide Challenge to Sustainable Development

Notwithstanding the great potential of ICT for sustainable development and the fact that many successes have already been achieved, there are significant global digital divide challenges that will continue to be serious barriers against successful development, especially in the countries that need it most. The most recent data and analysis come from the latest United Nations eGovernment Survey.[22] "The digital divide is omnipresent. In its multifaceted form, it is present in developed and developing countries in the form of a global divide; between upper and lower income groups within a country; between men and women as a gender divide; between highly skilled and nonskilled individuals; and between affluent and disenfranchised and vulnerable populations within an area."

There also is no doubt that the digital divide is closely linked to and often reflects other technology, socioeconomic, cultural, and political divides, as well as having an in-country geographic dimension between, for example, urban and rural areas or between core economic centers and remote locations.[23] The UN survey concludes: "… as such the digital divide in one form or another affects the majority of the populations of the world."

Some of the major digital divides highlighted by the United Nations include national differences in the use of the Internet as shown in Figure 1.5. Despite the progress noted above even in some of the world's least developed countries, the past 10 years have seen the leading countries increase Internet use at a steeper gradient than most others. There also has been a bifurcation within the least connected group of countries since 2000 resulting in a number of largely so-called emerging economies pulling away from the least developed nations, which thereby risk falling even further behind.

This pattern is reinforced by data on global functional digital literacy, using households with a computer as a surrogate measure, as shown in Figure 1.6. Again, Africa is lagging and also growing at a less steep gradient than most other global regions.

Using data from the International Telecommunication Union (ITU), Figure 1.7 illustrates a significant gender gap where there is a 16 percent difference in online access between men and women in the developing world compared with only a

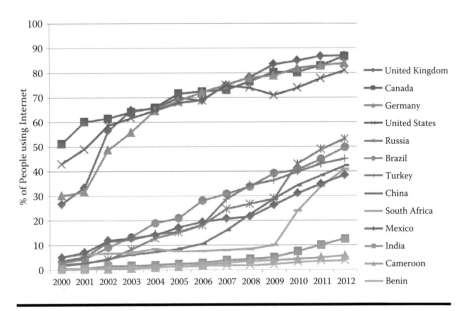

Figure 1.5 Global digital divide. (From the ITU World Telecommunication/ICT Indicators database: http:www.itu.int/en/ITU-D/Statistics/Pages/publications/mis2013.aspx.

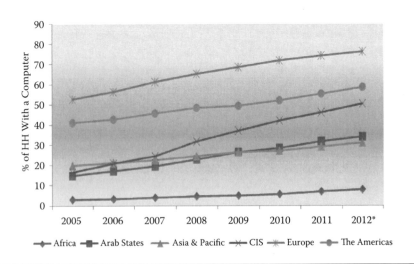

Figure 1.6 Global functional digital literacy. (From the ITU World Telecommunication/ICT Indicators database: http://www.itu.int/en/ITU-D/Statistics/Pages/publications/mis2013.aspx.[25])

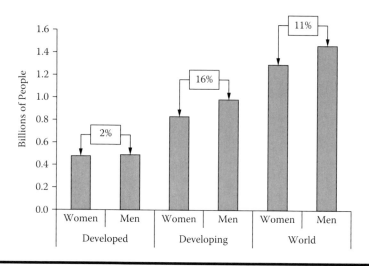

Figure 1.7   Online gender differences. (From ITU.[27])

2 percent gap in developed countries. This is largely due to gender differences in terms of education, access to resources, income levels, and social attitudes. It also likely reflects lack of content relevant to women's needs. According to the United Nations, this ultimately leads to poorer life chances and opportunities for the social and economic empowerment of women, and has potential implications for the post-2015 development agenda where gender issues are being highlighted.[26] Empowering women, especially in poorer countries, has been demonstrated to be a powerful tool for development purposes.

Other data from the United Nations 2014 report shows a very strong correlation between national income per capita and the provision of services for vulnerable groups (Figure 1.8). This highlights a difference in focus between groups of countries in using ICT to support vulnerable groups, and to some extent reflects the recognition of the needs of such groups and the ability to be able to prioritize resources to address them.

Also important are factors such as the cost and quality of ICT connection and related services available to users. Using fixed broadband prices as an example, Figure 1.9 shows that, despite the huge drop in ICT prices in developing countries since 2008, there remains a large disparity with the developed world. Almost one-third of average incomes are needed to subscribe to fixed broadband in the former compared to much less than 2 percent in the latter, signifying that much progress in addressing the affordability issue is still needed.

Comparable data on the availability and use of ICT within developing countries is difficult to find. However, relevant 2012 data from the United States that, because of its relatively high levels of income and socioeconomic inequalities, illustrates the likely digital divide challenges seen more widely, show that:[29]

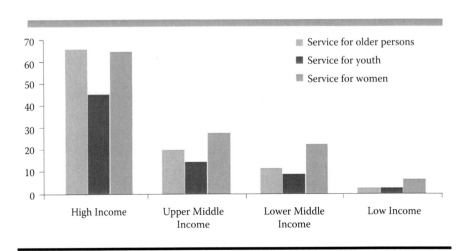

Figure 1.8 **Online services for the vulnerable by country income. (From the United Nations.** *e-Government survey 2014–e-Government for the future we want.* **(2014). With permission.)**

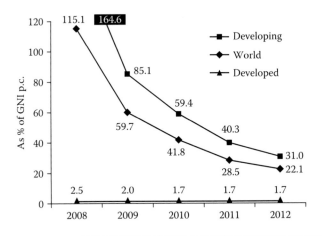

Figure 1.9 **Fixed broadband prices as a percentage of gross national income (GNI) per capita. (From ITU.[28])**

- 87 percent of households in the United States still lack high-speed Internet access.
- Almost half of the poorest households in the United States do not own a computer.
- Only 4 percent of the richest households in the United States do not own a computer.

- Minorities in the United States have significantly lower rates of Internet access than whites.
- Rural households are two times more likely to have dial-up Internet than urban households.

Finally, smartphone compared with "dumb" phone penetration 2011 data can perhaps be used as a surrogate for ICT service quality. Although Figure 1.4 dramatically shows Africa's mobile phone revolution, data from the Vision Mobile website (http://thenextweb.com/mobile/2011/11/29/report-smartphones-account-for-just-27-of-all-mobile-phones-worldwide/#!A80Ed) puts this into perspective by showing that, despite this remarkable growth, well over 80 percent of mobile sales in 2011 consisted of feature or "dumb" phones rather than smartphones, a long way behind the main developed countries in North America and Europe. This, of course, has a lot to do with price, but also illustrates developing countries' reduced access to sophisticated services and more advanced features and usage opportunities, including to smartphone apps.

The evidence presented above clearly highlights the fact that the least developed countries, despite the promise and real impact of ICT to date, still lag considerably in terms of usage, the digital literacy necessary to exploit that usage, gender differences, the focus they have so far been able to give to using ICT to support vulnerable groups, as well as price and service quality constraints. Moreover, there is little evidence that they are catching up in absolute terms with the more developed countries, although in relative terms their growth may sometimes be stronger given they are starting from a low base. It is probably safe to argue that the digital divide is deepest between developed and developing nations, and given the direct impact of ICT on development exemplified in this section, this raises serious issues for the post-2015 development agenda.

1.4 The Five Levels of the Digital Divide

From 2004 to 2009, the Internet alone contributed on average 21 percent to gross domestic product (GDP) growth in mature economies.[31] However, this potential will not be realized in the least developed countries unless access to and effective use of the Internet can become widespread, and this means mitigating as far as possible the drag effects of the global digital divide described above. In addressing this issue, it is important to recognize more systematically the different types of the digital divide and how these are related.

In 2006, the author recognized four levels of ICT usage and exploitation, whilst in 2012 he added a fifth level related to the active participation by users in developing ICT products, services, and content.[32] Each level cumulatively increases ICT's importance for development purposes and, thereby, is also subject to potentially greater digital divide constraints:[33]

1. Access to ICT, such as Internet, broadband, computers, mobile devices, relevant online services including social media, ICT content, etc. This is a supply side issue, so reflects the level of development of the country, government policy, and private investment in ICT infrastructure and services, and also includes the cost and quality of ICT.
2. Socioeconomic characteristics of the user, i.e., education, occupation, labor market status and income, plus demographics like gender and age.
3. Skills, motivation, opportunities, and needs of the user if he/she is to use available ICT products and services.
4. Beneficial use of ICT, i.e., whether and how the supplied ICT products, services, and content are appropriately used to provide benefits for the user.
5. Participation and co-creation of ICT, i.e., whether and how the user is actively engaged in contributing to or developing ICT products, services, and content, for example, using Web 2.0 tools that typically "have an 'architecture of participation' that encourages users to add value to the application as they use it; for example, using social media applications."[34]

Levels 2 to 5 basically represent demand side issues, and, like level 1, are subject to intervention initiatives. Figure 1.10 illustrates the cumulative nature of these levels, each one typically building on the level before, and, through the size of the oval, emphasizes that each level potentially has progressively greater development impact.

Unpicking each of the above levels will throw some light on how the digital divide can be mitigated and thereby achieve greater development outcomes. In this context, some European experience also is drawn upon given the relatively

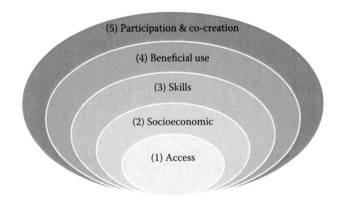

Figure 1.10   Levels of ICT usage and exploitation. (From Millard, 2006.[35])

successful efforts in that continent to increase e-Inclusion since the Lisbon Strategy in 2000.[36]

In terms of Level 1 access to ICT, the author showed that the two most important determinants of ICT use tend to be related to technology availability and user skills, and these are independently somewhat more important than the socioeconomic characteristics of the user.[37] This observation can provide a strong basis for policy design. Such nonsocioeconomic factors are, in principle, easier to tackle through policy intervention, at least over a relatively short time horizon. Thus, policies related to ICT supply in a country and individual skills can typically be designed and implemented over the short to medium term, whilst socioeconomic characteristics, such as educational level, occupation, income, and labor market status typically require much longer time scales and cooperation with a larger number of stakeholders, although both types of factors are important.

Level 2 socioeconomic characteristics, although largely only amenable to long-term policy interventions, are nevertheless important. In 2012, the author, using the 2006 data, showed that ICT users compared to individuals not using ICT are significantly more likely to:[38]

- be in employment
- be well educated
- have medium to high income
- be aged 25 to 34
- be male

These characteristics in themselves demonstrate the digital divide that tends to permeate all ICT-related usage, as also documented, for example, by the United Nations and Pew, an American research institution.[39] Further, looking at some of these individual characteristics in Europe, income emerges as the most important factor for using ICT, assuming it is available, whilst educational level is the most important for beneficial use and the intensity of use. This is a general conclusion also reached by the United Nations on a global scale.[40] According to a study quoted by the United Nations, the probability of an individual using the Internet every day increases by 2.4 times in Europe and by 3.6 times in South Korea if he/she has a university degree or above.

At Level 3, user skills, as mentioned above, are, alongside technology availability, the most important determinant of ICT use. For example, user skills can be learnt and developed relatively quickly given motivation, opportunity, and technology availability, and, as such, are only weakly correlated to socioeconomic characteristics.[41] The rapid take up and beneficial use of mobile phones in most countries around the world, regardless of such characteristics, tends to exemplify this.

An additional dimension of ICT skills is that there is strong evidence that, if an individual does not him/herself have the requisite skills nor indeed access, they might still benefit through an intermediary who uses ICT on their behalf. For example, intermediaries can be family members, friends, neighbors, the community, as well as more formal organizations, like NGOs or telecenters.

It was accepted in Europe in the mid to late 2000s that, given that still 20 to 30 percent of people would not be online at least for the next 10 years, that they could still benefit from ICT through such strategies, which also might include better use of ICT in back offices of governments and companies in order to better target services. In other words, not everybody needs to use ICT themselves straightaway to get the benefits of it, though, of course, there is a need to move toward that in the medium-to-longer term. Indeed, European data from 2006 showed that, in relation to e-government, only 53 percent of users use ICT for their own purpose, 51 percent as part of their job, and 42 percent on behalf of family or friends, the latter thus being termed "social intermediaries."[42]

Moreover, each social intermediary on average assists 2.6 other individuals who are not themselves direct ICT users, thereby dramatically extending the actual impact of ICT. Interestingly, the profile of social intermediaries also differs from that of ICT users generally who tend to be younger and/or in employment, in that they tend to be older and perhaps retired, often unemployed and living in a country with poor or expensive ICT availability. This seems to be because this group as a whole is generally less ICT literate, but that the small subset of them that are ICT literate are better able to relate to their peers and assist in ICT use.

The profile of individuals receiving assistance from social intermediaries also strongly mirrors that of non-ICT users generally, i.e., having low e-skills and e-attitudes, unemployed or in unskilled occupations, lower income and educational levels, in higher age groups including retired, and also living in countries with undeveloped ICT. Overall, it is clear that social intermediaries considerably extend the benefits of ICT to individuals who otherwise are not being reached.[43]

Level 4 is where ICT use starts to have developmental impacts. ICT is not a magic bullet. It is not the technology itself that provides benefits nor the user characteristics or skills, but if these are brought together and used in the right contexts it becomes a powerful tool for achieving developmental goals, as outlined in the earlier section. At Level 4, impacts are made through the beneficial use of ICT; simply having access to ICT and the skills and resources to use it, does not in itself guarantee benefits. In other words, in a developmental context, is ICT being successfully used to improve the quality of life, provide jobs and income, better services, better information, etc.?

The beneficial impacts of ICT typically require new mindsets, the ability to act innovatively, to create new business and financial models, etc., within a conducive framework of regulation, incentives, and open markets that allow local innovators to earn money, perhaps through developing micropayment reward systems as in Kenya. In particular, there is a need to think about how these contextual conditions will impact beneficial outcomes. It is often important as well to include a broad range of stakeholders, not only from government, but also from the ecosystem of commercial companies and especially small- and medium-sized enterprises (SMEs), civil society organizations, hacker communities, and interest groups, where there is huge potential for generating innovations using ICT.

Building on Levels 1, 2, and 3 to achieve impacts at Level 4 is the critical transition, not traditionally addressed by digital divide analyses. This shift has been more or less successfully achieved in Europe by political priority, adequate funding, and appropriate frameworks both at the EU as well as Member State levels.[44] This has been documented, for example, by the author in the context of e-government who showed the decisive shift over just three years between 2007 and 2009 between a preoccupation with access initiatives, to first an emphasis on skills training and then to a focus on beneficial service use for socioeconomic impact.[45] This resulted not in the neglect of access initiatives, but in a synergistic balance between all three aspects, as illustrated in Figure 1.11.

Level 5 in terms of participation and co-creation is an important step up from Level 4. It focuses on the proactive contribution by users to ICT products, services, and content, rather than their more passive use at Level 4. This can be, for example, in the form of adding/editing content, developing apps/widgets and even programming, and co-creating or creating new or enhanced products and services. This is very much a Web 2.0 phenomenon and one which builds on rapidly emerging technologies to develop innovation opportunities, such as mobile; social media and networks replacing other forms of web interaction; cloud computing and the advantages it can bring of agility, scalability, cost effectiveness, and security; big

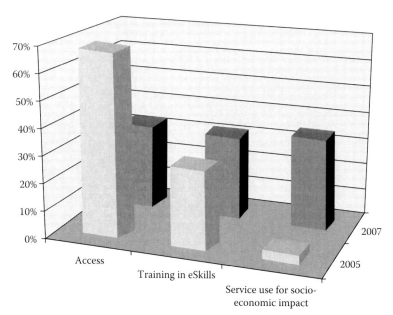

Figure 1.11 The shifting focus of inclusive e-government activities in Europe, 2005–2007. (From Millard, 2012.[46])

data, data mining, and analytics, and the potential this has for smarter products, services, and governance; as well as the growing need for cyber security to address the rapid increase in threats to identity and cybercrime.

Reaching Level 5 is where the greatest development "bang" for the proverbial "buck" is likely to be found. Of the many digital divide impediments described, most examples are from developed countries and the emerging economies. However, there also are outstanding instances from the developing world that, for example, capture citizen experiences through crowdsourcing and social media analytics techniques, such as sentiment analysis, opinion, and data mining. High impact initiatives include the low-cost, video-based, traffic congestion monitoring system using phones as sensors in Kampala in Uganda. There also are very successful "stop stock out" campaigns for pharmaceuticals where retailers and/or customers and other actors can, through crowdsourcing, provide data showing when a pharmacy or medical store temporarily has no medicine on the shelf, preferably in advance, in order to inform the supply chain when this is likely to happen. Access to this data by patients through mobile or a website also can prevent unnecessary journeys and point them to alternative sources in real time as well as providing enhanced transparency. Some current examples are in Kenya and Uganda.

In an African context, Kenya is often the leading example given that many of its home-grown ICT innovations are world beaters being used or copied globally. An early example is MPESA, the mobile money app and service enabling for the first time the vast majority of the population without a traditional bank account to transfer money by ordinary mobile phone both easily and safely. MPESA also acts as a microfinancing service for Safaricom and Vodacom, the largest mobile network operators in Kenya and Tanzania. As currently the most developed mobile payment system in the world, MPESA allows users with a national ID card or passport to deposit, withdraw, and transfer money easily with a mobile device. It is an outstanding example of partnerships between the nonprofit and profit sectors. Kenya has also developed many world-beating crowdsourcing applications like Ushahidi as a tool to easily crowdsource information using multiple channels, including SMS, email, Twitter, and the web, and is now being used in many countries globally. Social media analytics also have been slow to take off in the developing world, but examples are now appearing, such as the citizen sensor data mining and social media analytics initiative in Hyderabad, India.

Social media tools and analytics are being used and are altering the political process globally through enabling multisource, real-time coordination, and monitoring in civil society. In Brazil, Rio+ (http://riomais.benfeitoria.com/) is a platform where any citizen can create a project for Rio de Janeiro, to any scope provided it will improve the city. Presently, it has a huge range of ideas listed, from mobile apps to tunnels connecting areas of the city. Rio+ is easy to use, with projects split into categories and not too many details required for each listing. Just enter the idea and go! Once listed, *Benfeitoria*, along with partner organizations, will initiate a feasibility study, selecting the best ideas and identify resources and partners needed to make it happen. The remaining projects then go to the jury (i.e., they will be voted for online and by the city of Rio) where people can decide on the best design in each category. Once the winners are chosen, the city is responsible for realizing each of the projects, after which they will be monitored so that the impact can be measured, and in the future some may become public policy and be expanded.[47]

Moving back to Kenya, Kibera in Nairobi is one of the largest slums in Africa. Independent of the city authorities, a team of social activists started to develop the Map Kibera community information project in October 2009 as an interactive grassroots map. This appears to be the first ever comprehensive multifunctional interactive community map (ICM), and it took place in a developing country, perhaps because acute need drives the people involved to innovate in entirely new ways. Although many civil and international development organizations had been present and active in Kibera for many years, it had largely remained a blank spot on the map. This lack of openly available geospatial data and other public sources of information about the slum led a group of social activists to create Map Kibera. The underlying idea is that without basic geospatial knowledge, it is impossible to conduct an informed discussion on how life conditions in Kibera can be improved. The Map Kibera team found that the provision of such information would rapidly facilitate better coordination, planning, and advocacy efforts within the community, and between the community and the government.

In the first stage of its operation, the Map Kibera team recruited volunteer community mappers who reside in Kibera to map "points of interest" in the slum, using simple GPS devices and uploading the collected data to OpenStreetMap (OSM). The mappers collected data about the location of clinics, toilets, water points, places of worship, and more. On top of this basic geospatial information, the mappers added a "storytelling" layer, capturing personal accounts, stories, and news of Kibera residents. As part of the second stage, Map Kibera deepened its coverage of life conditions in the community, and collected more contextualized information in the areas of health, security, education, and water/sanitation. At this stage the city authorities saw the importance of what was happening and started to use the map itself and to cooperate with further enhancement. The Map Kibera team also introduced the Voice of Kibera website, an online news and information-sharing platform for the Kibera community.[48]

1.5 Implications and Recommendations

On top of the specific relationships between ICT use and access, socioeconomics, skills and benefits outlined above, there are also important interrelationships between them. For example, the higher the level of Internet and broadband coverage, the higher Internet use becomes even for lower educated and skilled individuals. In addition, analysis has shown that the likelihood of household Internet take-up increases the higher the educational attainment level of individual occupants, even if Internet coverage and GNI (gross national income) per capita in a given area is relatively low. It is also the case that economically more developed regions have on average higher ICT take-up than less well-endowed regions, regardless of other characters.[49] All this implies the need for comprehensive and coordinated, rather than piecemeal and separately focused policies.

There is a strong trend in Europe to move away from specially designed ICT purely for specific typically disadvantaged groups, except where absolutely necessary, toward "inclusion by design."[50] This means that all ICT is designed so anyone can personalize it for their own very specific purposes, given that literally everyone has some "special needs" at any of the digital divide levels, at least at some point in their life. This has two main advantages. First, it pushes ICT toward personalization, which, because this basically means only presenting content and functions that the individual user actually needs, leads directly to user friendliness with concomitant higher usage and satisfaction. Second, it broadens the market making it much more attractive to invest in R&D, rollout, and marketing than it does in comparison with a myriad niche products and services. This approach also recognizes that any digital divide disadvantage is multifaceted and that everybody is "disabled" in some way.

Thus, for example, all services should be designed to be easy and delightful to use, with plain short text, help features, etc., and users should be able, for example, to switch on or off such things as font enlargement, color adjustment, additional explanatory text, screen readers, etc. In other words, we should not design separate touch points in any service for disadvantaged groups, however defined, as everything should be embedded for personalization by the user whoever they are, by the intermediary, or by the provider in consultation with the user.

Experiences in developed countries suggest that strong economic growth helps to both maximize ICT use and the beneficial impacts it has. Part of this is to provide the right enabling conditions for open markets to develop ICT products, services, and content that both increase the variety and quality of home-grown competition, but also help to decrease the costs of technical infrastructure and bandwidth. Many developing country markets are relatively ripe for growth and should prove very attractive both for foreign and domestic providers, thereby helping to realize the "fortune at the bottom of the pyramid."[51]

At the political level, it is essential to promote awareness of the benefits of ICT and the importance of tackling the digital divide blockers that mitigate high impacts. Favorable conditions for so doing include a proactive national policy emphasizing broadband infrastructure rollout, as well as adequate funding for more general information society initiatives including the promotion of digital literacy. However, although ensuring Internet, mobile, and broadband infrastructure availability is a necessity, it is not a sufficient condition for higher take-up and beneficial use of ICT. Nor can it be concluded that lack of monetary, physical factors, and good socioeconomic conditions are the only barriers to Internet take-up and use. Creating appropriate incentives, awareness, reward systems, and provider and user ecosystems, with high levels of cooperation and co-creation in addition to competition, as outlined in Levels 4 and 5 in Section 1.4, are also required.

However, and as also mentioned above, ICT is not a magic bullet, and although it clearly delivers growth, jobs, better services, and more transparency if used well; how this takes place can be highly context dependent. According to Bevir, "… it is the mix that matters," i.e., the Indigenous mix of policy and program approaches related to a country's unique level of development, as well as to socioeconomic context and history, are precursors to good use of ICT for development.[52] And, ICT also can be badly or misused and damage development goals if, for example, governments use it to control and centralize power, if developing countries come too much under the sway of large multinational ICT corporations to purchase solutions they may not need or are not appropriate for them.

ICT for development works best when the above mentioned conditions are in place, when technology is not allowed to simply "blaze a trail" luring policy and procedure to try to play catch-up for its own sake. In this sense, technology's role in fighting poverty is still ripe for discussion. However, many observers do sense "a better understanding and appreciation of appropriate technology in the ICT4D field. People are beginning to make the right noises—local ownership of technologies and tools, local content, and projects where end users drive the process among them" is the way forward.[53]

At the same time and despite many exceptions, there remain many countries, localities, and people in danger of being left behind. As is the case with all forms of exclusion, the digital divide not only wastes the lives of those on the wrong side of it (the individual perspective), it also wastes assets and resources that can enrich us all rather than being a drag on us all (the societal perspective).

According to the eTransform Africa report, and drawing on the discussion above, experiences in the use of ICT for development offer many useful lessons for policy makers to overcome the global digital divide, for example:[54]

- The deployment of ICT and the development of applications must be rooted in the realities of local circumstance and diversity.
- The private sector will need to drive investment, but this may not be enough to ensure competitive markets or to reach rural areas. Public private partnerships (PPPs), such as the Burundi Backbone System consortium, can help.
- Governments have an important part to play in creating the enabling environment in which innovations and investments can flourish while serving as a lead client in adopting new innovations and technologies.
- The effective use of ICT will require cross-sectional collaboration and a multistakeholder approach, based on open data and open innovation.
- Most innovative ICT applications in Africa, as in other developing country contexts, have been the result of pilot programs. Now is the time for rigorous evaluation, replication, and scaling up of best practices.

This chapter has reviewed the undoubtedly large benefits that well-used ICT can bring to development. It also has shown that there are significant challenges involved in doing this, not least of which is a digital divide in which individuals, groups, organizations, sectors, or localities are more or less excluded from these benefits through no fault of their own. These challenges have been analyzed using the latest data and findings from both developing and developed countries. Designs for the post-2015 development agenda, being put together under the auspices of the United Nations, but to which many actors are contributing, are taking these issues, challenges, and opportunities very seriously. Well-used ICT is transforming the way our societies and economies are structured and function. Everybody needs to benefit and be included, or we will all be the poorer for it.

Endnotes

1. United Nations (2000). United Nations Millennium Declaration 2000. Online at: http://www.un.org/millennium/declaration/ares552e.htm
2. United Nations (2013a). Realizing the future we want for all. The UN Task Team Report. Online at: http://www.un.org/en/development/desa/policy/untaskteam_undf/report.shtml
3. Ibid; United Nations (2013b). Governance, public administration and information technology for post-2015 development. Discussion and findings of the Expert Group Meeting in Geneva, July 2013. Online at: http://workspace.unpan.org/sites/Internet/Documents/Governance_PA_Report.pdf; World Bank (2012a). ICT for greater development impact. The World Bank Group Sector Strategy 2012–2015, June 15.
4. *The Guardian.* (2013). Global Development website. Online at: http://www.theguardian.com/global-development/interactive/2013/sep/24/millennium-development-goals-data-interactive
5. United Nations, Realizing the future we want for all.
6. United Nations, Governance, public administration and information technology for post-2015 development; United Nations (2014). E-government survey 2014–E-government for the future we want. Online at: http://unpan3.un.org/egovkb/en-us/
7. United Nations, Realizing the future we want for all.
8. International Monetary Fund (2014). Redistribution, inequality, and growth. IMF Staff discussion note, February.
9. United Nations, Realizing the future we want for all.
10. World Bank website: http://web.worldbank.org/WBSITE/EXTERNAL/TOPICS/EXTINFORMATIONANDCOMMUNICATIONANDTECHNOLOGIES/0,,menuPK:282828~pagePK:149018~piPK:149093~theSitePK:282823,00.html
11. World Bank infoDev website: http://www.infodev.org/postconflict
12. World Bank, ICT for greater development impact.
13. World Bank (2010). eTransform Africa: The transformational use of information and communications technologies in Africa. The World Bank and the African Development Bank with the support of the African Union. Online at: http://www.eTransformAfrica.org

14. Crandall, A., A. Otieno, L. Mutuku, and J. Colaço (2012). Mobile phone usage at the Kenyan base of the pyramid. iHub research, November. Online at: https://blogs. worldbank.org/ic4d/files/ic4d/mobile_phone_usage_kenyan_base_pyramid.pdf
15. http://ict4gov.net/
16. http://odta.net/post/technology-drives-citizen-participation-and-feedback-in-rio-grande-do-sul-brazil-0
17. http://odta.net/post/participatory-budgeting-cameroon; http://blogs.worldbank.org/ic4d/mobile-enhanced-participatory-budgeting-in-the-drc
18. http://www.wsp.org/FeaturesEvents/Features/using-technology-track-how-citizens-experience-water-service-delivery-india
19. *The Guardian* (2014). Experts outline key ICT for development trends in 2014. Online at: http://www.theguardian.com/media-network/media-network-blog/2013/dec/04/ict-for-development-trends-2014
20. Prahalad, C. K. (2005). *The fortune at the bottom of the pyramid: Eradicating poverty through profits.* Upper Saddle River, NJ: Pearson Prentice Hall.
21. *The Economist* (2013). Poverty: Not always with us: The world has an astonishing chance to take a billion people out of extreme poverty by 2030. June 1.
22. United Nations, E-government survey 2014.
23. Millard, J. (2012a). E-government for all: From improving access to improving the lives of the disadvantaged. In *Public sector transformation through e-governance: Experiences from Europe and North America*, eds. W. Weerakkody and C. G. Reddick. New York: Taylor & Francis/Routledge.
24. 2013 figures are estimated. Source: ITU World Telecommunication/ICT Indicators database. Online at: http://www.itu.int/en/ITU-D/Statistics/Pages/stat/default.aspx
25. 2012 figures are estimated. Source: ITU World Telecommunication/ICT Indicators database. Online at: http://www.itu.int/en/ITU-D/Statistics/Pages/stat/default.aspx
26. United Nations, E-government survey 2014.
27. International Telecommuication Union (2013). Measuring the information society 2013. Online at: http://www.itu.int/en/ITU-/Statistics/Pages/publications/mis2013.aspx
28. Ibid.
29. http://ansonalex.com/infographics/2012-digital-divide-statistics-infographic/
30. http://thenextweb.com/mobile/2011/11/29/report-smartphones-account-for-just-27-of-all-mobile-phones-worldwide/#!A80Ed
31. INSEAD (2013). The Global Innovation Index 2012: Stronger innovation linkages for global growth. Online at: http://www.globalinnovationindex.org
32. Millard, J. (2006). eUSER conceptual and analytical framework. Part D: e-Government, a deliverable of the European Commission financed eUSER project, May; Millard, J. (2012b). Report on the development of online networking tools. A deliverable of the project: The theoretical, empirical and policy foundations for building social innovation in Europe. (TEPSIE), European Commission, 7th Framework Program, Brussels: European Commission, DG Research. Online at: http://www.tepsie.eu
33. Note these first four levels correspond, but with some variation, to the four levels recognized in United Nations (2014): (1) access, (2) sociodemographic, (3) cognitive, and (4) capability.
34. Millard, Report on the development of online networking tools.
35. Millard, eUSER conceptual and analytical framework; Millard, Report on the development of online networking tools.

36. European Commission (2000). eEurope 2002, Action Plan: An information society for all, June 14; European Commission (2010). A digital agenda for Europe. August 10, COM(2010) 245.

37. Based on telephone interviews with 10,000 randomly selected adults across 10 EU Member States, although also recognizing that these factors are often interdependent; see Millard (2006). eUSER conceptual and analytical framework.

38. Millard, E-government for all.

39. United Nations, E-government survey 2014; Pew (2012). Digital differences. Pew Internet & American Life Project, April 13. Online at: http://www.pewinternet.org/~/media//Files/Reports/2012/PIP_Digital_differences_041312.pdf

40. United Nations, E-government survey 2014.

41. Millard, J. (2006). eUSER conceptual and analytical framework. Part D: e-Government, a deliverable of the European Commission financed eUSER project, May.

42. Note the percentages total more than 100 percent because most ICT users act in more than one capacity.

43. Millard, E-government for all.

44. European Commission, eEurope 2002, Action Plan.

45. Millard, E-government for all.

46. Ibid.

47. World Bank (2013). Amplifying citizen voices through technology. Online at: http://odta.net/post/call-for-feedback-amplifying-citizen-voices-through-technology-0

48. World Bank (2012b). Getting on the map: A community's path to better services. Open Development Technology Alliance. Online at: http://www.worldbank.org/socialdevelopment

49. Meyerhoff-Nielsen, M., and J. Millard (2009). Broadband penetration gaps in thinly populated areas and less developed regions in Europe. Part of the study on the development of the information society in EU rural development and regional policies, prepared for the European Commission, February.

50. Millard, J., et al. (2010). Interim evaluation of the ambient assisted living joint programme: Unlocking innovation in ageing well. Independent panel report chaired by Meglena Kuneva for the European Commission, December.

51. Prahalad, *The fortune at the bottom of the pyramid.*

52. Bevir, M. (2013). *A theory of governance.* Berkeley, CA: University of California Press, September.

53. *The Guardian.* Online at: http://www.theguardian.com/global-development/poverty-matters/2011/jan/04/technology-poverty-development-policy-discussion

54. World Bank, eTransform Africa.

Chapter 2

The Digital Broadband and Gender Divides

Gary Fowlie and Phillippa Biggs[1]

Contents

2.1 Introduction: Why Gender Matters in Access to ICTs and Broadband

The Internet has transformed the lives of billions of people. It represents a gateway to new ideas and opportunities, a means of self-expression and empowerment, a driving force for innovation and, increasingly, sustainable growth. In many countries around the world, the Internet is helping people—men, women and youth—to acquire new skills, imagine new possibilities, and be active participants in deciding their own future.

To achieve greater digital inclusiveness, The Broadband Commission for Digital Development was launched by the International Telecommunication Union (ITU) and the United Nations Educational, Scientific, and Cultural Organization (UNESCO) in response to UN Secretary-General Ban Ki-Moon's call to step up efforts to meet the Millennium Development Goals (MDGs). Established in May 2010, the Commission unites top industry executives with government leaders, thought leaders and policy pioneers, and international agencies and organizations concerned with development. The Broadband Commission embraces a range of different perspectives in a multistakeholder approach to promoting the roll-out of broadband, as well as providing a fresh approach to UN and business engagement. To date, the Commission has published a number of high-level policy reports, best practices, and case studies.[2] For instance, to unlock the full potential of the Internet for sustainable development, women need to have the knowledge and freedom to have access to and use of information and communication technologies (ICTs).

Today, access to new ICTs and the Internet enable the exercise of human rights and freedom of expression, a sense of self-identity, cultural rights, and the right to assembly. Achieving gender equality in access to ICTs and the Internet would be fair, just, and appropriate, because the Internet is empowering stakeholders and an increasingly important catalyst for the delivery of education, healthcare, government, job opportunities, and financial services.

In theory, the Internet might be considered by some to be "genderless"— available and usable by anyone who has access to it. Unfortunately, this is not the case in reality. The numbers speak for themselves. Shockingly, in some countries, there are more than twice as many men accessing the Internet as women. Although the technology itself does not innately discriminate, the human context of its usage and application is not always so equal. Women face social barriers that make access more challenging, whether it be lower wages, lower levels of education, or cultural norms, which may discourage access. And, where women do manage to get connected, they may find content and services that are not as relevant to their lives because the content and services are mostly being produced by men. Even worse, women may face harassment or other safety issues online.

Equality in access to ICTs is not only a key human rights issue, it also makes sound economic and commercial sense. Recent research suggests that ICTs boost economic growth. The World Bank estimates that every 10 percent increase in access to broadband results in 1.38-percent growth in Gross Domestic Product (GDP) for developing countries.[3] Access to the Internet can enable women to increase their productivity, access new markets, improve their education, find better jobs, and contribute to the innovation economy. Intel* estimates that bringing 600 million additional women and girls online could boost global GDP by up to US$13–18 billion.[4]

Nations with greater gender equality and higher proportions of educated females also may be more resilient to withstand economic shocks. The World Bank found that eliminating discrimination against women in employment could boost worker productivity by up to 40 percent. The underutilization of female talent and perspectives dampens productivity and ICT innovation, and slows economic development. If women's paid employment rates rose to equal those of men, global GDP could increase by up to 14 percent by 2020.

Microsoft[*] points out that everyone is watching the economic potential of the emerging BRIC economies (Brazil, Russia, India, and China), but that the most exciting new emerging market in the world may well be women and their capability to generate tremendous economic value and social growth.[5] According to Ernst & Young, over the next decade, the impact of women on the global economy—as producers, entrepreneurs, employees, and consumers—will equal the impact of China's or India's 1 billion+ populations, if not exceed it.[6] More women online will result in greater economic growth due to increased efficiency/productivity in their daily work and businesses, improved access to markets both to buy and sell goods, improved education, wider networks, new innovations, and faster access to relevant information. Bringing girls and women online will expand the digital opportunities of the new online global economy.

With the global rise of the knowledge society, realizing the right of women to full access and use of ICTs also can help achieve the full potential of a nation for sustainable development. The full utilization of human resources is especially important in the global knowledge society, as underlined by the UN and ITU.[7] Indeed, the importance of gender and ICTs was specifically recognized by ITU Member States at the World Summit on the Information Society (WSIS), held in 2003 in Geneva, where Member States declared ICTs to be vital tools for women's empowerment.[8]

The availability of ICTs to the entire population, and a better understanding of their importance, can help communities learn about and better respond to development challenges. There is growing recognition for the role of broadband and ICTs in empowering women. Empowered women are better informed, more financially independent, able to make better decisions for themselves, their families, and their communities, and meaningfully participate in decision-making processes that can directly affect their future. It is little wonder that there is growing recognition of the importance of broadband-based ICTs as a tool of empowerment.

Women are often committed agents of family and community welfare. Studies show that women invest a large proportion of their income back in their families and communities, which can help reduce poverty, and improve health and education. Children can access improved nutrition and education, and their communities are healthier and safer, helping fuel economic growth. Expanding women's access to ICT can enhance the reach of policymakers to a far broader population base, as women are more likely to take time to inform others and reflect such knowledge in family and community planning. By the same token, increased access will also give women a distinct voice in development planning and allow them to be active participants in having gender-aware policies and programs at the local and national levels.

The ITU/UNESCO Broadband Commission for Digital Development has defined broadband as Internet access that is always on, high speed, and capable of the combined provision of services.[9] Broadband is a catalyst for fostering women's digital inclusion, which, in turn, can lead to gender equality in all social, economic, and political dimensions, by providing women with access to resources to educate themselves and their children, improving their own health and the health of their families and communities; starting their own businesses, keeping themselves safe, empowering them to have voice and effectively participate in governance processes, and innovating to build and shape the future they want. Empowering women and girls to access the online world could help them learn to read, write, and acquire other vital skills.

2.1.1 Less Access Leads to Fewer ICT Jobs

Unfortunately, current evidence suggests that women and girls are being left behind. They do not have equitable access to the Internet, which in itself hinders society's ability to unlock the full promise of new digital opportunities. As the Internet becomes more critical to modern life, there is a risk of leaving women farther behind, and failing to effectively leverage female productivity. There is a significant and pervasive gender divide in Internet use. This gap varies from region to region, but is particularly high in sub-Saharan Africa, where in 2011 there were twice as many men as women on the Internet.[10] As the Internet provides enormous economic, social, political, and professional value, this gender gap has grave consequences for women everywhere.

Evidence also suggests women hold fewer science, technology, engineering, and mathematics (STEM) jobs, which often tend to be better paid and more highly skilled.[11] This suggests that women may be in a weaker position to develop better-paid skills for future competitiveness. To close the gender gap, support for ICT skills training is needed at all levels of development.

Women are disproportionately underrepresented in ICT employment. In OECD (Organization for Economic Cooperation and Development) countries, women account for less than 20 percent of ICT specialists.[12] In other regions, the disparity may be higher and it is apparent that the women in the ICT gap is exacerbating the overall "e-skills" gap. Women may miss out on new opportunities of earning more income, starting a new business, accessing or selling products to new markets, participation in decision-making processes that affect their lives, finding or changing jobs, or forging new contacts and accessing information. In short, women may miss out on the new digital opportunities offered by access to the Internet and broadband. Closing the former will require equipping more women with the training and technical skills needed to be successful in ICT careers.

On the microeconomic level, empowering women through access to ICTs and the opportunity to acquire and use new ICT skills could help them better access more skilled jobs, earn more income from new sources (e.g., microworking), and raise the standard of living for themselves and their families. This is all the more important, as there is evidence to suggest that 70 percent of the world's poor are women and children.[13]

2.2 Quantifying the Global Gender Digital Divide

More than 20 years after the birth of the Internet, two-thirds of the planet's population still do not have regular access, and a greater proportion of these unconnected global citizens are women. In 2013, ITU estimated the size of the global digital gender gap for the first time, finding that some 200 million fewer women are online, compared with men. Women are coming online later, and, as a gender, more slowly than men. In March 2013, the ITU/UNESCO Broadband Commission for Digital Development endorsed a fifth broadband advocacy target, calling for gender equality in access to broadband by 2020.[14] Its report, Doubling Digital Opportunities: Enhancing Digital Inclusion in the Information Society for Women and Girls, made a number of key findings:

1. **There is no single ICT or Internet gender gap, there are several.** As early as 2000, Bimber cited two Internet gender gaps for the United States: "One in *access to the Internet*, and one in *use of the Internet* among those men and women [who are already equipped] with access."[15] Other "gaps" or differences in behavior become apparent for different uses. Although most of the available data focus on gaps in access to ICTs between men and women, such gaps are often reflected in a range of other differences, including female participation in the labor force, gender differences in career choices, and, ultimately, pay differentials.

2. **Further, there are a number of different ways to measure ICT and Internet gender gaps.** Methodological problems are exacerbated by differences in data collection methods and data availability issues. For example, methodological differences in gathering the data include:
   a. Government surveys/estimates (e.g. ITU)
   b. User surveys on the demand side (e.g., Research ICT Africa)
   c. Usage of actual services (e.g., data from Facebook)
   Hafkin draws attention to the significant lack of data available for many countries, especially official data.[16] Pyramid, a research company, observes that different institutions use different "methodologies, instruments, and data collection methods (including in-depth surveys to top-level estimates based on available data points)."[17] The Partnership on Measuring ICT for Development has defined various gender-relevant core ICT indicators.[18] ITU has collected sex-disaggregated data since 2007 through an annual questionnaire sent to its member countries. While data for developed countries are largely available, in the developing world, only a small (albeit, increasing)

number of countries collect ICT use statistics (which can be broken down by sex) as part of their regular household surveys. Today, one of the key barriers to measuring progress in achieving this target remains the lack of sex-disaggregated and gender-sensitive data and indicators.

3. **Although ex post ICT gender gaps are generally closing over time in the majority of countries for which data are available, ICT gender gaps may still be large in absolute terms, and remain significant and persistent.** Small percentages may still translate into large absolute numbers. Of the two-thirds or nearly 5 billion of the world's population who are not yet regular Internet users, ITU estimates that 59 percent of all men have yet to become Internet users, compared to 63 percent of women. Based on Internet usage data, by the end of 2013, ITU estimated that some 1.3 billion Internet users will be women (or 37 percent of all women worldwide were using the Internet) (Figure 2.1), compared to 1.5 billion men online (41 percent of all men), giving a global Internet gender gap of 200 million.

The gender gap is more pronounced in developing countries, where 16 percent fewer women than men use the Internet, compared with only 2 percent fewer women than men in the developed world.[19] According to Intel, in 2011, of a total Internet user population in developing countries of 1.4 billion, 800 million were men and 600 million were women. In terms of Internet user penetration, there are 21 percent of women and girls online and 27 percent of men and boys online. This gives a gender gap for all 144 developing countries of 23 percent (i.e., 23 percent fewer women than men were online in the developing world), and a total global Internet gender gap of 200 million

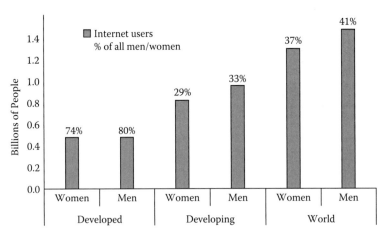

Figure 2.1 The gender gap: Men and women online, totals and penetration rates, 2013. (From ITU (2013). ICT facts and figures.)

in 2011. Without further action, Intel forecasts that the Internet gender gap could grow to a total gender gap of 350 million in three years' time.[20]

Women or girls may be choosing not to go online, or be prevented from going online, because there is a belief that women and girls cannot master technology. However, if women fail to go online, they may never master technology, and miss out on acquiring vital ICT skills, which are helpful in everyday life, and increasingly essential in the modern digital economy. The search is on to find policies and programs that can accelerate the rate of women logging on.

4. **Although gaps in ICT access reflect broader social and cultural divides, their roots are complex and multidimensional as are their consequences.** Digital gender gaps reflect gender inequalities throughout societies and economies, and a range of socioeconomic and political factors affect gender divides. It is widely and consistently established that women experience discrimination around the world in fields such as employment, income, health, and education, partly reflecting cultural biases and/or household decisions about relative reward/return on effort.[21]

Hilbert notes that it is not clear if existing background inequalities result in women making less usage of ICT or if being a woman, per se, has a negative effect on ICT usage (e.g., through "computer anxiety").[22] According to Hilbert's analysis, fewer women access and use ICT as a direct result of their unfavorable conditions with respect to employment, education, and income. After controlling for variation in these factors, women, in fact, emerge as more active users of digital tools than men.

The goal of equal opportunity to participate and benefit from the information society concerns affordability, accessibility, and the appropriateness of meaningful access.[23] Affordability, gaps in wages, and, therefore, gaps in purchasing power are major determinants of the different abilities of men and women to access ICTs. Endogenous, self-reinforcing, or circular causation is likely. Education and income gaps affect women's access to ICTs, while women's comparatively limited access to ICTs mean that they have fewer opportunities to access better paying skilled jobs. In particular, lower income hinders the purchase of equipment and payment of broadband fees.[24]

Intel notes the role of illiteracy in inhibiting access to the Internet, which poses a greater barrier to online access by women than by men.[25] Across all developing countries, only 75 percent of women are literate, compared to 86 percent of men, with far greater margins of difference in some countries. Without this fundamental skill, the Internet will remain out of reach—at least until computers can fully support natural language voice interfaces. Conversely, access to the Internet or even to a mobile phone could help improve literacy rates.[26]

5. **Women and men use ICTs in different ways, with quantifiable gaps increasing for more sophisticated uses.** Men and women may experience telecommunications/ICTs differently. For example, in 2008, men from the United States were more likely than women to surf the web daily (54 percent of men, compared to 41 percent of women), while men spent 1.5 hours more than women at their monitors browsing or reading.[27] In some Arab countries, consistent and measurable gender gaps are observed in the use of e-commerce and smartphones, with consistently more men choosing to purchase and use these services than women.

   Pyramid notes that gender and ICT indicators should go beyond sex-disaggregated statistics and provide gender-sensitive insights into the context and use of ICT for social and economic development.[28] It is important to note that gender equality in the use of ICTs should not necessarily mean that men and women should use ICTs in the same way; the differences between sexes, their behavior, and outlook are complementary, and should be celebrated.

6. **Gender gaps extend far beyond gaps in basic access to ICTs; gender gaps also are strongly evident in terms of the content accessed.** Today, broadband networks are increasingly serving as key platforms for delivery of films, TV, and other rich-content resources, which people—men, women, teenagers, and children—consume every day. In addition to reliable, affordable, and fast access, access to content that is relevant to specific contexts and languages is also critical. This entails being able to use and interact in online spaces without fear of surveillance, data retention, threats, harassment, intimidation, or violence. This may not be the case for many women and, increasingly, for women's human rights activists, in particular.[29] Disproportionately low participation of women and girls in education, employment, and decision making in technology, policy, and legislation may be compounded by discrimination and violence against women, including sexual harassment and bullying, affecting how the Internet and ICT are shaped and used by everyone.[30]

   In a number of countries with high Internet penetration, such as the United States, Canada, and the United Kingdom, attention has recently focused on the issue of cyberbullying and "Internet trolls," with a number of tragic suicides by young people bringing this issue to public attention. There is currently only limited research into the phenomenon of cyberbullying, which clearly affects both vulnerable young men and women. There are some early indications that cyberbullying might vary by gender, although young men may be more reticent to admit to or report a past bullying experience.[31] Nevertheless, this represents a worrying new development, with the extension of sexual content and violence in the real world into new forums online, with worrying implications for men and women.

   The origin, evolution, and role of content in shaping people's aspirations and outlooks is the subject of a growing body of research. Recent research by the Geena Davis Institute on Gender in Media, its programming arm See

Jane, and the Annenberg School for Communication at the University of Southern California found stark inequalities in the representation and gender of characters on screen. Currently, only one in four characters in family films is female. In crowd scenes, only 17 percent of the crowd is female, while only 11 percent of movies have a woman as the lead. Despite making up half the population, the message sent to children is that women and girls do not take up half of the space in the world, and women and girls have far less value to society than men and boys. This suggests that gender stereotyping remains deeply entrenched in today's entertainment media, which is a cause for major concern, as the influences children are exposed to may shape their outlook and notions of identity and aspirations from an early age.

These potential negative influences ignore the very positive influence online content and apps can have in educating Internet users against sexual violence. For instance, UN Habitat studies show that women in urban areas are twice as likely as men to suffer some form of violence, especially in developing countries.[32] In Brazil, as in many other countries, sexual violence is a significant problem. Although reported cases reflect only a fraction of actual occurrences, in 2012, there was a 23.8-percent increase in estupro (including rape and other violence) reported in Rio de Janeiro, compared to 2011. On International Women's Day, March 8, 2013, UN Women, UNICEF, and UN Habitat launched an online website that also works as a smartphone app that brings together information on support services for women and girls who are survivors of violence. With a large part of the population using mobile technology and computers in the favelas (shanty towns), an online tool was created so that anyone with a smartphone or computer and Internet access can use it to get information about assistance and services for survivors of violence. It provides abuse hotline numbers, information about rights, as well as the responsibilities and locations of Specialized Women's Attention Centers, which provide psychological, social, and even legal support. The tool also details steps to take after being raped, along with geographical positioning systems so users can locate the closest women's center, police station, medical center, and public prosecutor's office.

Basic access to the Internet and ICTs is just the starting point for gender equality in access to ICTs. Due consideration must be given to meaningful content for women online, as a trigger to promote demand for ICT services by women. Gender-appropriate content also must be considered as an integral part of ICT policies.

2.3 Policy Development, Gender, and Broadband

Policy plays a vital role in shaping ICT for development agendas as well as uptake and demand for broadband services.[33] Now more than ever, ICTs are ubiquitous and pervasive, permeating our everyday activities (and objects), and are indeed "socially embedded." At the same time, ICTs are key enablers for development and, thus, have the potential to impact most sectors of society. Historically, however, governments have tended to regard ICT policy development as mostly a technical matter.

There is a need to consider technology policies, as well as approaches to policy development, through a more holistic lens, and to introduce the social implications of ICT policy on all development areas, including gender.[34] ICT policy development does not stand alone, but is closely linked to education, health, governance, inequality, agriculture, finance, science, and many others, all having direct impact on gender equality issues. An innovative approach—and mindset—for policy development, therefore, is needed.

In general, ICT policies and policy development should be readily linked to other national development and strategic policies. In most cases, when we look at developing countries in particular, we find that policies and strategies for many sectors and areas are already in place, from national development and e-governance plans to national competitiveness policies and sustainable development strategies. The issue here is that most of these policies and strategies are seemingly disconnected and, in many cases, they actually compete against each other for scarce resources. So, the first step in innovating and changing mindsets is to foster the creation of *integrated policy development frameworks* where key national development goals and targets can lead the pack.

Here, ICTs have a distinctive advantage as they are crosscutting. Broadband is an enabler that can help address key service delivery gaps, enhance the participation of people in policy making, and foster transparency and accountability of public institutions and private sector entities, among others. ICT and broadband policies should strive to have direct links to other national socioeconomic development policies, and be seen as enablers that can help achieve agreed targets within a national or local context.

A similar argument can be made in the case of gender equality. Gender-specific policies have been promoted in many countries, especially since the 1995 Beijing World Conference on Women and the promotion of the National Gender Machineries in many countries. Since 2000, there has been significant growth in National Gender Policies, which complement or supplement these machineries. Being that as it may, these policies do not systematically take into account ICTs and, thus, remain oblivious to their potential as enablers for development. By the same token, most ICT and e-governance policies do not openly tackle gender. On the contrary, there seems to be an assumption that ICTs, somehow or automatically, will promote gender equality, implicitly assuming that ICTs are gender-neutral.

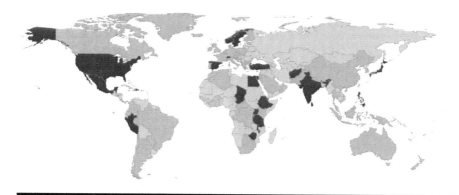

Figure 2.2 Inclusion of gender in countries' National Broadband Plans, mid-2013. (From Broadband Commission research, based on analysis of 109 plans.) Note: Light gray–no data, NBP not analyzed; Medium gray–NBP with a gender reference; Dark gray–no reference to gender.

Integrating gender perspectives into national ICT policies is a key aspect in policy development, which is readily measurable and is the subject of recent research by the Broadband Commission. Gender concerns are largely absent from ICT policies, just as ICT is largely absent from gender policies. Recent Broadband Commission research demonstrates that in 2012 only 30 countries or 29 percent of 119 countries included reference to gender as an issue in their National Broadband Plan (NBP).[35]

Figure 2.2 shows which countries did and did not include gender as a consideration in their plan. Bangladesh, Finland, India, Japan, Norway, Spain, Sweden, Switzerland, Turkey, and the United States all included references to gender in their plans. A large number of Asian, European, and Latin American countries did not, as well as Australia and Canada.

In fact, many countries have yet to extend their broadband policy to include gender, and some of the critical aspects include:[36]

■ Many countries/states do not yet treat affordable, pervasive/ubiquitous access as a basic right for the entire population, especially including women.

■ Many countries/states are not yet proactive in implementing broadband development and policies that promote the coordination of efforts among the public sector, businesses, and civil society.

■ Most broadband policies omit gender (aside from identifying women as an untapped market for mobiles).

■ There is little investment to enlarge the social impact of the Internet, especially in terms of awareness-raising and building information literacy, particularly amongst more excluded members of society.

■ There is little consideration of the digital gender gap between households with male heads and households with female heads. Digital literacy programs targeted to this segment should take into account the particular characteristics of households with female heads and their specific needs, mainly caused by lower income that hinders the purchase of equipment and payment of broadband fees.

National plans that did include gender aspects heavily focused on ICT training for women, which was included in 17 plans or 57 percent. Such references demonstrate countries' willingness to remove gender barriers to ICT education and training and to eradicate digital illiteracy among women and girls. Furthermore, half of the countries formulated measurable targets in this area. One example is the Dominican Republic, which aims to achieve a 50-percent digital literacy rate for women within four years. Other country-level targets are more focused, and refer to the development of specific ICT training centers and programs. For example, Chad's National Broadband Plan aims at developing 18 such training centers within a four-year timeframe. Egypt outlines actions to equip girls' schools with PCs. Chad has defined concrete goals to measure progress in this area by outlining administrative and fiscal measures to achieve ICT gender equality, and to develop a favorable legal framework within two years.

Fourteen countries refer to ICTs for women's empowerment. ICTs create new avenues for improving the situation of women as they provide them with access to knowledge and pedagogic content, and facilitate telecommuting to allow better family–work balance. In this regard, Gambia commits to increasing the proportion of women involved in the ICT sector and industry, targeting their level of involvement in terms of ownership and management of ICT businesses.

Only four countries included elements related to the use of ICTs to promote women's role in the decision-making and governance process. Malawi aims at putting in place policy instruments to ensure the participation of women in the formulation of ICT policies, and to ensure these policies are geared toward meeting specific developmental needs of women. Mexico indicates that achieving digital inclusion will be a vehicle to increase women's role in politics.

The good news is that country approaches to broadband policy is becoming more comprehensive. From a narrow focus on ICTs at the start of this century, national plans and policies are shifting to broader considerations of the digital and development agendas, with more countries including socioeconomic and political considerations in their national policies.[37]

For instance, in June 2013, the World Bank sponsored a hackathon where more than 80 young techies and civil society representatives joined forces to find a way and address the problem on how technology could be used to end violence against women in Nepal, where patriarchy is a deeply rooted problem.[38] One-third of married women have experienced some form of emotional, physical, or sexual violence from their spouses in their marital relationship. Nepal is a landlocked country in South Asia that is still recovering from a decade-long civil war. It ranks 157th out of 187 countries in terms of human development, according to *UNDP's Human Development Index Report 2013*. However, there is cause for optimism. Nepal has not only achieved the MDG on reducing maternal mortality, but it is also on track to achieve gender equality in education. Educating girls will not only help end poverty, but also help a historically patriarchal nation become a more equal, open-minded, and fair society.

The key to Nepal's transformation is its youth, who are using technology to shape their own futures and that of their country. Just eight years ago, only 0.4 percent of Nepal's population used the Internet. Today, one in every four Nepalese has access to the Web, and some Nepalese are using it to address societal challenges.

2.4 Conclusions and Policy Recommendations

Gender equality and women's empowerment are not just nice principles, they are vital building blocks for nations' economic competitiveness and long-term sustainable development. Gender issues are of key importance not just because they address basic human rights of billions of women and girls in the world, but also because they have positive economic, social, and political impact throughout society. And new ICTs and broadband, as enablers of development, play a central role by furnishing new tools and solutions to core gender gaps.

The report, Doubling Digital Opportunities: Enhancing the Inclusion of Women and Girls in the Information Society,[39] lists some of this work and makes policy recommendations as a means of inspiring policymakers to consider this issue further and, ultimately, initiate action in five areas, which are discussed below.

2.4.1 Integrate Gender and National ICT and Broadband Policies

Policymakers need to introduce strong gender perspectives into ICT policies, to devise strategies with clear goals, and to put in place measurement systems and practices to ensure these are achieved. Policy needs to cover universal access, regulatory frameworks, privacy and security, licensing, spectrum allocation, infrastructure, ICT industry development and labor issues, and draw upon available expertise, frameworks, and tools that provide relevant guidelines.

Policymakers designing ICT and broadband-related strategies also should be well aware of existing or planned national gender strategies and machineries that openly tackle gender equity issues, but do not usually include any ICT or broadband components. Furthermore, governments also should strive in having integrated policy frameworks that include key development goals and targets, in addition to gender. Only in this fashion can governments break down the policy silos that currently exist. Different ministries should be involved in the policy-making and implementation process. Governments should consult regularly with gender experts, allow broad-based participation of women's groups, and account for diversity to enable genuine multistakeholder involvement. Gender considerations and a gender perspective should be included in National Broadband Plans, based on a multistakeholder consultation process with women's representatives to ensure that women's needs are included. This also may involve:

- Annual audit and reporting of gender inclusion in published plans
- Taking stock of existing or planned national gender equality policies
- Engaging technical experts to educate, advocate, and recommend changes
- Including women's program in Universal Service Funds (USFs)[40]

2.4.2 Improve Sex-Disaggregated ICT Statistics and Measurement

ICT statistics on gender should be coordinated with overall national planning efforts and be part and parcel of broader efforts to target ICT outreach efforts. Similarly, gender advocates must become knowledgeable about ICT/telecommunications, science, and technology. ICT gender statistics must be seen in context of overall gender equality. Reliable and consistent, further sex-disaggregated data and indicators are needed on access and usage, skills, content, employment, education, consideration of gender issues in telecommunications policy, representation in ICT decision making, and impact of ICTs on women. Further resources and support from other stakeholders are needed to improve the availability and comparability of data. Better evidence-based analysis on the economic impact of ICT access on women's empowerment is urgently needed.

2.4.3 Take Steps to Boost the Affordability and Usability of ICT Products and Services

Communities, and especially women, need access to affordable, pervasive broadband services, and the equipment necessary to use it. Generally, the cost of a useful broadband connection may be more than the income of someone at the bottom of the pyramid, and broadband services are not uniformly available, except in major cities and towns. Industry and policymakers need to consider how Internet access can become more affordable, for example, through a review of taxation requirements within broader fiscal policy reforms. Competitive markets and market efficiencies (including infrastructure sharing) have been shown to result in reductions in the cost of most services.[41] Equipment often costs more than double what it would if taxes and duties were exempted on ICT devices.

This also can be achieved through support for public access facilities for those who cannot afford their own broadband connection or equipment (such as tele-centers, libraries, multimedia and community services centers, or similar social initiatives) providing high-quality connectivity at affordable or subsidized prices. These social initiatives also should offer equal opportunities to access ICT training and participation in content development, promoting the digital inclusion of young and adult women and girls. Specific actions that can be taken along these lines include:

- Engage with device manufacturers to promote more affordable devices, including from the Global South with innovative solutions to reach bottom of the pyramid populations.
- Foster local innovation on low-cost devices and connectivity plans.
- Incentivize development of smartphone, tablet, and computer user interfaces geared toward low literacy and limited resource environments.
- Support innovators in developing user-friendly interfaces in local languages.

2.4.4 Improve Relevant and Local Content Online

There is an urgent need to address the lack of relevant content and services for people in marginalized areas or areas far from a country's commercial or industrial centers. Billions of people only speak a local language. The creation of local content and applications should be stimulated (such as development of websites, software and mobile tools in Indigenous languages, or information systems for rural women and men). To raise awareness, policymakers can:

- strengthen local capacities for digitizing existing content and creating new relevant information
- encourage more women/girls into the ICT sector; only when women and girls are fully involved in producing the content and services, will more content and services designed for and relevant for women appear
- foster partnerships to encourage collaboration between tech providers, manufacturers, and content providers to provide women-tailored content
- incentivize development of services and apps geared toward women's needs and priorities
- support the creation and development of online content that is relevant to women and girls, and especially content developed by women and girls

■ incentivize local developers and social entrepreneurs to develop gender-relevant content that is easily accessible and understandable by local users, especially those at the bottom of the pyramid
■ promote use of local and Indigenous content that communities hold, and share it online and via other means of communication
■ consider launching online campaigns to address online harassment and other Internet safety issues

2.4.5 Initiate an Action Plan to Achieve Gender Equality in Access to Broadband by 2020

In order to help achieve gender equality in broadband access, governments may wish to study all of the previous recommendations, package them together, and consider their implementation on a sustained basis. Key entry points can include some of the following measures:

■ Digital literacy training for women and girls:
  - Familiarity is a key obstacle to greater use of the Internet by women, who may not understand what it is for and how it can be used.[42]
  - Governments may wish to consider supporting digital literacy campaigns targeted toward women and, specifically, training that can be applied to their lives.
  - Digital literacy should go beyond how to use a computer/technologies, and focus on how it can be used as a gender-equality tool for empowerment, and to access new job opportunities and information.
■ Empower women to participate in policy and decision-making processes and hold key policymaking positions within government:
  - Create capacity building initiatives using ICTs to allow women to meaningfully participate in policy discussions.
  - Launch access to information (via ICTs) programs targeting women and girls.
  - Support e-leadership initiatives customized for women.
■ Environment/Improve outreach to women/girls:
  - Policymakers should work with ICT ecosystem stakeholders (such as operators and tech companies) on public service campaigns on benefits of the Internet to women; how/where to access and direct them toward digital literacy campaigns, telecenters, government-sponsored programs.
  - Cultural organizations should be consulted and involved on how to address cultural norms around girls'/women's empowerment, and norms around technology use.

These recommendations are not exhaustive, but present a range of policy and implementation options. It is hoped that by following these five policy recommendations, governments working in concert with civil society and the private sector can increase digital opportunities, achieve digital inclusion for all, and address the core socioeconomic and political barriers and challenges that many women face in their daily lives.

Endnotes

1. This chapter is an adaptation based on the Report of the Broadband Commission Working Group on Gender & Broadband (2013, September). Doubling digital opportunities: Enhancing the inclusion of women & girls in the information society. Online at: http://www.broadbandcommission.org/documents/working-groups/bb-doubling-digital-2013.pdf

2. More information about the commission is available at: http://www.broadbandcommission.org

3. World Bank (2009). Information and Communication for Development Report.

4. Intel (2013). Women and the Web, January. Online at: http://www.intel.com/shewill/

5. Ayala, O. (2013). Women: Talent and potential are boundless, opportunity should be too … . Microsoft, March 6. Online at: http://blogs.technet.com/b/microsoft_on_the_issues/archive/2013/03/06/women-talent-and-potential-are-boundless-opportunity-should-be-too.aspx

6. Girls in STEM and ICT careers: The path toward gender equality. Online at: http://download.microsoft.com/download/E/6/5/E6523A39-82DF-4330-A216-AA520EB4FEB7/Girls In STEM and ICT Careers_WP_FINAL.pdf

7. UN ECOSOC Resolution E/2001/L.29. (2001). Social and human rights questions: Advancement of women, which calls for mainstreaming a gender perspective into all policies and programs of the UN system; ITU Marrakesh Resolution 70 (Rev. Marrakesh, 2002) calls for incorporation of a gender perspective in ITU's work programs, management approaches, and human resource development activities.

8. WSIS (2003a). *Declaration of Principles.* "We are committed to ensuring that the Information Society enables women's empowerment and their full participation on the basis of equality in all spheres of society and in all decision-making processes. We should mainstream a gender equality perspective and use ICTs as a tool to that end. Online at: http://www.itu.int/dms_pub/itu-s/md/03/wsis/doc/S03-WSIS-DOC-0004!!PDF-E.pdf

9. Broadband Commission for Digital Development Report (2010). A 2010 leadership imperative: The future built on broadband. Online at: http://www.broadbandcommission.org/Reports/Report_1.pdf

10. Intel (2013). Women and the web. January 2013. Online at: http://www.intel.com/shewill/

11. U.S. Department of Commerce (2011). Women in STEM: An opportunity and an imperative. Online at: http://www.esa.doc.gov/Reports/women-stem-gender-gap-innovation and http://www.commerce.gov/blog/2011/08/03/women-stem-opportunity-and-imperative

12. ITU (2012). A bright future in ICTs opportunities for a new generation of women, February. Online at: http://www.itu.int/ITU-D/sis/Gender/Documents/ITUBrightFutureforWomeninICT-English.pdf

13. UNDP (1995). Human Development Report. Online at: http://hdr.undp.org/en/content/human-development-report-1995

14. ITU (2013). UN Broadband Commission sets new gender target: Getting more women connected to ICTs 'critical' to post-2015 development agenda. Press release, March 17. Online at: http://www.itu.int/net/pressoffice/press_releases/2013/08.aspx

15. Bimber, B. (2000). Measuring the gender gap on the Internet. *Social Science Quarterly* 81 (3): 2. Online at: http://www.dleg.state.mi.us/mpsc/electric/workgroups/lowincome/internet_gender_gap.pdf

16. Hafkin, N. (2012). Gender and ICT statistics: The policy perspective. Paper presented at the 10th ITU World Telecommunications/ICT Indicators Meeting (WTIM), September 25–27, Bangkok, Thailand.

17. Jorge, S. (2012). Gender and ICT: Identifying sources of data and proposed indicators. Paper presented at the 10th ITU World Telecommunications/ICT Indicators Meeting (WTIM), September 25–27, Bangkok, Thailand.

18. ITU (2014). Partnership on measuring ICT for development. Online at: http://www.itu.int/en/ITU-D/Statistics/Pages/intlcoop/partnership/default.aspx

19. ITU (2013). ICT Facts and Figures 2013. http://www.itu.int/en/ITU-D/Statistics/Documents/facts/ICTFactsFigures2013-e.pdf

20. Intel. (2013). Women and the web, http://www.intel.com/content/dam/www/public/us/en/documents/pdf/women-and-the-web.pdf.

21. Anand and Sen. (1995). Quoted in the World Economic Forum's Global Gender Gap Report 2013. Available at: http://www.weforum.org/reports/global-gender-gap-report-2013.

22. Hilbert, M. (2011). http://www.martinhilbert.net/DigitalGenderDivide.pdf.

23. Gurumurthy, A. (2012). A new goal to ensure equal participation of all in the network society: Beyond the horizon of MDGs. Online at: http://www.bit.ly/13VH3Aa

24. CEPAL/ECLAC. *Banda ancha en América Latina: más allá de la conectividad.* Online at: http://bit.ly/14O3MRs

25. Intel, Women and the web.

26. Remarks by Mohammed Yunus to the Sixth Meeting of the Broadband Commission, September 2012.

27. World Internet Project, cited in Martin Hilbert (2011). http://www.martinhilbert.net/DigitalGenderDivide.pdf.

28. Jorge, Gender and ICT.

29. Note recent problems in the United Kingdom where women's rights advocates have been targeted via social media networks.

30. Commission on the Status of Women 55. (2011). E/2011/27-E/CN.6/2011/12. Agreed Conclusions.

31. Based on a 2010 study involving a random sample of 2,212 teen males and 2,162 teen females, females reported a higher percentage in all categories, with the male to female ratio varying across the following three areas: victimization within a person's lifetime (16.6 percent for males versus 25.1 percent for females), admitted to a cyber-bullying offense within a person's lifetime (17.5 percent for males versus 21.3 percent for females), and had a hurtful comment posted about oneself online (10.5 percent for males versus 18.2 percent for females), according to Hinduja and Patchin (2010), p.1; also see https://www.elon.edu/docs/e-web/academics/communications/research/vol3no1/04DoneganEJSpring12.pdf

32. UN Women (2013). In Rio de Janeiro's favelas, a new online tool tackles violence against women and girls. June 6. Online at: http://www.unwomen.org/en/news/stories/2013/6/rio-de-janeiro-apps-to-end-violence-in-favelas#sthash.D1RUQYNe.dpuf

33. ITU/Cisco. Planning for progress: Why national broadband plans matter. Online at: http://www.broadbandcommission.org

34. Hafkin, Gender and ICT statistics. Presentation by Dr. Nancy Hafkin to the World Telecommunications/ICT Indicators Meeting (WTIM), 25–27 September 2012, in Bangkok, Thailand.

35. Broadband Commission (2013). Gender in national broadband policies. Discussion paper by the Broadband Commission Secretariat, March. Online at: http://www.broadbandcommission.org

36. APC Women's Rights Program, Association for Progressive Communications (APC), quoted in the report of the Broadband Commission Working Group on Broadband and Gender (2013). Doubling digital opportunities: Enhancing the inclusion of women and girls in the information society. Available at www.broadbandcommission.org.

37. ITU/Cisco, Planning for progress: Why national broadband plans matter. Available at www.broadbandcommission.org.

38. World Bank. (2014). *Huffington Post,* July 23. Online at: http://www.huffingtonpost.com/ravi-kumar/young-people-use-ech-to-_b_3612004.

39. Report of the Broadband Commission Working Group on Broadband and Gender (2013). Doubling digital opportunities: Enhancing the inclusion of women and girls in the information society. Available at www.broadbandcommission.org.

40. Currently, very few USFs include gender considerations, and USF policy could be adjusted to enable the use of USFs for expanding access for underrepresented groups such as women (in addition to rural areas).

41. ITU (2002). World Telecommunication Development Report 2002. Online at: http://www.itu.int/ITU-D/ict/publications/wtdr_02/

42. Intel. (2013). Women and the web. Available at: http://www.intel.com/content/dam/www/public/us/en/documents/pdf/women-and-the-web.pdf.

Chapter 3

Challenging the Digital Divide in a Developing Country: Ghana Case Study

Johanna Ekua Awotwi

Contents

3.1 Introduction

The terms *digital divide* and *technological divide* refer to the differences in resources and capabilities to access and effectively utilize information and communication technology (ICT) for development that exists within and between countries, regions, sectors, and socioeconomic groups. This divide has remained an important public policy debate that embraces social, economic, and political issues.

Poverty, illiteracy, lack of computer literacy, and language barriers are among the factors impeding access to ICT infrastructure, especially in developing countries.[1] The divide could also be argued to be a form of discrimination as with gender, race, or religion without the use of which livelihoods hardly improve.

A brief look at studies and articles on the subject highlights the multifaceted nature of the subject matter. Currently, there is literature covering as many kinds of digital disadvantages as there are identified excluded or disadvantaged groups, from remote rural communities to every kind of disabled community to ethnic groups and developing countries. Interestingly, it is becoming commonplace to talk of "a continuum of digital divides."

Earlier research defined the digital divide broadly, either the disparity between people in their access to ICTs or, more specifically, the differences in their access to the Internet. However, as noted by Srinuan and Bohlin,[2] "From the end of the 1990s onward, attempts to accurately define the digital divide are frequently seen." According to van Djik,[3] "Scholarly literature and that of international organizations pointed out that the divide should be defined in terms of both access and the use of ICT."

Research work during the following decade saw ICT researchers conclude that ICTs had great potential as essential tools in international development and also confirming that both access to and the benefits of ICTs are unevenly distributed.[4] During this period, the digital gap concentrated on the imbalance in the access to information technology on a number of levels, for instance, that between rural and urban areas and also between developed and developing countries or globally between the Northern Hemisphere and the Southern Hemisphere.

The overall best definition for the digital divide may have been given by Kofi Annan, the past Secretary-General of the United Nations. In his statement to the World Summit on the Information Society (WSIS) in Geneva on December 10, 2003, he emphasized that "… the so-called digital divide is actually several gaps in one. There is a technological divide—great gaps in infrastructure. There is a content divide. A lot of web-based information is simply not relevant to the real needs of people. And nearly 70 percent of the world's websites are in English, at times crowding out local voices and views. There is a gender divide, with women and girls enjoying less access to information technology than men and boys. This can be true of rich and poor countries alike."[5]

However, defined another way, it is clear that developed nations with the resources to invest in and develop ICT infrastructure are reaping enormous benefits from the information age, while developing nations are trailing at a much slower pace. This difference in rates of technological progress is widening the economic disparity between the most developed nations of the world (primarily Canada, the United States, Japan, and Western Europe) and the underdeveloped and developing ones (primarily Latin America, Africa, and Southeast Asia), thus creating a digital (i.e., digitally fostered) divide. This global divide is often characterized as falling along what is sometimes called the north–south divide of "northern" wealthier nations and "southern" poorer ones.[6]

This chapter discusses how Ghana has faced the new challenges of this chasm and the strategies it has employed for bridging them in order to capture the benefits, especially for women. The chapter begins with a background where Ghana fits into the digital divide equation followed by an analysis of its ICT environment and usage levels. The second half of the chapter provides an overview of the challenges of access to ICTs, especially by women, and current opportunities of ICTs' usage and their benefits in the future.

3.2 Background

The level of ICT readiness in sub-Saharan Africa is still very low, with most countries evidencing strong lags in connectivity because of an insufficient development of an ICT infrastructure, which remains too costly. Low level of skills that do not allow for an efficient use of the available technology add to the challenges these countries face if they are to increase ICT uptake to close the digital divide. Moreover, most countries still suffer from poor framework conditions for business activity that, coupled with the other weaknesses, result in poor economic impacts, which hinder the much-needed transformation of the region toward less resource extraction-oriented activities and higher value-added production.[7]

Three in five of the world's population are not connected to the Internet. This digital divide hampers economic and social progress.[8] Low levels of development, low levels of knowledge and physical infrastructure, and limited benefits (such as employment creation and productivity growth) are always associated with lack of ICTs' usage in most developing countries; Ghana being no exception. ICT networks may either lead to inclusion or exclusion and the digital divide acts as the gap that separates the information rich and the information poor.[9] The OECD (Organization for Economic Cooperation and Development) definition of the digital divide breaks the term down as the difference between individuals, households, businesses, and geographic areas with regard to:

1. their opportunities to access ICTs
2. their use of the Internet for a wide variety of activities

Other measurements of the gap include citizen/population access to ICT with indicators for measuring access being:

1. Telephone density (teledensity)
2. Personal computer (PC) deployment and penetration
3. Number of Internet users

In absolute terms, the number of Internet users in Africa is abysmally low. Latest statistics from the International Telecommunications Union (ITU) shows that, in 2013, over 2.7 billion people worldwide were using the Internet, which corresponds to 39 percent of the world's population.[10] In the developing world, 31 percent of the population is online, compared with 77 percent in the developed world. Europe is the region with the highest Internet penetration rate in the world (75 percent), followed by the Americas (61 percent). In Africa, 16 percent of people are using the Internet, only half the penetration rate of Pacific Asia.

Unfortunately, 90 percent of the 1.1 billion households *not* connected to the Internet are in the developing world, even though between 2009 and 2013, Internet penetration in households grew fastest in Africa, with an annual growth of 27 percent.[11]

Research by the World Economic Forum with collaboration from the World Bank, confirms that, generally, access to the Internet in Africa is expensive and skewed in favor of urban areas. The penetration rate is much higher in North Africa (where 27 percent of the population have Internet access, on average) than in Southern Africa (13 percent), East Africa (12 percent), West Africa (9.5 percent), and Central Africa (4.5 percent).[12]

Fairchild and Quansah elaborate that one of the problems faced by those trying to find a solution to the digital divide in sub-Saharan Africa (SSA) is that the divisions are themselves fragmented.[13] The vast majority of the population simply lacks access to basic infrastructure for Internet access, for instance, but there is also a minority who could get Internet, but fail to grasp the opportunity. The researchers point to Ghana as one SSA nation that has overcome some of its internal problems to successfully increase access and participation in information and communications technology, even if minimally. However, even though Ghana was an early adopter of the Internet among African nations, having been online since 1993, there is still a vast digital divide in this country. Just as other countries, Ghana has supportive policies that are supposed to narrow the digital gap through its Ghana ICT for accelerated development (ICT4AD Policy 2003). Additionally, its policy to become a developed nation by the year 2020 as spelled out in the country's economic plan, Ghana Vision 2020, aims to achieve newly industrialized status by 2030. An important factor to these goals is the country's intent to improve its ICT infrastructure and penetration rate. In a recent report on Ghana's attempts to "diminish" its digital divide, KPMG, an international accounting firm, points out that Ghana, by 2013, had an unemployment rate of 1.9 percent, and a mere 3 percent lived below the poverty line.[14] Bridging the digital divide, however, is integral to Ghana reaching the next level of its socioeconomic development. According to the same source, a central component to its ICT advancement is mobile telephony.

This chapter places emphasis on whether developing countries, with Ghana as a country case study, have realized the unlimited opportunities offered by bridged technology gaps and are implementing supportive and relevant policies that place focus on universal access funding, for instance; and also whether these policies are flexible enough to encourage technological growth. Strict regulatory policies can easily have a direct negative impact on technology usage in these countries and the desired benefits of bridged technology gaps may not be felt.

The benefits offered by bridging the digital divide include Internet usage that, as a gateway, puts millions of people together in order to communicate ideas and act as potential buyers and sellers in a global economy. Indeed, the Internet also has created a worldwide platform for dialogue and has "generated a revolution of innovation and entrepreneurship through e-commerce."[15] With free access to information by all strata of a society, the following positive developments take place in a country:

1. Knowledge acquisition, through better teaching methods
2. Inclusiveness in global community that:
   a. Attracts tourists and investors
   b. Provides better healthcare facilities
   c. Promotes e-governance, which enhances better policy making

Countries with stagnant digital vacuums are unable to compete economically on an international scale and are partially excluded from international dialogue, apart from the likelihood of potential demonstrations by the affected population to demand a redistribution of information and technological resources, where demands may lead to unstable governments—socioeconomic stress.

A major policy by developing economies for harnessing access and availability of ICTs for their citizens is through universal access and funding. Universal access or services, Intelecon Research states, aims "at increasing the number of individual residences with telecommunications services and providing telecommunications services to all households within a country, including those in rural, remote, and high-cost locations."[16] The research also stressed focus on affordability of telecommunication services especially to underserved and nonserviced areas.

To improve digital access to all areas, The Ghana Investment Fund for Electronic Communications (GIFEC), an implementing agency of the Ministry of Communications, was established in January 2004, to facilitate the spread of ICTs and their use in rural Ghana. The agency is helping to promote research and reading culture, through ICT use, thereby empowering the people in nonserviced and underserved communities to directly participate in development and decision-making processes at local and national levels.[17] Therefore, GIFEC is recognized as the foremost government institution expected to bridge the different levels of the digital chasm in the country.

What is topical now is Ghana's recognition of the importance of achieving universal access and funding to bridge different levels of the digital divide without overburdening its financial reserves with a suggestion by this author to Ghana's policymakers to use innovative options, such as mobile telephony to address efficient governmental service delivery, especially in the interest of women who are marginalized at all socioeconomic levels of the society.

3.3 State of Ghana's ICT Environment

Ghana lies in the center of the West African coast, shares 2,093 kilometers of land borders with the three French-speaking nations of Burkina Faso (769 km) to the north, Côte d'Ivoire (424 km) to the west, and Togo (171 km) to the east. To the south are the Gulf of Guinea and the Atlantic Ocean.

With a total area of 238,533 square kilometers, Ghana is about the size of the United Kingdom, or slightly smaller than the American state of Oregon. Its southernmost coast at Cape Three Points is 4° 30′ north of the equator. From here, the country extends inland for some 670 kilometers to about 11° north. The distance across the widest part, between longitude 1° 12′ east and longitude 3° 15′ west, measures about 560 kilometers. The Greenwich Meridian, which passes through London, also traverses the eastern part of Ghana at Tema.

Ghana ranked 135th out of 186 countries in the 2013 Human Development Index (HDI) released by the United Nations Development Program (UNDP) on March 14, 2013, and the country's rate of life expectancy at birth rose to 64.6 years from 64.2 years in 2011. Ghana's HDI was valued at 0.558 compared to the globally ranked no. 1, Norway's 0.955. The UNDP said between 1980 and 2012, Ghana's HDI rose by 0.9 percent annually from 0.391 to 0.558. "The HDI of sub-Saharan Africa as a region increased from 0.366 in 1980 to 0.475 today, placing Ghana above the regional average," the UN agency added.

According to the 2013 index, which conducted innovation studies among 142 countries globally, Ghana made a score of 30.6 out of 100, which moved it from sixth in 2012 to fifth in 2013 in SSA.

3.3.1 Information and Communication Technologies in Ghana

Since the 2003 ICT4AD, Ghana's developmental agenda includes a policy document to guide the implementation and use of ICTs. This is a policy statement for the "realization of the vision to transform Ghana into an information-rich, knowledge-based society and economy through the development, deployment, and exploitation of ICTs within the economy and society," according to the Republic of Ghana in 2003. The policy takes into account provisions of key socioeconomic development framework documents including:

1. Vision 2020: Achievement of middle income status
2. Ghana Poverty Reduction Strategy (GPRS 2002–2004)
3. Coordinated Program for Economic and Social Development of Ghana (2003–2012).

According to a report from Budde Internet Research, an Australian research company, Ghana was among the first countries in Africa to have connected to the Internet and to have introduced ADSL (asymmetric digital subscriber line) broadband services. The sector is highly competitive with more than 140 licensed Internet service providers (ISPs), although the bulk of the market is in the hands of only a few. Internet penetration is still very low mainly due to the poor condition of the national fixed-line network and the high cost of connectivity. The emergence of wireless and mobile broadband technologies is now speeding up developments and has put pressure on the current monopolistic pricing of international bandwidth. The reprivatized national carrier, Ghana Telecom, is expected to be more effective in the future in driving the broadband market by expanding its retail as well as wholesale offerings under the Vodafone banner.

Although ICT infrastructure development has not progressed rapidly, Ghana compares favorably with other low-income countries, particularly those in sub-Saharan Africa, in terms of bridging the global divide between it and the developed world.

3.3.2 Comparative ICT Environment in Ghana

The 2013 Networked Readiness Index part of the World Economic Forum's (WEF) Global Information Report shows that Ghana was 95th in the 2013 edition, up from 97th in 2012.

The Networked Readiness Index, calculated by the WEF and INSEAD, an international business school based in France, ranked 144 economies based on their capacity to exploit the opportunities offered by the digital age. The ranking capacity is determined by the quality of the regulatory, business, and innovation environments; the degree of preparedness; the actual usage of ICTs; as well as the societal and economic impacts of ICTs. According to the annual report, eight countries in Africa were ahead of Ghana:

Mauritius (55th, with a score of 4.12)
South Africa (70th, with a score of 3.87)
Seychelles (79th, with a score of 3.80)
Egypt (80th, with a score of 3.78)
Cape Verde (81st, with a score of 3.78)
Rwanda (88th, with a score of 3.68)
Morocco (89th, with a score of 3.64)
Kenya (92nd, with a score of 3.54)

Category	Score	Rank
a. Availability of latest technologies	4.7	86
b. Firm-level technology absorption	4.2	115
c. FDI and technology transfer	4.5	82
d. Individuals using Internet %	14.1	109
e. Broadband subscriptions/100 pop.	0.3	115
f. Int'l Internet bandwidth, kb/s per user	0.2	142
g. Mobile broadband subscriptions/100 pop.	23.0	42

Figure 3.1 Ghana's technological readiness/144 economies. (From The World Bank/WEF.[18])

Additionally, in the Africa Competitiveness Report for 2013 (Chapter 3), the Competitiveness Profiles section indicates Ghana's technological readiness under different headings with rankings and scores that show marginal progress in filling in the digital gap (Figure 3.1).

According to this report, "Internet users" refer to people using the Internet from any device (including mobile phones) in the past 12 months and "Mobile broadband subscriptions" refer to active SIM cards with connections being used in any type of device able to access mobile broadband networks, including smartphones, USB modems, mobile hotspots, and other mobile broadband connected devices. Not excluding CDMA (code division multiple access) networks, connections accessing the Internet at consistent broadband speeds of over 512 kb/s, including cellular technologies, such as HSPA (high speed packet access), EV-DO (evolution-data optimized), and above.[19]

While Ghana has moved up in the world digital rankings, it is important to note that ICT usage and impact are not encouraging. As Figure 3.1 illustrates, Ghana has some way to go and the march to bridging the digital divide is slow.

3.3.3 Ghana's Digital Divide Challenges

More men than women use the Internet—globally, 37 percent of all women are online compared with 41 percent of men, according to the ITU. This corresponds to 1.3 billion women and 1.5 billion men. The gender gap is more pronounced in the developing world, where 16 percent fewer women than men use the Internet, compared with only 2 percent fewer women than men in the developed world. The developing world is home to about 826 million female Internet users and 980 million male Internet users, whereas the developed world is home to about 475 million female Internet users and 483 million male Internet users.

Yet, it is widely known that "gender equality is essential for growth and poverty reduction," and "in the developing world, women suffer disproportionately from poverty and its related ills, such as malnutrition, poor health, and illiteracy."[20] Illiteracy is one area of inequality that has led to more women not benefitting from the use of technology in developing countries. In recognizing the limitations faced by women all over the world, many international conferences and other declarations have sought to promote women's use of ICT. Some of these declarations include the 1975–2000 Conferences on Women, which sought to address the gender digital divide gap. The 1995 World Conference on Women in Beijing delineated a strategy to promote greater access to communication by women internationally. The United Nations' millennium development goals (MDGs) include the eradication of extreme poverty, universal access to primary education (age 7–14), and the promotion of gender equality as their top three objectives. All three of these involve the education of girls. These international declarations are clear manifestations that there is a problem with equal access by women to ICTs, which has to be addressed in order to fully realize the benefits of ICTs.

Available Ghana national-level data collected by the ITU and others indicates that women's rate of Internet use will not automatically rise in tandem with national rates of Internet penetration. In a well-researched and peer-reviewed conference paper on women and access challenges to ICTs, the author noted the following challenges that continue to prevail in Ghana:[21*]

1. There is a lack of consideration of the role of women and girls in ICTs in the planning and implementation of programs.
2. Minimal women's education and skills enhancement in ICTs are limitations in many African countries, including Ghana.
3. The biological and social roles of women circumscribe their ability and opportunity to function on an equal basis with men in most economic spheres.
4. Women are overwhelmed in meeting local and family needs in developing countries, hence, not linked to a global digital economy.
5. Women's lack of access to family property or institutional finance make it difficult to engage in self-employment in the ICT sector, such as establishment of businesses in telecenters or cybercafés.
6. The effect of discrimination against women restricts their access to the professions and jobs that would provide access to high-end ICTs, which have a higher gain and economic status.
7. There exists a general pay inequality between men and women due to women's inadequacy in ICT skills.

---

* Awotwi, Johanna E. and George Owusu (2008). "Lack of Equal Access to ICTs by Women: An e-Governance Issue," 2nd International Conference on the Theory and Practice of Electronic Governance, ACM.

Generally, even though women make up over 51 percent of the Ghanaian population, they remain barely visible in the public arena. Discrimination against girls/women starts at an early age. Social customs often give preference to boys. Female children often have domestic work and responsibilities that leave little time for school. Even when girls make it to school, they often drop out, because the schools do not meet their needs. The teachers, curriculum, and textbooks frequently reinforce gender stereotypes. Also, female students are especially susceptible to sexual and emotional harassment. Very few females, therefore, are able to continue schooling to levels that would enable them to understand ICTs.

Although the government in Ghana has reversed the discrimination policies through the ICT4AD, the 2003 Strategic Document on Gender and ICT acknowledges, "We, as a nation, must appreciate the fact that ICT has become the threshold of national development and, therefore, it is important we involve all citizens to avoid any technological divide between men and women." It also acknowledges that inequity still exists because of the assertion that "… if access to and use of these technologies is directly linked to social and economic development, then it is imperative to ensure that women and children in Ghana understand the significance of these technologies and use them. If not, they will become further marginalized from the mainstream of the country and the world. Many people may not appreciate the concern for gender and ICT in Ghana on the basis that development should deal with basic needs first. However, it is not a choice between one or the other. ICT can be an important tool in meeting the basic needs of all and can provide the access to resources to lead women out of poverty."

As recently as 2013, GIFEC commissioned a study on the digital divide in Ghana through the Institute of Statistical, Social, and Economic Research (ISSER) of the University of Ghana, and it was confirmed that more men than women use the Internet as in most of sub-Saharan Africa. Figure 3.2 shows that far fewer Ghanaian women than men use the Internet either directly through proxy, by themselves as a premium with their own fast and reliable access, as regular Internet users in the past three months, or users of fast and reliable connections to the Internet.

	Male (%)	Female (%)
Premium	9.9	4.6
Reliable	11.6	5.2
Fast	12.0	5.5
Internet	19.0	8.9
Proxy	19.0	8.9

Figure 3.2 Ghana's gender digital divide. (From Ghana Investment Fund for Electronic Communications (GIFEC).[22])

Even though the government has focused, since 2003, on closing the ICT gender gap, the figure indicates that not much has been achieved in closing the divide. Maybe the challenges are too many and need to be tackled one step at a time or through ICT tools other than fixed telephone lines and computers.

3.3.4 Community Information Centers

A 2009 conference paper entitled, "Ghana's Community Information Centres (CiCs): An e-Governance Success or a Mirage?" asserted that:[23]

> Many developed countries have exploited ICTs successfully for the development of their remote and hard to reach communities. Taking a cue from their experience, developing countries have used these technologies, with varying degrees of success. Many of us are both witness and participants to the exploitation of ICTs to further the goals of development. It is therefore instructive to note, that Information Technology (IT) and telecom are only means to an end and not an end in themselves. IT is an enabler and, if not well utilized effectively for socioeconomic benefits, its phenomenal growth is of very little relevance in any country, especially the developing ones.

And, so even though Ghana is not on the list of most-connected African countries, the country is currently on course to get as many of its citizens as possible to join the information highway in the realization of digital gap closure.[24]

However, the following have been known to hinder progress in bridging the divide, especially in low-income countries such as Ghana:

- Weak telecommunications infrastructure
- Generally low level of economic activity
- Irregular or nonexistent electricity supplies
- Lack of human resource capacity, lack of skills, and brain drain

A study on rural access in Ghana commissioned by the Institute for Information and Communication Development (IICD) in 2008, revealed that a rural community in Ghana is a deprived community that lacks telecom infrastructure, electricity, and sometimes appropriate buildings. It further showed that the absence of meaningful economic activity and skilled personnel make these locations unattractive for investors.[25] Rural communities, therefore, generally have had limited access to technology, and the cost of a PC is typically more than what the average villager can afford. Due to poor connectivity, inadequate infrastructure, and human resource limitations, most of the telecenters provide extremely limited services.

The Community Information Centers (CiCs) project falls within the framework of World Summit on Information Society (WSIS), where all nations strive to attain certain targets, including the provision of ICT access and skills to the underprivileged and rural dwellers globally.

The project also operates within the context of the MDGs whose set targets address structural concerns that impede economic growth and human development. Ghana's own Poverty Reduction Strategy (GPRS) represents comprehensive policies, strategies, programs, and projects at macro and micro levels to support economic growth and poverty reduction. Within these broad frameworks, ICT is being deployed within the CiCs as an integral tool.

Government, through its regulators, has placed "universal access" requirements on telecommunications providers. These requirements have resulted in infrastructure investment—CiCs—that have made access available to some degree. However, these centers typically operate at a loss.[26]

ICTs through the CiCs should play an essential role not only in reaching marginal/and underserved communities, but also in scaling up the services at affordable costs, creating new markets and new demand for additional products and services. This, however, is still not happening on any scale, substantive or otherwise.

Ghana's CiC gap-bridging option, for instance, still has very limited access of the rural population to social and economic information and transformation. Apart from those noted above, challenges continue to include lack of enough and consistent revenue to support running expenditures for connectivity, lack of local content and content development for the mainly illiterate rural population, technical problems that linger on for months because of inadequate technical staff, and insufficient skills and awareness to fully optimize the use of ICTs.

The slow pace of CiC development also may be due to its lack of positive socioeconomic impact, lack of centralized standards, and also the fact that there may be an alternative to empowering and informing the underserved and nonserviced more effectively and with less financing.

Unless people have other venues for building their awareness of and confidence in using ICTs, the CiCs have not proved a robust method of overcoming the multiple barriers to access that many people face.

The recent report by GIFEC, entitled Study of the Digital Divide in Ghana, confirmed "significant gaps in Internet and broadband access and quality along multiple sociodemographic dimensions. Most notably, geography, age, gender, and income all appear to be aligned with the digital divide."[27] Analysis of this research showed that the digital divide exists along several dimensions in Ghana and suggests interventions to be based on location, gender, age, and income that may be effective in narrowing the divide between users and nonusers.

In recognition of the challenges faced by GIFEC with its initial attempts, other more meaningful attempts have been introduced to enhance the mandate of this singular, digital, gap-building unit of Ghana's government.

3.3.5 ICT Usage Opportunities

The GSM Association, which reports the growth rate of mobile penetration and its necessity as an alternative to encourage universal access, explained that "approximately half of African countries face a great challenge to bring greater geographical and population coverage to markets where penetration and affordability are low. These are generally low-income countries, mostly with large geographical areas or topographical barriers and weak transportation and electricity supply infrastructures, which contribute to high operator costs."[28] This is illustrated by the inability of GIFEC to provide as much access through its CiCs as first planned.

A change in tactic has led GIFEC to projects that include the use of mobile phones to provide access to important government departments as an initial step.

Projects to assist GIFEC realize its vision include the following: the Common Telecommunication/Rural Telephone, the Last Mile Initiative, Community Information Centre, Information Communication Technology (ICT) Capacity Building, the School Connectivity, Rural Pay Phone, Easy Business Centre, Library Connectivity, and Security Connectivity Projects. The others include the Disability, Post Office Connectivity, ICT for Sustainable Fishing, The e-Learning, e-Health, Community Initiative, Content Creation, and Public Education on Electromagnetic Fields Exposure and Health.

Making these projects sustainable require effective monitoring and evaluation that should not take away attention from other equally important developmental projects, such as good roads, school structures, health centers, and markets. The e-Health project, for example, has recorded an incredible improvement with respect to the infrastructure and ICT facilities in the country.[29]

Currently, many Ghanaians use phones, not PCs, to access the Internet because broadband connectivity is incredibly slow and the nation lacks a decent fixed-line network. This has led to growth in the number of people who use mobile phones to access the Internet. The National Communications Authority claims there are 10 million Ghanaians who access Internet services on their mobile devices. *The Ghana Business and Financial Times* reported that the data market, which is considered as the next frontier for network operators, grew by 19.5 percent last year from 8.6 million access lines in January to 10.3 million at the end of December 2013. This puts the rate of data penetration at almost 40 percent in a population of 26 million. Growth in the mobile data market has been helped by the proliferation of cheap smartphones, which have helped to drive mobile data traffic to social media platforms and other Internet applications, such as Facebook, WhatsApp, and Twitter.[30]

Mobile phones, which were not widely available in most of the developing world, have reached every segment of society and this has "completely changed the game with regard to ICTs and development," said Laurent Elder, program leader for Pan Asian Networking at an International Development Research Center (IDRC) forum at Harvard University on September 23 and 24, 2013. He went on to ask a very important question that explains why mobile telephony has taken the center stage as an ICT tool, which, when well used, bridges the digital divide faster than PCs. "Once you assume that access to technology is a given, after that, what is the means to ensure that you can actually get access to the knowledge conveyed by those technologies," asked Elder.[31] Mobile telephony does convey knowledge, and it is an illustration of an identified tool for policy intervention to improve ICT take up and usage. With this technology, it is suggested that recommendations are made for policy interventions and regulatory measures, which would decrease access and usage costs.

With the staggering penetration figures in a country such as Ghana, there are opportunities in tackling the bridging mission on a different level. GIFEC, realizing the importance of mobile telephony, has lately supplied the following government agencies with many phones in order to make their work more efficient and responsive: Ghana Prison Service, Ghana National Fire Service, the Ghana Armed Forces, National Disaster Management Organization, and the Bureau of National Investigation.

Other suggested interventions based on location, gender, age, and income will be effective in narrowing the divide between users and nonusers as noted by GIFEC.[32] The interventions include Public–Private Partnerships that reduces the government burden in bridging the divide by itself.

3.3.6 Future Benefits of Closing the Digital Divide

In developing countries such as Ghana, ICT dissemination and adoption facilitates the achievement of major development goals in the areas of health, education, governance, and others. Thus, easier and cheaper access to ICTs are now being encouraged.

However, policies and strategies that have been adopted have not been successful in addressing the question of how such countries can catch up with global levels of ICT access and usage and how the poor can join the newly developing information societies.[33] In order to combat the digital obstacles and to achieve knowledge acquisition and global inclusiveness, better health awareness, and e-governance, the use of mobile phones have been encouraged through public private partnerships.

Within governance, mobile technologies can offer new means for empowering citizens and stakeholders through greater mechanisms. Mobile governance initiatives that expand access to information and communications channels are creating new venues for people's participation and giving new voice to those who have historically been marginalized, especially women. Mobile technology services in some countries have proved informative; have more inclusive citizen participation and monitoring, which in turn demand more accountability and transparency on the part of major local stakeholders.

Through private partnerships, Ghana's government introduced various mobile interventions that help to bridge the divide. Examples include the Mobile Technology for Community Health (MoTeCH) initiative by the Ghana Health Services, in partnership with Columbia University's Mailman School of Public Health, and the Grameen Foundation. It is funded by the Bill and Melinda Gates Foundation. Begun on a pilot phase in the upper east region of Ghana because it is one of the smallest and least urbanized regions in the country, with 85 percent of the population living in dispersed communities throughout the rural areas, the low population density and infrastructure barriers create a challenge for information dissemination in all forms, necessitating a community-based approach. Mobile phone ownership is not ubiquitous in rural Ghana.[34] Some pregnant women own their own mobile phone, but it is more common for a phone to be shared in the family (in which case, it is frequently controlled by the male in the household) or for there to be a single phone used by many members of the community.[35]

The use of the mobile phone has improved access to and use of information by pregnant women thereby reducing their search for better health facilities and reducing their exposure to risk. When women gain information about their needs, it leads to higher empowerment because it increases their choices. Specific benefits for women created by the access to a mobile phone include:

1. Opportunity to access resources
2. Empowerment by way of participating in various trading activities
3. Ability to negotiate with customers
4. Sharing vulnerability risks with the network of women formed through access to mobile phones
5. Reacting faster to arising opportunities
6. Maintaining contact data[36]

Mobile phones also have made a huge difference in the lives of farmers in a continent where the agriculture sector is one of the largest employers. Most of these people are without access to financing or technology.

However, recently, with the aid of private intervention, Ghana's government started piloting an e-agriculture mobile application program that is a free, multilingual, interactive voice response system and audio conferencing and free messaging service that has currently attracted over 40,000 active subscribers and an average daily usage of 2,000 accessing each day on their standard mobile phone in various Ghanaian languages.

Farmers can get weather alerts and identify the most competitive prices for their cash crops or learn how to combat a specific crop disease. This service allows direct access to information in real time from subject matter specialist as well as experts to farmers through standard phones at zero cost to the farmer.[37] Governments gain when they integrate such support for vulnerable groups into existing public reform and decentralization frameworks because they assist in diminishing the techno-logical divide since such integration promotes low-cost mobile phones accessible to the poor and also develops capabilities to support the delivery of information and services.

3.4 Conclusion

This chapter has tried to give an outlay of the digital divide of a low income coun-try with its numerous challenges and various efforts at trying to diminish the gap, especially for women. It also pointed out the benefits that go with the opportunities in having a digitized economy. The chapter also has presented the limited initia-tives of Ghana's efforts to close the digital divide. To enjoy the benefits of bridging the digital gap, governments have to be able to identify which ICT tool will be financially viable while giving access to its most vulnerable citizens. In Ghana, more people are accessing mobile telephony, with personal computers out of range for average Ghanaians. Internet charges are still high, and bandwidth remains a major issue. Although ICT infrastructure development has not progressed rapidly, Ghana compares favorably with other low-income countries, particularly in sub-Saharan Africa. It is suggested that, due to the current limited availability and use of Internet facilities, any broad-based digital closing gap program should involve mobile phones as a primary information and delivery channel. The wide penetra-tion of mobile phones and the ever-increasing coverage makes it more accessible to a large proportion of the population.

Best practices to benefit the poor, especially women, include new business mod-els that would lead to expanding access to networks through low-cost phones and low-tariff models, making sure that the services provided are relevant and tackle local problems. It's glaring, from the analysis, that GIFEC is leading the way to make sure these are achieved.

Endnotes

1. United Nations—Division for the Advancement of Women. Department of Economic and Social Affairs Women2000 and Beyond—Gender equality and Empowerment of Women through ICT [Report]. New York: UN Division for the Advancement of Women. Department of Economic and Social Affairs, September, 2005.
2. Srinuan, C. and E. Bohlin (2011). Understanding the digital divide: A literature survey and ways forward. Paper presented at the 22nd European Regional Conference of the International Telecommunications Society: Innovative ICT Applications–Emerging Regulatory, Economic and Policy Issues. International Telecommunications Society, September 18–21, Budapest, Hungary.

3. van Djik, A. (2002). Framework for digital divide research. *The Electronic Journal of Communication* 12 (1 & 2); Norris, P. (2001). *Digital divide: Civic engagement, information poverty and the Internet worldwide.* Cambridge, U.K.: Cambridge University Press; OECD (2001). Understanding the digital divide.

4. Loges, W. E. and J. Y. Jung (2001). Exploring the digital divide: Internet Connectedness and Age. *Communication Research*, pp. 28, 536–562; Light, J. S. (2001). Rethinking the digital divide. *Harvard Educational Review* 71 (4): 710–734; Gumpert, G. and S. Drucker (2002). Digital divide and digital cities. Online at: http://www.portalcomunicacion.com/bcn2002/n_eng/programme/prog_ind/papers/g/pdf/d_g017wg15_gumpe.pdf; Warschauer, M. (2003). Dissecting the "digital divide: A case study in Egypt. *The Information Society,* pp. 19, 297–304; Mossberger, K., C. J. Tolbert, and M. Stansbury (2003). *Virtual inequality. Beyond the digital divide.* Washington, D.C.: Georgetown University Press.

5. Annan, K., UN Secretary-General (2003). Statement to the United Nations, December 10.

6. Wordiq.com. Global Digital Divide. Online at: http://www.wordiq.com/definition/global_digital_divide; Lu, M.-t. (2001). Digital divide in developing countries. *Journal of Global Information Technology Management*, 1–4.

7. Awotwi, J. E. (2012). ICT-enabled delivery of maternal health services. Paper presented at the 6th International Conference on Theory and Practice of e-Governance, ACM, October 22–25, Albany, New York; Dutta, S. and B. Bilbao-Osorio (2012). The GITR 2012: Living in a hyper-connected world. World Economic Forum. http://www3.weforum.org/docs/Global_IT_Report_2012.pdf

8. ICTWORKS (2014). The 4 barriers to affordable Internet in 46 emerging and developing countries. February.

9. OECD (2003). The e-Government imperative.

10. ITU (2013). The world in 2013 ICT: Facts and figures.

11. Ibid.

12. The World Bank/WEF (2013). Africa Competitiveness Report 2013.

13. Fairchild, A. M., and E. A. Quansah (2007). Approaching the digital divide across Africa. *International Journal of Knowledge and Learning* 3: 6, 612–627.

14. KPMG Africa (2014). Ghana's diminishing digital divide, February.

15. FCC&TRAI (2001). Equality and the digital divide.

16. Intelecon (2004). Universal access funds.

17. Attor, K. (2012). Overview of USF in Ghana. Paper presented at the United Nations Commission on Science and Technology for Development Conference, May 21–25, Geneva.

18. The World Bank/WEF (2013). Africa Competitiveness Report 2013.

19. ITU. (2014).World Telecommunication/ICT Indicators database. Online at: http://www.itu.int/en/ITU-D/Statistics/Pages/publications/wtid.aspx

20. EU Development and Cooperation (EUROPEAID) (2013). Gender equality. European Commission.

21. Awotwi, J. E. and G. Owusu (2008). Lack of equal access to ICTs by women: An e-governance issue. Paper presented at the 2nd International Conference on the Theory and Practice of Electronic Governance, ACM, December 1–4, Cairo, Egypt.

22. GIFEC (2013). Study of the digital divide in Ghana.

23. Awotwi, J. E. and G. Owusu (2009). Ghana's Community Information Centres (CiC): An e-governance success or a mirage? Paper presented at the International Conference on Theory and Practice of Electronic Governance, ACM, November 10–13, Bogota, Colombia.

24. GICT (2012). Network Africa's 10 most connected countries.

25. Akakpo, J. (2008). Rural access: Options and challenges for connectivity and energy in Ghana. GINKS & IICD.

26. Awotwi, and Owusu, Ghana's Community Information Centres (CiC).

27. GIFEC, Study of the digital divide in Ghana.

28. GSM Association (2007). Universal access. How mobile can bring communications to all.

29. The Republican (2012). GIFEC raises the standard of ICT in Ghana…and calls on government for increment.

30. B&FT (2014). 10 m Ghanaians now on mobile Internet. February 17. Online at: http://www.peacefmonline.com

31. Kavur, J. (2009). Mobile gap closes, but digital divide grows in South Africa. IT *World Canada*, September 19. Online at: http://www.itworldca.com

32. GIFEC, Study of the digital divide in Ghana.

33. Chabossou A., C. Stork, A. M. Stork, Z. Zahonogo (2009). Mobile telephony access and usage in Africa. Research ICT Africa. Online at: www.whiteafrican.com

34. Weinstein, J. (2011). MoTeCH's mobile apps bridging rural gaps for pregnant women.

35. Columbia University Mailman School of Public Health, Ghana Health Service, Grameen Foundation MoTeCH (2011). A comprehensive overview.

36. Awotwi, J. E., A. Ojo, and T. Janowski (2011). Mobile governance for development: Emerging strategies and possibilities in the Ghanaian context. Paper presented at the 5th International Conference on the Theory and Practice of e-Governance, ACM, September 26–28, Tallinn, Estonia.

37. *Ghana News Agency* (2014). Government develops 24/7 free call e-extension platform. February 27.

Chapter 4

China's Digital Divides and Their Countermeasures

Yuanfu Jian

Contents

4.1 Introduction

Information technology (IT) enables new national and social development, but at the same time it also leads to digital divides. It is a complex concept that goes beyond technology alone as it is also a social problem. Today, technical, content, and personal factors all contribute to digital divides.

Technical factors, such as infrastructure and information channels, are key reasons for China's current digital divide. Information infrastructure is necessary to provide a platform for access to information. However, even if it is in place, there also must be information channels in order to obtain information through data devices, such as mobile phones. Therefore, in technical terms, information channels and information infrastructure are interdependent and indispensable. In the information society, transmission channels primarily include the Internet, but also mobile networks, as well as radio and television devices. To take advantage of the information society, people must have the ability to afford them and also be capable of using them to obtain and make use of the information that they can provide. Those who cannot are at a disadvantage and become vulnerable to the digital divide.

Content is another key factor in China's digital divide and refers to access to, and use of, information. Even if people can afford access and have the necessary devices, they also need appropriate information. If information providers do not produce the requisite information, access is meaningless. The amount of relevant information available to people also affects the size of the digital divide. Historically, information producers were limited to government agencies and media outlets. However, in the information society, there are a lot of information producers, which now include citizens. In a traditional society, information regulations are also quite few as well. For instance, all dynasties in ancient China were practicing an obscurantism policy that the rulers "would rather make people to do, but keep the public from knowing what they are doing," and they implemented government administration by virtue of information asymmetry between government and the public. However, in the information society, although information regulation still exists, it is mainly for the considerations of national and public interests and for protecting the safe and smooth information environment. The availability of content is directly related to the digital divide, although it can be resolved if availability is improved.

Personal factors also play a significant role in the digital divide as information literacy—both awareness and skills—is key to utilizing available infrastructure and content. Whether one has the knowledge to obtain and use information is an important criterion in determining whether there is a digital divide or not. Those who have no idea or know very little about where to get information or how to make use of it, suffer from weak information awareness and poor information skills and, hence, suffer from a digital divide.

Based on the technical, content, and personal factors underlying the digital divide, this chapter will review China's situation in greater detail, whereby the conclusion will provide suggestions for overcoming current deficiencies.

4.2 The Status Quo of China's Digital Divide

Due to a lack of information infrastructure, the lack of information resource and funds, and the large gap in education, quality of life, and the disparity in wealth, China has a digital divide compared with other countries, especially developed ones.

However, after years of catching up, China is still behind developed countries, but has gained remarkable achievements in narrowing its technical digital divide with other countries. As of July 2013, the total number of telephone subscribers reached 1.457 billion and the total number of Internet broadband users were 183 million. Mobile phone subscriptions increased to 820 million with a penetration rate of 69.2 percent. The new 3G mobile phone users exceeded 100 million, with a penetration rate of 28.2 percent. The total mobile phone subscribers arrived at 1.185 billion, accounting for 81.3 percent[1] of the total number of telephone subscribers.

Despite the rapid growth of China's Internet users and an annual increase in Internet penetration, the overall level is still relatively low. On Jan. 15, 2013, China Internet Network Information Center (CNNIC) released the 31st Statistic Report on China's Internet Network Development[2] in Beijing. At the end of December 2012, the number of China's netizens (persons actively using the Internet) reached 564 million, which means that Internet penetration was 42.1% percent. This is higher than the global average; however, compared with more developed countries, such as the United States, Japan, and South Korea (where Internet penetration is over 74% percent), the gap is still large. If you add more indicators, such as national economy information technology investment, the number of Internet hosts per 10,000 people, education, and income levels, then the gap between China and the world would be more significantly obvious.

However, there is also another divide—that within China. The difference between urban and rural areas, between cities, and between government agencies themselves is particularly sharp.

4.2.1 The Digital Divide between Regions[3]

There is no evidence of a rapid reduction in China's domestic digital divide; to the contrary, it appears to deepen and widen in certain areas, especially between regions. China's level of IT development is relatively strong in its eastern regions, but weakens in the central, and even more so in its western areas. For example, according to statistics[4] on the level of IT development, no western province or municipality is in the top five, but the last four are all in the west. Digital utilization, the level of

IT application for public and private usage, is relatively high in the eastern coastal cities, but lower in the central and western regions.

Statistical data illustrates the regional discrepancy. Out of China's 1.457 billion subscribers (272.219 million fixed line and 1185.229 million mobile), the eastern region accounted for 54 percent of fixed-line subscriptions (147.752 million), and 50 percent of mobile (595.482 million) as of July 2013. In comparison, the central region had 67.788 million fixed line subscribers (accounting for 24.9 percent) and the western region 56.679 million (20.82 percent). The number of mobile phone subscribers in the central region was 303.751 million (25.62 percent) and 285.96 million (24.12 percent) in the western region.[5]

Whether measured in fixed line or mobile telephone penetration, then this illustrates the divide between the eastern and western regions. As of June 2013, the overall telephone penetration rate in China reached 107.3 per 100 people, of which fixed line penetration was 20.2 and the mobile phone was 87.1 per 100 people. However, out of the six provinces and cities nationwide where mobile phone penetration has exceeded 100 per 100 people, all are in the eastern region except for the Inner Mongolia province.[6]

The same trend is reflected in the Internet penetration level. According to the statistics by CNNIC, a nonprofit organization, at the end of December 2012, there were eight provinces and cities where more than half of residents were Internet users. Of them, the Internet penetration rates in Beijing and Shanghai have reached about 70 percent, which is the same level as many developed countries in North America, Western Europe, as well as Japan and South Korea. The Internet penetration rate in Guangdong Province, Fujian Province, Zhejiang Province, and Tianjin is around 60 percent, and Liaoning Province and Jiangsu Province reached 50 percent in 2012, which is about the same as two other emerging market countries,[7] namely Russia and Brazil. Meanwhile, the Internet penetration rate is between 40 and 50 percent in central regions, such as Shanxi Province, Hebei Province, Shaanxi Province, Hubei Province, and Chongqing. The Internet penetration rate of Inner Mongolia Province, Jilin Province, Heilongjiang Province, Guangxi Province, Hunan Province, Tibet, Sichuan Province, Anhui Province, Gansu Province, Henan Province, Guizhou Province, Yunnan Province, and Jiangxi Province is less than 40 percent, of which, seven provinces are in the west and four provinces are in central China, further illustrating the gap between the eastern and western regions.

If the digital divide between regions is measured in terms of websites and the number of domain names, then the gap is even more pronounced. At the end of December 2012, according to CNNIC, the total number of domain names in China was 13.41 million. Out of those, 75.8 percent (or 10,152,164) were attributed to Zhejiang Province, Guangdong Province, Beijing, Shanghai, Fujian Province, Jiangsu Province, and Shandong Province, which are all in the east. Meanwhile, the last seven provinces were Inner Mongolia Province, Guizhou Province, Xinjiang Province, Gansu Province, Ningxia Province, Qinghai Province, and Tibet, which are all in the west, and accounted for only 1.1 percent (160,268) of all domain

Rank	Province	Number of Domain Names	Percentage of the Entire Country
1	Zhejiang	3,429,977	25.6
2	Guangdong	2,815,805	21.0
3	Beijing	1,255,887	9.4
4	Shanghai	843,503	6.3
5	Fujian	815,661	6.1
6	Jiangsu	522,351	3.9
7	Shandong	468,980	3.5

Figure 4.1 **The number of domain names in the top seven provinces (all in the east).**

Ranking	Province	Number of Domain Names	Percentage of Entire Country
1	Tibet	4,798	0.0
2	Qinghai	12,396	0.1
3	Ningxia	14,577	0.1
4	Gansu	23,794	0.2
5	Xinjiang	32,447	0.2
6	Guizhou	33,002	0.2
7	Inner Mongolia	39,254	0.3

Figure 4.2 **The number of domain names in the last seven provinces (all in the west).**

names in the country. This tremendous gap between different regions is reflected in Figures 4.1 and 4.2.

4.2.2 Digital Divide between Cities

Beyond a regional divide, there is also a digital divide between cities. The reasons for this phenomenon are the different levels of the urban economic development and the different administrative levels of different cities, and the income difference between urban residents. The difference resulting from an economic development level leads to the consequence of more government investment in e-government in economically developed cities and rapid growth in e-government, for instance, in Shanghai, Beijing, and Guangzhou, which are located in the eastern region, while, in Xining, Lhasa, and Lanzhou, the capitals of the western provinces, the development and input in e-government is lagging far behind. The difference resulting from the administrative levels of different cities leads to the digital divide among Shenzhen city, Zhuhai city, Zhaoqing city, and Meizhou city, although they are in the same province, and many other provinces are facing the same problems, such as Suzhou city and Xuzhou city in Jiangsu Province.

According to the statistical data released by ZDC[8] in 2013, it demonstrated that, in different administrative level cities, the number of computers owned by the users is significantly higher in municipalities. Twenty percent of the households in municipalities possess more than three PCs, while in the provincial capitals, prefecture-level cities, county-level cities, and towns, the figures were 18.4 percent, 12.1 percent, 11.9 percent and 7.4 percent,[9] respectively, which indirectly shows that the digital divide problem appeared in different cities as well.

4.2.3 The Digital Divide between Urban and Rural Areas

As in most countries, there is a tremendous digital divide between urban and rural areas in China. The inadequacy of investment and construction to rural information and communication infrastructures leads to enormous differences between public services provided by e-government to urban and rural residents. The gap in the level of Internet development is quite large. The rapid rise in the number of Internet users, for instance, is mainly attributed to cities. According to CNNIC, by the end of 2012, the Internet penetration rate in cities had reached 60 percent, but only 23.7 percent in rural areas. As of the end of December 2012, the rural population accounted for 27.6 percent of China's netizens, reaching 156 million and with a slight increase compared to 2011.[10] This has a practical impact as, for example, a considerable number of farmers suffer from the digital divide, becoming the "Digital Poverty" population of the digital society.

The basic reasons leading to a digital divide between urban and rural areas are gaps in income and educational levels. For example, in terms of information infrastructure, the lack of Internet access and the low computer penetration rate reduces the proportion of rural access to the Internet. Although, China's telecommunication industry had made rapid progress since the 1990s, it is not a balanced development and the fixed telephone penetration rate in rural areas is far lower than in cities. As of July 2013, according to the Chinese Ministry of Industry and Information Technology, the total number of fixed telephone lines in China reached 272.219 million, of which 68.67 percent (186.944 million) served urban areas, while rural areas accounted for only 31.33 percent (85.275 million). At the same time, the total number of Internet broadband users in China were 183 million, of which rural areas accounted for only 25.1 percent (45.766 million).[11] China is currently actively promoting "fiber to the home" (FTTH) connections and the number of subscribers were 31.595 million, and with a proportion of all broadband users increasing to 17.3 percent. FTTH is currently mainly carried out in cities, which also results in a widening of the digital divide between urban and rural areas.

Although the number of China's mobile communication users are in rapid expansion, it is concentrated to urban areas. A market survey conducted by the Telecommunications Research Institute of the Ministry of Industry and Information Technology showed that by the end of 2012, China's mobile phone penetration rate in urban areas was 104.2 percent, while in the rural area it was only 39.2 percent.[12] Take the main Internet access terminal equipment, computers, as an example, according to the survey data publicized by the National Bureau of Statistics in the end of 2008, the number of home computers owned by rural families was 5.4 units per 100 households, far below the 59.3 units per 100 households in cities and towns, and an even greater gap with the eastern cities. According to the sample survey data by Guangdong Survey Team of the National Bureau of Statistics, it demonstrated that, by the end of 2009, the number of home computers owned by Guangdong city and town residents was 91.54 units per 100 households, of which, 69.54 units had access to the Internet. Although the environment of Internet utilization in rural areas has been improved, there is still a considerable gap between rural and urban areas.

4.2.4 The Digital Divide between Government Agencies

The swift development of information technology also has led to China's rapid progress in e-government, which greatly improves public sector efficiency. Since 1999, China has improved its government IT infrastructure very quickly and its ranking in the UN e-government development index increased over 10 years. However, since 2008, due to a lack of information sharing and cooperation among government departments, China's ranking in the UN index has dropped.

Moreover, in the past two decades, China's e-government development has mainly focused on central ministries, and provincial and municipal governments, but (as in many countries) is lagging at the local level. Further, the development in this area attaches greater importance to construction than application, and pays more attention to hardware than software and places greater emphasis on investment than integration. As a result, China's e-government development has resulted in a digital divide between government agencies.

4.2.5 The Digital Divide between Individuals

There is a digital divide between individuals in terms of their digital skills, especially the difference in capabilities in regards to IT applications, stemming from various education levels. Uneven digital skills is a digital divide problem that further deepens the divide for vulnerable groups. In addition, occupation, income, and age factors lead to further divides in terms of the use of digital services.

CNNIC also analyzes the attributes of China's netizens, from a gender, age, education, occupation, and income perspective. At the end of December 2012, the ratio of male to female in China's netizens was 55.8 to 44.2. From an age point of view, China's main netizens are still young, with 68 percent at the age of 20 to 49, of which the netizens between the age of 20 and 29 accounts for 30.4 percent, and 25.3 percent between the age of 30 and 39. From an educational perspective, the majority of netizens have an high school education or above (accounting for 53.4 percent of the total), of which, high school, technical secondary school, and polytechnic school accounts for 32.3 percent, while 9.8 percent have a college degree and 11.3 percent a graduate degree. Students represent the largest group of netizens, accounting for 25.1 percent, followed by the self-employed and freelancers, at 18.1 percent. In the enterprises, managerial staff accounts for 3.1 percent of overall netizens in China and staff accounts for 10.1 percent. In the party and government organizations and institutions, the leading cadres and the staff account for 0.5 percent and 4.2 percent, respectively. In addition, the professional and technical personnel account for 8.1 percent. In regards to income, people whose monthly income is over ¥3000 (about US$500) account for 28.8 percent of netizens.

These numbers all illustrate that in China, as elsewhere, there are multiple digital divides, including between young and old, high and low educational groups, as well as between high and low income groups.

4.3 Conclusion: Countermeasures to China's Digital Divides

Domestic scholars have conducted in-depth discussions on the countermeasures to resolve the information gap; however, these measures are mostly in generalities with not much operability. Instead, China should start from the following aspects to bridge its digital divides.

4.3.1 Enhance the Level of National Information Technology

According to the Global Information Technology Report by the World Economic Forum, China was no. 37 in 2010, but decreased to 51 in 2011, and 58 in 2012, indicating a widening gap with developed countries. Although the 2012 statistical bulletin of the electronic information industry showed that China was above its size with sales volume of ¥8504.4 billion, representing 12.6 percent of the year-on-year growth. This includes 1.18 billion units of products, such as mobile phones (350 million units), computers (130 million units), color TVs (82.31 million units), and integrated circuits with 4.3 percent, 10.5 percent, 4.8 percent, and 14.4 percent year-on-year growth, respectively. The shipment of mobile phone, computer, and color TV also accounted for over 50 percent of total global exports, making China the largest producer in the world.[13] However, its IT industry is "big, but not strong" and lacks core technology, which leads to an insufficiency of fundamental capabilities to promote the entire nation's information technology.

Therefore, China should enhance its IT research and development to drive industrialization. During the 12th Five Year Plan period from 2011 to 2015, China should shift its IT industry from scale toward an innovation-driven era. In this effort, it should promote the integration of advantageous resources, break through a batch of key technologies, improve relevant institutional mechanisms, create an atmosphere conducive to independent innovation, support enterprises with innovative capability, and encourage key enterprises to master the key core technologies including cloud computing and the "Internet of Things," thereby improving the overall level of national information technology and provide basic conditions for shrinking the digital divide.

4.3.2 Narrow the Information Infrastructure Gap between the West and the East, and between the Urban and Rural Areas

A key digital divide issue lies in the gap between information infrastructure and performance, in particular, the lack of access to telecommunication facilities, such as the Internet in the central and western regions as well as in rural areas.

Thus, institutional policies should focus on the central and western regions where the information technology is lagging behind. Specifically, the government needs to provide more preferential policies and support for the central and western regions as well as the vast rural areas in terms of increased investment into its information channels and information infrastructure and narrowing the gap in telecommunication infrastructure between the east and the west as well as between urban and rural areas, thereby shrinking the digital divide within the country.

4.3.3 Increase Education and Improve the Public Information Literacy

Personal factors, such as physiological, occupational, family, income, and educational, all affect China's digital divide. Therefore, the government should take the necessary actions to improve public information literacy for all.

In bridging the digital divide, education must be first to improve knowledge and skills. Therefore, China should invest in the universal education of information technology and develop a multilevel and interactive network educational training system. In this effort, it should educate the public in general, but also provide education and training opportunity for the vulnerable groups to enable people to have more opportunities and choices. In particular, the advance of modern distance education enabled by IT can bring high-quality educational resources and scientific knowledge to rural areas to improve their education quality, thus enhancing information literacy and make them master the fundamental skills of information technology utilization, and to provide intelligent support for narrowing the digital divide.

4.3.4 Reduce Telecommunications Charges

The official release of China's 3G license[14] in 2009 led operators, such as China Telecom, China Mobile, and China Unicom, to decrease their charges, including data services. Yet, many user—and potential users—still find telecommunication charges too high, including many low-income people. At present, the main reason is that telecommunications, radio/television, and computer networks are operated independently in China, and their investment in information infrastructure construction are completely separate, which leads to higher operating costs. This results in higher charges to subscribers and decreases utilization, leading to continuously increasing operation cost and shrinking the number of users. It also results in the tardy development of China's telecommunication facility manufacturing industry and affects the Internet and e-businesses.

Therefore, China should integrate telecommunications by actively advancing the integration of the three networks, decreasing telecommunication operating costs, lowering the charges for communication (such as the Internet), and promote the healthy development of the telecommunication industry. In the fields of information channel and information infrastructure, the government may build a public–private partnership with telecommunication operators, including China Mobile, China Unicom, and China Telecom, and work together to make improvements in information channel improvement and information infrastructure provision, and use subsidies to lower the standard of telecommunication charges for central and western region users, thereby narrowing the national digital divide.

4.3.5 Vigorously Push the Government Information Publicity

The Regulation of the People's Republic of China on the Disclosure of Government Information officially began on May 1, 2008. Since then, the government has made great progress in information disclosure. However, local governments have made or modified the Local Regulation on Disclosure of Government Information, and there are a few remaining problems as the information disclosure of government departments of all levels show that it cannot be resolved by law alone and also needs the safeguard of relevant measures.

Therefore, government departments should implement the initial consultation system and include the government information disclosure work into the important schedule. This entails regularly listening to the briefing, timely solving of the problems encountered during work, and providing effective safeguards in human resources, financial, and material aspects. By implementing the accountability system in government information disclosure, the government should link the effectiveness of information disclosure with the political achievements of government staff, so as to encourage the public functionaries to actively and initiatively disclose government information, establish the concept of initiative disclosure that turn "let me disclose" into "I should disclose," and provide strong and powerful information resources for solving the digital divide problem.

4.3.6 Energetically Advance e-Government

China's 20-year e-government development has made certain achievements and effectively improved the working efficiency and the level of disclosure in all levels of governments; however, it still has a long way to go. China needs to vigorously continue its e-government development in order to break down digital divides between departments, realize the interdepartmental integration of business, information, and service, as well as form an interdepartmental network collaborative office environment, and reengineer the business process for government.

Thanks to the Internet, e-government has become the most convenient and efficient way to disclose governmental affairs and, without a doubt, it is the most direct resource for people to understand government and access information. At of the end of 2009, China had more than 45,000 government portals, including 75 central and national agencies, 32 provincial governments, and 333 prefecture-level city governments. More than 80 percent of county governments also had established websites, providing all types of online public services.[15] China should vigorously continue to advance e-government in order to propel information sharing and exchange between different government agencies, and allow citizens timely and effective access to relevant information of government agencies. It also will help people's understanding of the government's work and may provide important support for solving the digital divide.

4.3.7 Enhance the Public Service for Information Vulnerable Groups

China should provide high-quality public service for the public, especially for information vulnerable groups, and the most important is to improve the personal information literacy of information-vulnerable groups. Therefore, the government needs to strengthen the dissemination and training for the public in information awareness and information skills, and make efforts to enhance the information literacy of information-vulnerable groups by information technology dissemination and education.

In addition, the government should play the role of existing information literacy channels, such as the function of information assistant and the university student village official in the new rural construction. Firstly, the government may conduct training in information awareness and information skills for the rural information assistants and improve their information awareness and information skills. Secondly, the government should let them train the vast number of farmers for the sake of improving their information awareness and information skills. In some provinces of western China, due to the complex geographical environment and ethnic factors, there exist some information technology blind spots. To eliminate these, the government should rely primarily on the rural information assistants. In addition, because most of the university student village officials have received high education with higher information literacy, the government should play their roles, for instance, under the aid of the village committee. It could open the course for the villagers on information technology and let the university student village officials teach them, so as to enhance the information literacy of the public in rural areas. This would teach them on how to use modern information infrastructure and how to use this to obtain and make use of government information, thus, to enhance the information awareness and information capabilities of the information vulnerable groups, and make efforts to alleviate the digital divide.

References

1. Chinese Ministry of Industry and Information Technology. Online at: http://www.miit.gov.cn/n11293472/n11293832/n11294132/n12858447/15610697.html
2. China Internet Network Information Center (CNNIC) (2013a). Statistic report on China's Internet network development. Online at: http://www.isc.org.cn/download/fz0726.pdf
3. According to the difference of geographical locations and the level of economic development, China is divided into three regions, the eastern region includes 11 provinces and municipalities: Beijing, Tianjin, Hebei province, Liaoning province, Shanghai, Jiangsu province, Zhejiang province, Fujian province, Shandong province, Guangdong province, and Hainan province. The central region includes eight provinces: Shanxi province, Jilin province, Heilongjiang province, Anhui province, Jiangxi province, Henan province, Hubei province, and Hunan province. The western region includes 12 provinces, autonomous regions, and municipalities: Inner Mongolia, Guangxi province, Chongqing, Sichuan province, Guizhou province, Yunnan province, Tibet, Shaanxi province, Gansu province, Qinghai province, Ningxia province, and Xinjiang province.
4. Yang, J., and X. Youda (2009). Research on IDI of China in 2009. *Journal of BUPT* (Social Sciences edition) 11 (6), December.
5. Chinese Ministry of Industry and Information Technology: http://www.miit.gov.cn/n11293472/n11293832/n11294132/n12858447/15594387.html
6. Chinese Ministry of Industry and Information Technology: http://www.miit.gov.cn/n11293472/n11293832/n11294132/n12858462/15523389.html

7. China Internet Network Information Center (CNNIC) (2013b). "31st Statistic Report on China's Internet Network"
8. ZDC is a survey center based at ZOL (http://www.zol.com.cn). ZOL is a professional IT website with the most commercial value in Greater China, providing domestic computer DIY knowledge, hardware, offers information, shopping guide information and e-commerce service as the business cores.
9. See details in the 2013 China's Home Computer Utilization Report launched by ZDC survey center.
10. There is little change in China's urban and rural netizens' structure, which relates to the rapid advancement of China's urbanization process. In 2011, the scale of China's urban resident population exceeded the rural resident population for the first time, with the urbanization rate breaking through 50 percent, in which the urban resident population increased to 690.79 million and the rural resident population decreased to 656.56 million but with no significant improvement in the proportion of rural netizens.
11. Chinese Ministry of Industry and Information Technology (MIIT): http://www.miit.gov.cn/n11293472/n11293832/n11294132/n12858447/15610697.html
12. China Academy of Telecommunication Research of MIIT: http://www.catr.cn/kxyj/catrgd/201304/t20130422_918783.html
13. Chinese Ministry of Industry and Information Technology (MIIT): http://www.miit.gov.cn/n11293472/n11293832/n11294132/n12858387/15173031.html
14. On January 7, 2009, Chinese Ministry of Industry and Information Technology announced the approval of China Mobile's 3rd generation mobile communication business license based on TD-SCDMA technical standard, China Telecom's 3rd generation business license based on CDMA2000 technical standard, and China Unicom's 3rd generation business license based on WCDMA technical standard.
15. Press Office of China's State Council (2010). "White Paper of Chinese Internet," June 2010: http://news.cntv.cn/special/baipishu/shouye/index.shtml

Chapter 5

Spatial and Social Aspects of the Digital Divide in Russia

Tatiana Ershova, Yuri Hohlov,
and Sergei Shaposhnik

Contents

5.1 Introduction

In Russia, as elsewhere, information and communication technology (ICT) development and usage progress inconsistently in different regions and among social strata. The information society resulted in a new kind of geographical and social polarization—digital divide—and has become a factor of separation between regions and marginalization of certain community groups. These distinctions are more conspicuous than in the European Union (EU) and other developed economies. For example, computer and Internet use by young people in Russia is practically the same as that in the EU, but among senior age groups (55+) there is more than a twofold gap in the percentage of ICT users between the EU and Russia. A similar picture can be seen in what refers to geographical differentiation of information society development, in terms of key ICT use indicators because differences between Russian regions, cities, and rural settlements are considerably higher than in European countries, and can exceed differences between developed European countries and developing ones. Russian regions that have poorly developed ICT infrastructure and low ICT use are falling behind in a quickly developing system of information, economic, and social relations.

To analyze the digital divide level of different social groups of the Russian population, we used results of representative opinion polls held by the Institute of the Information Society (IIS) in autumn 2008, and in April and May 2012, with authors of this chapter managing and participating in the survey.[1] The noncommercial organization, All-Russian Nongovernment Public Opinion Fund (www.fom.ru), conducted the field studies on behalf of IIS. A similar methodology was employed including questionnaires developed on the basis of reference questionnaires of OECD (Organization for Economic Cooperation and Development) and Eurostat (a statistical office of the EU) in order to conduct ICT use surveys of population and households. Other data include preliminary results of the federal statistical monitoring of ICT use by individuals that was first held in 2013, by Rosstat, the Russian Federal State Statistics Service, using statistical monitoring form that coordinated with Eurostat reference questionnaires. Data from Eurostat database were used for international comparisons.

To illustrate the particular spatial and social aspects behind the digital divide in the country and to delve deeper into the reasons for Russia's current position, the chapter uses data from the Russian Regions e-Readiness Index, published by the IIS. For context, this chapter first compares the extent of the digital divide in Russia with the EU and finds that, although it is on par with some countries, it lags the northern European leaders by a significant amount in certain areas. In conclusion, the chapter provides an overview of current policies to help close these gaps.

5.2 Comparing the Digital Divide in Russia with the EU

In 2012, the IIS conducted research on behalf of the Microsoft Corporation to find out the impact of ICT competences on development. Based on the data of this research, an analytical report was prepared disclosing, among other things, computer and Internet use by individuals in Russia, including residential Internet use, and illustrating the tendency of Russia to catch up with other countries and continue to bridge these digital divide gaps.[2] The results from a survey carried out in April and May 2012 was compared to the EU population opinion poll held in autumn of 2011.

One of the most important conclusions of the research is that the number of computer and Internet users in Russia is growing mostly due to residential use, with use intensity increasing. Demand of the Russian population for acquiring (developing) ICT skills is quite high (18 percent of the population claimed the need to improve their skills, though this is only half as much as in EU member states). In addition to the desire to enhance work skills, the main reasons for ICT training were extending communication opportunities and obtaining information and services required in everyday life. Enhancing people's motivation to use computers and the Internet, therefore, is undoubtedly one of the most important factors for overcoming the digital divide in Russia.

The percentage of Russia's population that had been using computers for a year before the survey amounted to 65 percent (Figure 5.1). This coincides with a similar

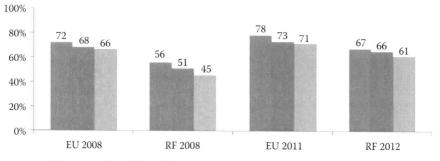

Figure 5.1 Percentages of population that used computers in the Russian Federation (2008 and 2012) and EU member states (2008 and 2011).

EU indicator in 2007 and corresponds to the levels of Poland and Lithuania in 2011 (67 percent and 65 percent, respectively), while exceeding a number of countries in eastern and southern Europe, such as Italy (57 percent). However, it is considerably lower than the numbers for the northern European countries (where indicator values exceeded 90 percent). Overall, the gap between Russia and EU member states has declined compared with 2008 levels. For example, in the past five years, there has been a difference of 5 to 7 percentage points between the EU population that have ever used computers and those that have been using computers during the past three months. In Russia, this gap has declined from 11 to 6 percentage points since 2008 and now matches the European level.

Growth of computer use intensity in the Russian Federation is confirmed by the data of computer use frequency. In 2008, only 68 percent of users used computers daily (or almost every day), but in 2012 this figure reached 82 percent.

The situation with Internet use is similar. At the end of April 2012, the number of people who had accessed to the Internet in Russia comprised 60 percent of the population aged 16–74, which approximately corresponds to the level of Poland in 2011 (62 percent). However, this is somewhat lower than the EU average in 2008 (64 percent) and considerably lower than that of the northern European countries in 2011, such as Norway (93 percent) and Iceland (95 percent).

Growth of Internet use intensity in Russia is illustrated by Internet use frequency between 2008 and 2012. Among those who use the Internet, 81 percent now do it daily, whereas in 2008 their share was only 59 percent.

Though the Russian level of using computers and the Internet is 10–12 percentage points lower than the average European level, this gap is declining as Internet usage is an aspect in which Russia has developed quickly. Since 2008, the gap with the EU has been cut in half. Today, 58 percent of the Russian population aged 16–74 use a computer at least once a week, while in Europe this value is 69 percent; the Internet is used by 56 percent of the Russian population and 68 percent of those in EU. Hence, Russia is in line with average European levels of 2008 and surpass current indicators of the entire range of countries in eastern and central Europe.

Younger populations (including students) are most active in using ICT, while unemployed and retired people are the least active groups of users. Computer and Internet use by Russian youth has approached the average European levels. At the same time, a considerable gap remains among elderly groups. While the percentage of Russian youth aged 16–24 that use a computer daily amounts to 87 percent (92 percent in EU), the percentage of the elderly people aged 55–74 is only 18 percent in Russia (42 percent in EU). The "age divide" in Russia, therefore, remains unacceptably high and concerning, as illustrated in Figure 5.2.

An ICT use gap also is observed in population groups having different educational levels as education is correlated with higher numbers of computer and Internet users. The education and age correlations with usage apply in both the Russian Federation and EU, but is more prominent in Russia.

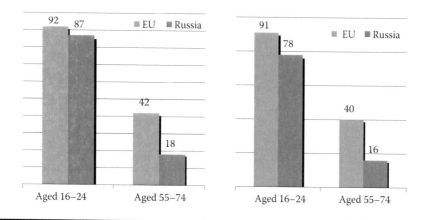

Figure 5.2   Percentage of computer and Internet use on a regular basis (at least once a week) in different age groups of the Russian and EU population.

Another indicator of ICT development is Internet access from mobile devices. In 2012, the percentage of the Russian population that accessed the Internet using mobile phones or smartphones based on 3G and higher standards was 5 percent, whereas that of those using portable computers (laptops, netbooks, or tablet PCs) with enabled wireless access (3G and higher modem, WiFi, or WiMAX public networks) was 12 percent. In 2010, such indicators are at comparable levels in the EU member states where they equal 4 percent and 19 percent, respectively. Of particular note is also that access to the Internet using second-generation (2G) cellular communications are quite high in Russia (19 percent of the population).

Based on the survey results, a set of actions and operations the respondents have performed using computers and the Internet were analyzed. Percentages of computer and Internet users in Russia and the EU who performed different operations are provided in Figures 5.3 and 5.4.

In comparison to the EU, the operations performed by a much lower percentage of computer and Internet users in Russia included using copy/paste tools for duplicating or moving information, moving files between a computer and other devices, using main arithmetic formulae in spreadsheets, and creating presentations and modifying software configuration parameters. Conversely, as compared to EU users, Russian users more frequently updated operating systems and developed software products using specialized programming languages as shown in Figure 5.3.

Fewer Russians than Europeans send e-mails with attached files, use search engines, and modify web browser security settings. On the other hand, Russian users outpaced EU users in such ICT skills as uploading texts, games, images, films or music; chatting, messaging in forums or social networks; sharing films, music etc. (Figure 5.4). The explanation is evident: Most operations Russian citizens perform are often related to using social media, the domain where Russia is leading

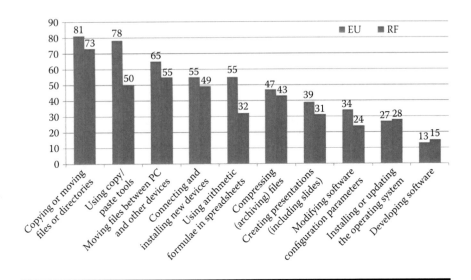

Figure 5.3 **Actions and operations computer users have ever performed in EU member states (2011) and the Russian Federation (2012); percentage of total users.**

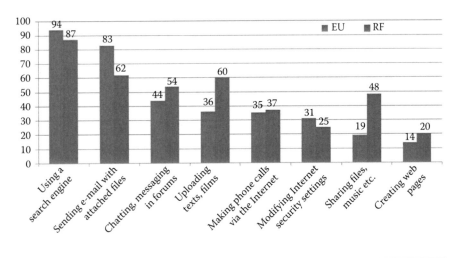

Figure 5.4 **Actions and operations Internet users have ever performed in EU member states (2011) and the Russian Federation (2012); percentage of total users.**

in (see below), socializing and entertaining; ways of Internet use that have been traditionally preferred in Russia.

According to the research, the entire range of Internet use by the Russian population has increased considerably compared with 2008, but it still lags behind EU member states in most areas, as indicated in Figure 5.5. Comparable indicators (with differences less than 10 percentage points) are observed only in using VoIP

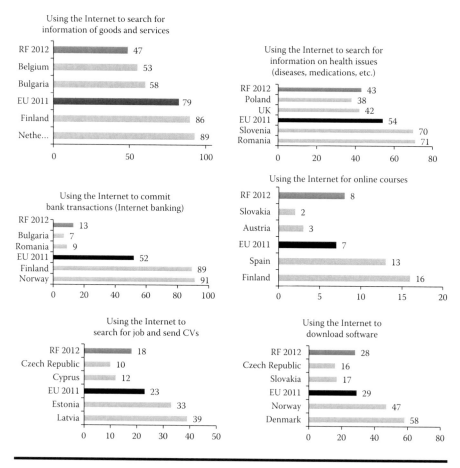

Figure 5.5 Percentage of users (three months' audience) in the Russian Federation (2012) and EU (countries with the best and worst indicators in 2011) that used the Internet for different purposes.

(voice over Internet protocol), downloading software, using online courses and searching for a new job, or sending a curriculum vitae (CV).

It's worth mentioning that Russian users lag behind in using Internet banking. Only 8 percent of the population (13 percent of the three months' Internet user audience) use the Internet to perform banking transactions, while the percentage of EU users is six times higher. At the same time, the smallest gaps in Internet use are demonstrated by such groups of the Russian population as people aged 16–24, students, and people with higher education.

The exception is social networking, where Russia considerably outperforms EU member states (even countries with the best indicators) as 81 percent of the three months' Internet audience in Russia use social networks, about 30 percent above the average EU level as shown in Figure 5.6.

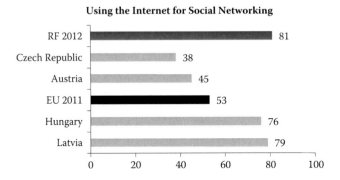

Using the Internet for Social Networking

RF 2012 — 81
Czech Republic — 38
Austria — 45
EU 2011 — 53
Hungary — 76
Latvia — 79

Figure 5.6 Social networking in the Russian Federation (2012) and EU (countries with the best and worst indicators in 2011); percentage of three months' Internet audience.

One of the top priorities of information society development in Russia is enhancing e-government. In this area, the situation in Russia differs considerably from Europe: only 10 percent of the Russian population received information of public and municipal services via the Internet, which is at least three times less than in the EU; 8 percent of the population downloaded forms of applications and other documents (in EU, 25 percent); only 5 percent (in EU, 21 percent) submitted filled-in documents electronically; and only 4 percent of the Russian population was provided public and municipal services electronically (by e-mail or via user account).

In response to the suggestion that all known ways of applying to the authorities would be available to the population, respondents chose the most convenient methods from their point of view (not more than two methods). The range of answers to this question is illustrated in Figure 5.7. According to Russian users, the most convenient method is Internet access from the computer.

When asked about the reasons for failure to use e-government services, 7 percent of the Internet users said that they had not submitted online forms to public and municipal authorities via websites because of a lack of skills and knowledge in how to use them, or because such operations turned out to be too complicated. Lack of knowledge as a barrier that hampers use of e-government services is confirmed by the data of the 2011 Public Opinion Fund surveys,[3] according to which this is one of the main obstacles in obtaining the services.

However, demand for these services in Russia is quite high: 42 percent of adults consider the Internet to be one of the most convenient methods of applying to authorities, while more than half of young people, if they had such an opportunity, would prefer to interact with the authorities via the Internet.

A special area of concern is a lack of ICT competences in the elderly age groups, which is a barrier in their using e-government services and further contributes to the digital divide between generations. These groups face higher need to interact

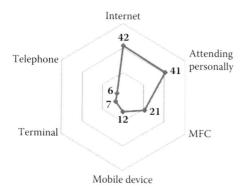

Figure 5.7 The way the Russian population prefers applying to public and municipal authorities in 2012; percentage. (From MFC—multifunctional center for delivery public and municipal services.[4])

with authorities and social services, while their level of ICT use is considerably lower as compared to that of young people.

5.3 Spatial Polarization of the Information Society in Russia: Measurement and Its Origins

Measurement of the digital divide in the Russian regions that are understood as differences of the constituent entities of the Russian Federation (called "federation subjects" here) by level of telecommunication infrastructure access and ICT use in different fields of activities, as well as analysis of factors contributing to appearance of this gap, is both of scientific and practical interest. With the Strategy of Information Society Development in the Russian Federation adopted in 2008, the task of reducing the e-development gap of Russian regions became a political objective. One of the Strategy's targets is "double reduction of differences between federation subjects in integral indicators of e-development by 2015."

This section provides results of measuring the digital divide of the Russian regions and, based on statistical methods, analyzes social and economic factors of spatial polarization of information society development.

The research is based on indicators and composite indices calculated for annual reviews of the Russian Regions e-Readiness Index (the first index was published in 2005).[5] This composite index is built on over 70 indicators that characterize social and economic development of the region and level of ICT use in different sectors. To calculate the index and its components, the indicators are normalized and, consequently, aggregated for different factors and areas of ICT use. The Russian Regions e-Readiness Index is built on indicators that characterize three key factors of e-development (human capital, economic environment, and ICT infrastructure)

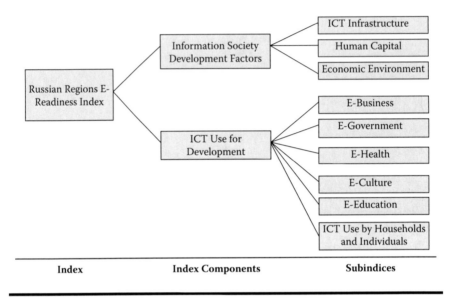

Figure 5.8 Structure of the e-Readiness Index.

and indicators of ICT access and use in six areas: business (e-business), public administration (e-government), public health, culture, education, and ICT use by households and individuals, as shown in Figure 5.8.

Each of the six areas (subindices) consist of a set of indicators that are grouped. As an example, Figure 5.9 shows the structure of the e-business subindex that was determined based on 16 indicators.

5.3.1 Measuring Digital Divide of the Regions

By the time the Strategy and the State Initiative intended to implement the strategy were adopted, the only integral indicator (composite index) of e-development in Russia that was regularly published was the Russian Regions e-Readiness Index, but its methodology did not measure the digital divide.

To resolve this issue, in 2010, a new index methodology was developed.[6] Now, normalization is performed in comparison with the "reference" normalization value: normalized value of the regional indicator Nx = Rx/Rn, where Rx is the indicator value for region x, while Rn is normalizing the "reference" value. To assess indicators whose value increase has negative character (e.g., "percentage of household spending on food"), another formula was used: normalized value (estimate) of the region indicator Nx = Rn/Rx.

Thus, if the region has a reference indicator value, its evaluation for this indicator is equal to 1, while if the value is less than the reference one, then its normalized value varies from 0 up to 1, and the figure of its normalized value allows to determine to what extent the region lags behind the reference value. As for the

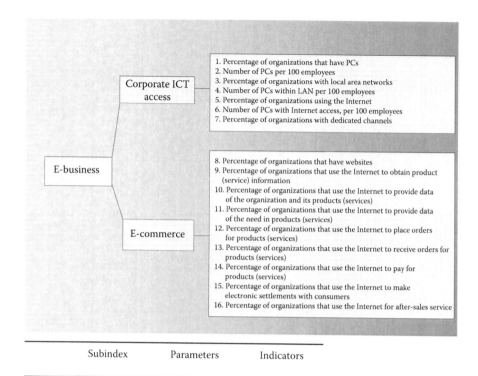

Figure 5.9   e-Business subindex structure.

percentage-based indicators, which constitute the majority of indicators, the maximum value of the index (100 percent) was taken as a reference. The digital divide between constituent entities of the Russian Federation considering individual and integral indicators is calculated by dividing values of indicators of these regions by each other (to determine how many times one value is greater than the other one), while digital divide is determined by dividing the maximum indicator value across Russia into the minimum one.

The gap was measured for each of the integral indicators. Figure 5.10 provides maximum and minimum values of integral indicators of information society development in the Russian regions, and gaps between them, according to the data of 2009–2011.

The data provided in the table show that the gap exceeds targets specified in the Strategy (two times) for all integral indicators. At the same time, most indicators tend to gradually reduce the gap; some e-development areas show growth of maximum gaps of integral indicators or differently directed movement: e-Culture, Human Capital (continuous growth), e-Education, ICT Use by Households, and Individuals (overall growth of the gap during four years, but gap reduction in the last year). The most troubled area of e-development, both in terms of overall ICT use and differences in informatization levels, is culture (libraries and museums).

Integral Indicator	Max and Min Index 2008– 2009	Max and Min Index 2009– 2010	Max and Min Index 2010– 2011	Max and Min Index 2011– 2012	Gap, 2008– 2009	Gap, 2009– 2010	Gap, 2010– 2011	Gap, 2011– 2012
Russian Regions E-Readiness Index	0.617 0.190	0.627 0.220	0.683 0.244	0.696 0.274	3.25	2.84	2.80	2.54
Information society development factors	0.749 0.199	0.724 0.210	0.755 0.230	0.786 0.224	3.77	3.44	3.28	3.52
Human capital	0.855 0.084	0.871 0.078	0.976 0.077	0.941 0.054	10.15	11.21	12.6	17.31
ICT infrastructure	0.645 0.104	0.618 0.108	0.606 0.151	0.654 0.189	6.23	5.75	4.01	3.45
Economic environment	0.856 0.329	0.840 0.323	0.856 0.347	0.828 0.357	2.6	2.6	2.46	2.32
ICT use for development	0.551 0.185	0.578 0.226	0.612 0.254	0.651 0.293	2.97	2.56	2.40	2.22
E-Government	0.593 0.174	0.630 0.162	0.704 0.279	0.713 0.317	3.42	3.89	2.52	2.25
E-Health	0.519 0.143	0.531 0.140	0.537 0.162	0.563 0.171	3.64	3.79	3.32	3.29
E-Education	0.582 0.224	0.591 0.266	0.637 0.159	0.692 0.205	2.59	2.22	4.01	3.38
E-Culture	0.476 0.024	0.503 0.053	0.608 0.027	0.649 0.027	20.17	21.96	22.52	24.04
E-Business	0.569 0.178	0.587 0.210	0.624 0.209	0.619 0.232	3.19	2.8	2.99	2.67
ICT use by households and individuals	0.745 0.324	0.734 0.331	0.791 0.313	0.817 0.334	2.30	2.22	2.53	2.45

Figure 5.10   Maximum difference in integral indicators of the informational development between constituent entities of the Russian Federation.

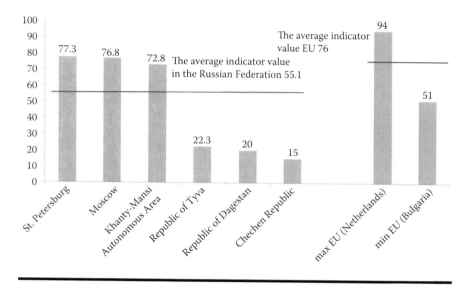

Figure 5.11 **Percentage of households with Internet in Russia and EU member states (maximum and minimum values); percentage 2012. (From Rosstat and Eurostat.)**

According to calculations (forecast), with the current rates of changes of the respective integral indicator, the target gap reduction will not be reached until 2015.

It's worth mentioning that integral indicators smoothen the existing gaps for individual indicators. There is a number of indicators for which the gap reaches hundreds of times, and the differences between the Russian regions correspond to these of developed countries and outsiders of the e-development. Figures 5.11 and 5.12 show a typical picture of the digital divide of the regions regarding such important indicators as percentage of households with Internet (Figure 5.11) and number of broadband Internet subscribers per 100 inhabitants (Figure 5.12). Similar indicators for EU countries and the world are provided for reference.

5.3.2 *Statistical Analysis of the Factors Contributing to the Digital Divide of the Russian Regions*

Factors affecting the information society development in Russian regions were analyzed based on statistical methods using indicators that reflect levels of social and economic development and ICT use in different fields of activities (there are 83 constituent entities in the Russian Federation). In particular, indices (and subindices) published in annual issues of the Russian Regions e-Readiness Index were used as integral indicators characterizing main lines and factors contributing to information society development.[7] Pirson's correlation coefficients of these indicators to each other and ICT use composite index were calculated.

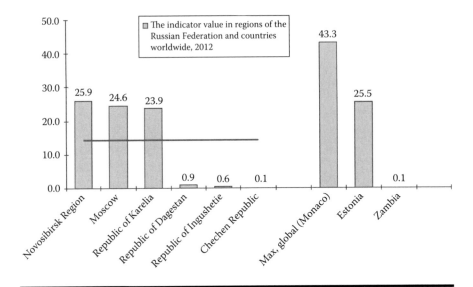

Figure 5.12 **Penetration of fixed broadband access (number of subscribers per 100 people) in the Russian regions and foreign countries, 2012. (From Rosstat and the International Telecommunications Union (ITU).)**

5.3.2.1 Multiple Factors of Information Society Development

Information society development is conditioned by a number of factors that include, for example, human capital and economic environment. According to the analysis, each of these factors correlates with index of ICT use in Russian regions individually to a considerably lower extent than the composite indicator of these factors, whose correlation coefficient reaches 0.74, as shown in Figure 5.13.[8] It means that human capital and economic environment are independent factors of ICT use and, taken collectively, considerably impact information society development.

An important factor—under otherwise equal economic possibilities—is the population density and urbanization level, which is quite understandable as a region with larger territory and lower population density finds itself in a less favorable situation, given it faces higher infrastructure development costs.

If we build the composite index consisting of indicators of economic development of regions, human capital, population density, and urbanization level, the correlation coefficient of this composite index with ICT infrastructure development index is equal to 0.89. Correlation of this composite index with the general index of ICT use is 0.84. Therefore, the three groups—human capital, economy, population density and urbanization—determine ICT infrastructure development opportunities and information development in constituent entities of the Russian Federation to a great extent.

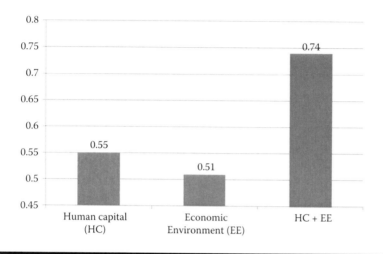

Figure 5.13 Correlations of human capital and economic environment indicators with the overall level of ICT use in the Russian regions.

5.3.2.2 Role of Economic Factors

Large-scale ICT use is not possible without sufficient economic development and household income. Indicators that reflect the level of the economic development of the region also demonstrated an expected high degree of correlation with indicators of ICT use.

According to results, the percentage of household spending on food for private consumption is related, to a great extent, with the level of ICT use in the Russian regions. This indicator manifests consistently high correlation with the composite index of ICT use in the Russian regions that integrates indicators of ICT use in different areas.[9] This is accounted for by the fact that the household spending structure reflects both overall level of economic development of the region that impacts ICT use in business and the public sector, and ICT spending capacity of the population. Thus, this indicator seems to integrate the main economic premise of ICT demand in the economy and is a good measure of the economic development level (the lower the percentage, the higher the e-development level).

While playing an important role in e-development of the regions, economic premises are a necessary, but not a sufficient condition of purposeful ICT use for developing different fields of activities, which is demonstrated by the results of human capital indicators.

5.3.2.3 Human Capital as the Factor Contributing to Information Society Development

According to the classical definition, human capital is understood as a set of knowledge, skills, and capabilities that a person has and uses during his/her work and that

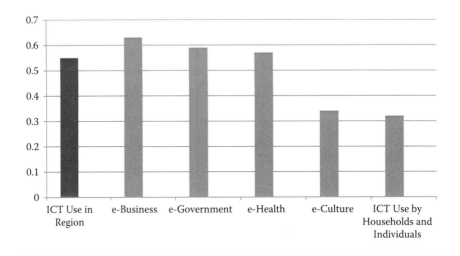

Figure 5.14 Correlation of human capital with indices of ICT use in different fields of activities.

impact his/her economic performance. Components of the human capital indicator here includes, but is not limited to, education level, graduation of ICT specialists, and percentage of researchers in the population.

Results confirm that human capital is one of the most important e-development factors in Russia. The higher the population education, ICT skill levels, graduation rates of ICT specialists, and percentage of researchers in the region, the higher are indicators of ICT use in different fields of activities, as illustrated in Figure 5.14.

Analysis of interrelations between human capital development level and ICT use in different fields of activities leads to the following conclusions:[10]

- In an entire range of information society development areas, the human capital impact on ICT use level surpasses that of economic factors. Thus, interconnection of e-business development in the region with human capital is quite high and surpasses correlation with economic factors (correlation coefficient of any economic environment indicators, including integral ones, is considerably lower).[11] A similar situation is observed in public health. Economic environment indicators (both integral and individual) have much lower correlation with ICT use level in healthcare facilities than human capital indicators.

- The situation is different with households. ICT use strongly correlates with economic indicators, in particular, with income of households in the region, and is related with human capital development level to a lesser extent. This is generally accounted for by low household income, which is currently a considerable barrier in equipping households with ICT equipment.

■ The situation of ICT use in education is specific; correlation of the respective index with both economic factors and human capital is equally low. The likely reason is likely the external federal-level initiative of Internet connectivity and computer classes for all Russian schools. Implementation of this federal project has reduced differentiation of the regions in terms of ICT equipment for schools and decreased dependency on this level of conditions in the regions.

To calculate an integral indicator of human capital development in the Russian regions, we used indicators that characterize level of the population's education (population's percentage of students and people with higher education), training of ICT specialists (enrollment and graduation), scientific personnel (percentage of researchers among population), as well as ICT skills of the working population. Interconnection between the level of ICT use in terms of both individual indicators and the integral indicator of human capital shows that all human capital components are important to shape favorable conditions for information society development in the Russian regions. This is confirmed by the fact that each human capital component taken separately demonstrates weaker correlation with the ICT use index than the integral indicator of the human capital in general, as shown in Figure 5.15.

According to the data, the level of ICT skills of the working population in a region strongly correlates with ICT use level. The less often companies' CEOs specify lack of employees' skills as the main factor counterstaining ICT use, the higher is the integral indicator of ICT use in the region. Among human capital components, the level of ICT skills has its own value in developing the information

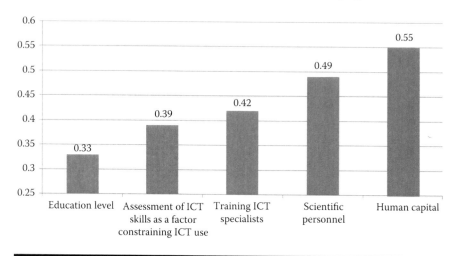

Figure 5.15 **Correlation of the integral indicator and individual components of human capital with ICT use level in the Russian regions.**

society. If this indicator is added to the integral human capital domain, it further increases the correlation coefficient between human capital and ICT use level (from 0.48 to 0.55).

Statistics from 2003 provided similar results for both individual indicators and the integral indicator of human capital development. These results may be articulated as follows. While ICT access of organizations and households of the region (availability of computers and network access) is to a larger extent determined by the economic development level of the region and household income, indicators of ICT purposeful use (indicators to what extent e-commerce or e-government applications are deployed in the region) to a greater degree depend on the level of human capital development.[12]

It is interesting to compare these results with those of 2009. While in 2003, correlation coefficients of human capital with corporate ICT access (0.575) were lower than that with corporate ICT use for e-commerce (0.691) in 2009, these coefficients were approximately equal (0.563 and 0.595, respectively). They considerably surpass similar correlation coefficients of economic environment and the most significant indicator—percentage of food products in household spending—with corporate ICT access and use. While in 2003, correlation of percentage of household spending on food with corporate ICT access amounted to 0.626 (which is higher than the human capital correlation), and that with e-commerce (0.521), in 2009, these coefficients fell to 0.506 and 0.456, respectively. One can conclude from these data that the relative role of human capital has increased, and economic factors lose their significance as an e-development barrier.[13] This is largely due to the fact that basic ICT—Internet access, computers, local area networks—have become more affordable for businesses; the role of economic barriers to their use decreases, while human capital factors remain relevant.

5.3.2.4 Role of the Academic Community

Quite an unexpected result of the interconnection of the level of social and economic development and the use of ICT in the Russian regions is that the "percentage of researchers in the population" indicator turned out to have the highest correlation with ICT use in the Russian regions (both with general index of ICT use and Internet penetration in the regions) among all indicators that characterize human capital as an information society development factor. This small population group (on average, about 0.3 percent of the country population) happens to be an important indication of distribution and use of new technologies in Russian regions.[14] The hypothesis accounting for this fact consists in the idea that the academic community has played an important role in initial deployment and distribution of such new information technologies as the Internet in the Russian regions; the first computer networks used to be implemented in research institutions and universities and acted as the catalyst and the source of development of the Internet as a public network of the region.[15]

These results indicate that:[16]

- interconnection of percentage of researchers in the population and Internet penetration in the Russian regions demonstrate consistency and repeatability on time-series data, which proves that the interconnection is not accidental
- correlation coefficient between the indicators in question is gradually decreasing, which is an indirect proof of the hypothesis, under which the academic community was a significant factor at initial stages of Internet development in the Russian regions, with its impact subsequently declining as Internet development is more affected by other factors after its initial introduction

To exclude the possibility of the identified interconnection being determined by a joint correlation of the indicators ("percentage of researchers in the population" and "percentage of Internet users among adult population") with any other indicator (factor), i.e., the indicator interconnection being conditioned, e.g., by the state of economy, percentage of people with higher education, etc., partial correlations of these indicators were calculated less the role of possible "mediators." According to the results of partial correlation calculations:

- In the beginning of the examined period (in 2003), partial correlations of the indicators ("percentage of researchers in the population" and "percentage of Internet users among adult population") excluding impact of the economic situation and level of population education (percentage of people with higher education) remain significant, which proves direct interconnection of these indicators.
- The partial correlations in question, as calculated according to data of 2011, demonstrate considerable reduction, which is the evidence of decreasing influence of the academic community and confirms the hypothesis of the "initial impact" of this factor.[17]

Based on the results obtained, one can speak of the social function of science, which is not usually mentioned and is practically not investigated; in this case, the academic community plays the role of the pioneer advancing social technology innovations and a guide that delivers them in the social environment. Identifying and substantiating significance of this function, alongside with those traditionally attributed to science (such as, supplier of new knowledge of nature and society, source of research-based technology and technology innovations, a participant in training and proliferating qualification through the educational system, scientific investigation) allows us to shape a new approach to the role of science and academic community in modern Russia as the most important and underestimated component of its modernization potential.[18]

5.3.2.5 State Policy and Regulation as e-Development Factor

Though in today's environment much is determined by economy, demographics, and social situation, an active policy of the constituent entity of the Russian Federation and federal authorities is very important for e-development.

Both in ratings of 2010–2011, and in previous Index publications, one can note a specific peculiarity. The Republic of Karelia, the Republic of Tatarstan, the Leningrad Region, and the Chuvash Republic, all of them having high ICT use rates (from 6 up to 9), hold relatively low places in terms of information society development factors (33rd, 23rd, 49th, and 44th places out of 82, respectively). This can be accounted for by purposeful and efficient efforts made by the authorities of these regions toward ICT use in different fields of activities. This conclusion is indirectly confirmed by the data provided in Figure 5.16. The table presents regions leading in the indicator that may be termed "efficient use of available e-development background." This indicator is calculated as quotient of ICT use index by the index of factors.

As expected, the Leningrad Region and Chuvashia retain leadership in this indicator, while the Republic of Karelia moved down to the fifth position (from the second place held in the previous Index publication). The Krasnodar Krai (Territory) and the Kemerovo Region are also referred to as federation subjects, where ICT use somewhat outstrips the available prerequisites of information society development.

Federation Subject	Index Ratio
Leningrad Region	1.433
Chuvash Republic–Chuvashia	1.407
Krasnodar Territory	1.400
Kemerovo Region	1.369
Republic of Karelia	1.354
Altai Territory	1.277
Lipetsk Region	1.263
Belgorod Region	1.262
Vologda Region	1.259
Kurgan Region	1.259

Figure 5.16 The regions leading in the ratio of the integral indicator of ICT use and the integral indicator of information society development factors.

An interesting situation is observed in the Republic of Tatarstan. In the first publication of the Index in 2005, Tatarstan had a large gap between high values of e-development factor indicators (available funds, well-developed human capital, etc.) and low values of ICT use indicators. The region was among underperformers in terms of these indicators. However, purposeful efforts the authorities made in recent years resulted in dramatic improvement of the situation. Currently, progress of e-development factors matches ICT use level in this region and Tatarstan has become one of the information society development leaders.

Another important point is the policy of federal authorities aimed to smoothen disproportions in information society development in the Russian regions. Above, we have already mentioned the federal-level project of deploying Internet connectivity and computer classes in general education schools implemented in 2006 and 2007. After the project had been implemented, differentiation of the regions in terms of ICT use in education has reduced considerably.

To sum up, one can conclude that the digital divide of the Russian regions to a greater extent results from the social and economic stratification of constituent entities of the Russian Federation and differences in demographic situation (population density and urbanization level). One should understand, though, that market vehicles and processes of gradually smoothening social and economic development of constituent entities of the Russian Federation are not the key to resolving all issues. Some territories are not able to deploy either up-to-date infrastructure or modern services based on market mechanisms. Investments in them will not return or make profit. Therefore, the solution lies in activating the policy of all level of authorities, and this is where highly coordinated, dedicated problem-solving efforts are needed.

5.4 Social Aspects of the Digital Divide in Russia

In October 2013, Rosstat conducted the first federal statistical monitoring of ICT use by individuals. The monitoring was held in all federation subjects based on sampling method of observation, covering the same range of households that was subject to a population survey devoted to employment issues.[19]

5.4.1 Digital Divide in Different Types of Populated Areas and Age–Sex Groups

Figure 5.17 presents data from the survey that discloses availability of important components of ICT infrastructure in urban and rural households.

Based on the data, one can see that the digital divide between urban and rural households remains high and is the most explicit in what refers to use of broadband Internet access. It is explainable. Deployment of broadband Internet access

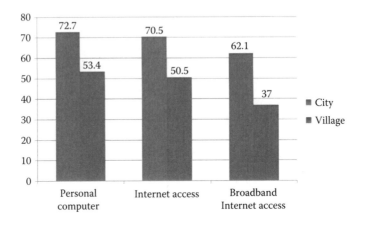

Figure 5.17 ICT use in households of the Russian Federation, by types of populated areas (October 2013); percentage. (From Rosstat.[20])

infrastructure in remote and underpopulated settlements is not always technically feasible and requires high costs that often are not profitable for Internet service providers. Lower levels of education of the rural population is another contributing factor.

Figure 5.18 shows data that characterize gender differences in Internet use by urban and rural population. Interesting is the fact that, while men slightly prevail in ICT use when considering the population, in general, or urban population, in rural settlements women are currently more active Internet users than men (according to some indicators by 1–1.5 percentage points). As for Internet shopping, women are more active in both cities and rural areas.

It's worth mentioning that overcoming the gender gap in Internet use and smoothening differences in ICT use between other social demographic groups is a recently observed phenomena. According to results from a survey of Moscow held by IIS in 2005, the digital divide between specified groups was much higher, as shown in Figure 5.19. At that time, Internet users included 40.8 percent of male Muscovites and only 24.4 percent of female Muscovites. Larger gaps were observed in population groups that differed in age and financial situation attributes, as well as social status.

5.5 Conclusion: State Policy in the Field of Overcoming Digital Divides in Russia

The federal policy of reducing information society development level differences of constituent entities of the Russian Federation was developed more than 10 years ago. A series of measures aimed to resolve the issue were implemented under the first initiative of information society development in the Russian Federation, the federal

Russian Federation			
	Percentage of Population		Number of Internet Users per 100 Inhabitants
	Active Internet Users (Weekly Audience)	Using the Internet to Order Goods and/or Services	
Total	61.4	15.3	64.0
Men	62.0	14.0	64.9
Women	60.8	16.4	63.3
City	66.8	17.9	69.4
Men	68.2	16.8	71.0
Women	65.5	18.8	68.0
Village	45.2	7.5	48.1
Men	44.4	6.2	47.6
Women	45.9	8.7	48.5

Figure 5.18 Internet use by urban and rural population aged 15–72 (October 2013). (From Rosstat.)

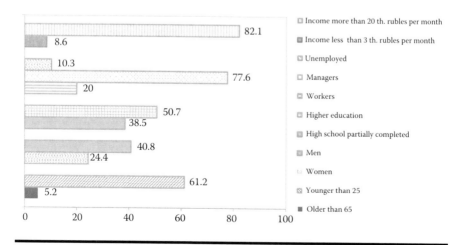

- Income more than 20 th. rubles per month
- Income less than 3 th. rubles per month
- Unemployed
- Managers
- Workers
- Higher education
- High school partially completed
- Men
- Women
- Younger than 25
- Older than 65

82.1
8.6
10.3
77.6
20
50.7
38.5
40.8
24.4
61.2
5.2

Figure 5.19 Differences in Internet use by different social demographic groups of Moscow (2005, percentage of users per group).

target program "Electronic Russia (2002–2010)." In 2006, the Concept of Regional Informatization up to 2010 was adopted, which defined goals, tasks, main lines, and tools of the information society development policy in the Russian regions.[21] In 2008, as noted above, the Strategy for Information Society Development in the Russian Federation was signed by the president.

The policy of reducing regional differences in information development may be conditionally split in two directions. These directions are similar to approaches of overcoming the social economic gap of the regions. The first approach is focused on the region, its support, etc. (strong regional policy); while the second one is oriented at an individual, a budget institution, and other end users of provided support (strong social policy).

Both strategies were implemented in Russia when dealing with ICT. For example, education informatization includes three large-scale federal projects related to the strategy focused on the end user of ICT goods and services that differ in implementation mechanisms.

The first is the Internet connectivity of schools under the "Education" national project in 2006–2007. This project was not actually related with regional support as such, but was focused to directly support educational establishments by providing Internet access (at least 128 kbps) and equipping classrooms with computers. This centralized project turned out to be efficient in resolving the digital divide issue in terms of general education institutions using ICTs, primarily the Internet. The project of supplying free software packages was implemented in the similar manner. The "Education for Children with Disabilities" project used a somewhat different mechanism. With the budget being central, and project infrastructure being both federal and regional, federal subventions intended to provide required equipment for such children and were distributed on the dedicated basis.

A certain problem of the Internet connectivity for school projects was that centralized obligations of payment for channel and technical support of ICT infrastructure were valid for only two years after the connection had been provided. When this period expired, some regions did not find enough funds, technology infrastructure, and personnel to ensure the required level of schools' Internet access and efficient use of computers and the Internet during the teaching process, and the differentiation of regions in this important field of ICT use grew larger again. Thus, direct federal investment turned out to be insufficient without creating proper infrastructure, school informatization support, personnel training, etc.

The example of more efficient centralized end user-focused resolution of digital divide issues is the project of telephone penetration in populated areas and establishing public Internet access points. Implementation of this project employed another approach based on the universal service mechanism—providing universal communications services while performing the "On Communications" law adopted in 2005. The universal service mechanism includes two basic services: (1) stationary telephone communications provided in all populated areas (telephone boxes) and (2) Internet access points available within walking distance in all settlements with population of over 500 people.

This range of measures includes development of model programs of regional informatization and other documents, the tender held in 2012–2013 for providing the Russian regions with federal subsidies on information society development that resulted in joint funding of regional projects in line with three top-priority focuses, this ensuring interdepartmental interaction of federal agencies and regional and municipal authorities; delivering state and municipal services to citizens and legal entities electronically; and enhancing quality of "one-stop principle" state and municipal services in multifunctional centers.

In general, the policy of overcoming differences of the Russian regions in ICT use level may be deemed insufficient; so far, no significant success was achieved as high levels of digital divides remain. The last, but not the least, of what hampers reaching the set goals is lack of a fine-tuned system of federal-level bodies for administration and coordination of regional informatization, stable institutionalized sources of funding, and a new conceptual document that defines tasks and mechanisms of information society development in the Russian regions.

On January 31, 2013, under the chairmanship of the president of Russia, the extended meeting of the government of the Russian Federation was held, where overcoming the digital divide of the Russian regions was discussed as one of the main lines of activities of the government for the period until 2018. Taking into account the size of the country, it was emphasized that the issue was to be resolved at all levels—federal, regional, and municipal—and to replicate best practice of the regions across the country, including that dealing with enhancing computer literacy of the senior generation. By 2018, an absolute majority of Russian citizens are supposed to use advantages of broadband Internet access.

On January 24, 2014, the State Duma of the Russian Federation adopted draft No 297374-6 of Amending the Federal Law "On Communications" in revision of the mediation committee between the State Duma and the Federation Council. This draft is aimed at reforming the system of universal service, which is intended to overcome the digital divide. The law establishes a single operator of the universal communications service (UCS) that will undertake to support the existing UCS infrastructure including coin box telephones and public Internet access points, and providing a new UCS, broadband Internet for settlements with population of over 250 people. The reform is intended to ensure more efficient use of the existing funds of the UCS Foundation and will contribute to solving the task set by the president of the Russian Federation, to resolve the issue of digital divide in Russia by 2018. By that year, broadband Internet access connectivity is planned to be provided to 97 percent of the population of the country. It is planned to perform main construction operations of laying fiber optics communications lines for the first three years of providing universal communications service in the new environment. In fact, funds of the UCS Foundation are used to create the brand new optic fiber-based telecommunications infrastructure that will interconnect virtually the entire country.

5.6 Appendix

Индекс готовности регионов России к информационному обществу 2004–2005. Под ред. Т.В. Ершовой, Ю.Е. Хохлова, С.Б. Шапошника. М.: Институт развития информационного общества, 224 с, 2005. [Index of Russian Regions' e-Readiness 2004–2005. Ed. by T. V. Ershova, Yuri E. Hohlov, Sergei B. Shaposhnik. Moscow: Institute of the Information Society, p. 224, 2005.]

Индекс готовности регионов России к информационному обществу. 2005–2006. М.: Институт развития информационного общества, 244 с, 2007. [Index of Russian Regions' e-Readiness 2005–2006. Moscow: Institute of the Information Society, p. 244, 2007.]

Индекс готовности регионов России к информационному обществу 2007–2008. Под ред. Ю.Е. Хохлова и С.Б. Шапошника. М.: Институт развития информационного общества, 256 с, 2009. [Index of Russian Regions' e-Readiness 2007–2008. Ed. by Yuri E. Hohlov and Sergei B. Shaposhnik. Moscow: Institute of the Information Society, p. 256, 2005.]

Индекс готовности регионов России к информационному обществу 2008–2009. Под ред. Ю.Е. Хохлова и С.Б. Шапошника. М.: Институт развития информационного общества, 296 с, 2010. [Index of Russian Regions' e-Readiness 2008–2009. Ed. by Yuri E. Hohlov and Sergei B. Shaposhnik. Moscow: Institute of the Information Society, p. 296, 2010.]

Индекс готовности регионов России к информационному обществу 2009–2010. Под ред. Т.В. Ершовой, Ю.Е. Хохлова, С.Б. Шапошника. М.: Институт развития информационного общества, 360 с, 2011. [Index of Russian Regions' e-Readiness 2009–2010. Ed. by T. V. Ershova, Yuri E. Hohlov, Sergei B. Shaposhnik. Moscow: Institute of the Information Society, p. 360, 2011.]

Индекс готовности регионов России к информационному обществу 2010–2011/Под ред. Т.В. Ершовой, Ю.Е.Хохлова и С.Б.Шапошника. М.: Институт развития информационного общества, 462 с, 2012. [Index of Russian Regions' e-Readiness 2010–2011. Ed. by T. V. Ershova, Yuri E. Hohlov, Sergei B. Shaposhnik. Moscow: Institute of the Information Society, p. 462, 2012.]

Endnotes

1. The autumn 2008 survey sample covered 2,000 household members. The survey was held in the territory of 44 constituent entities of the Russian Federation among adult population aged 16 and over, permanently residing in the territory of Russia. The sample included 160 election districts out of 103 populated areas (44 rural areas and 59 urban areas). Household respondents were selected taking into account quotas for gender, age, and higher education. The survey questionnaire was developed taking into account reference questionnaires of OECD (Organization for Economic Cooperation and Development) and Eurostat, and consisted of 64 questions. The April–May 2012 survey was held in the territory of 46 constituent entities of the Russian Federation in 103 populated areas (44 rural areas, 59 urban areas). The survey covered 1,800 people, with population of analysis being urban and rural population of the Russian Federation aged 16–74. A multistage, stratified area-based random sample was used. The method of face-to-face interview at the place of residence was used to hold the survey; household respondents were selected taking into account quotas for gender, age, and higher education.
2. Hohlov, Y.E. and Shaposhnik, S.B. eds. (2012). ICT Competences as a Factor in the Socio-Economic Development of Russia. Institute of the Information Society, Moscow, p. 80. Online at: http://e-competences.iis.ru
3. http://runet.fom.ru/Elektronnoe-pravitelstvo/10221
4. MFC—Multifunctional Center for Delivery Public and Municipal Services.
5. See Appendix for the complete list as well as native Russian titles (translated into English in the endnotes).
6. Yuri E. Hohlov and Sergei B. Shaposhnik, eds. *Index of Russian Regions' e-Readiness 2008–2009* (Moscow: Institute of the Information Society, 2010), 296.
7. See Appendix.
8. Shaposhnik, S.B. (2006). Role of Human Capital in Russian Regions' E-Development. In: *Science.* Innovation. Education miscellany. Executive editor: E.V. Semenov. M.: Parade, 368–377.
9. Pearson product-moment correlation coefficient between them equaled to 0.695 in 2003, 0.681 in 2009, and 0.653 in 2012.
10. Shaposhnik S.B. Spatial Polarization of of the Information Society Development in Russia: Role of Human Capital // S.I. Vavilov Institute for the History of Science and Technology of the Russian Academy of Sciences. Yearly Scientific Conference 2012. Executive editor: Yu.M. Baturin. M.: Annonce Media, 2012.
11. Pearson product-moment correlation coefficient is 0.63.
12. Shaposhnik, "Role of Human Capital in Russian Regions' E-Development."
13. Shaposhnik, "Spatial Polarization of the Information Society Development in Russia."
14. Shaposhnik, "Role of Human Capital in Russian Regions' E-Development"; Sergei B. Shaposhnik. "The scientific community as a factor of information society development in Russia," S. I. Vavilov Institute for the History of Science and Technology of the Russian Academy of Sciences. Paper presented at the yearly Scientific Conference 2013, LENAND, pp. 184–187.

15. True to form, Pearson product-moment correlation coefficient between such indicators as "percentage of researchers in the population" and "percentage of Internet users among adult population" demonstrate consistently high values based on data of 2003–2008 (exceeding 0.5). In 2009, its value started decreasing and in 2011 amounted to 0.396. Shaposhnik, "Role of Human Capital in Russian Regions' E-Development."

16. Shaposhnik, "The scientific community as a factor of information society development in Russia."

17. Ibid.

18. Shaposhnik, "Role of Human Capital in Russian Regions' E-Development"; Shaposhnik, "The scientific community as a factor of information society development in Russia."

19. The survey was held in the second week of October, with about 69,000 people polled, which amounts to 0.06 percent of the population aged 15–72.

20. Russian Federation, Federal State Statistics Service. Online at: http://www.gks.ru/wps/wcm/connect/rosstat_main/rosstat/ru/statistics/science_and_innovations/it_technology

21. Online at: http://www.inforegion.ru/ru/main/goverment/reg_inform_concept/reg_inform_concept_text/

Chapter 6

Broadband Policy and Rural and Cultural Divides in Australia

Scott Ewing, Ellie Rennie, and Julian Thomas

Contents

6.1 Introduction

The benefits of being online are already being enjoyed by most Australians, and are likely to attract almost everyone in the near future. However, although the number of nonusers across Australia is declining, it appears to be doing so increasingly slowly. As of 2013, around 14 percent of the Australian adult population, mostly in older age groups, did not have home access to the Internet. In this chapter, we explore Australia's evolving digital divide. While the divide may be narrowing, it also is deepening. Those who are not connected now, and in the future, may be fewer, but they will be missing out on far more—in education, health, e-government, commerce, communication, and entertainment—than the nonusers of previous decades. As the group of nonusers gets smaller, the consequences of exclusion are likely to increase as more public and private services are delivered online. This particular dynamic is considered in the context of larger national information policies, especially the National Broadband Network (NBN), which is the Commonwealth government's major investment in network infrastructure that is likely to drive a wave of new applications across all areas of life, transforming Australia's service economy in fundamental ways.

The example of Australian broadband policy touches on a central concern of digital divide debates, namely the relationship between socioeconomic factors and Internet adoption, which scholars and experts have long argued determine the digital divide, leading them to conclude that infrastructure provision will not, on its own, solve the problems created by unequal take-up. Here we suggest that infrastructure provision can make a significant difference if it responds to the preferences of consumers and users; understood within the local context. Australia's NBN is an instance where a national-level strategy aimed at the majority may struggle to meet the needs of those most excluded unless local factors are addressed.

We use the example of broadband adoption amongst Australia's Indigenous households, where uneven patterns of adoption reflect consumer preference for mobile over satellite services that arises from the particular geography, culture, and economy of remote Indigenous Australia. Although disadvantage is likely to influence the sociality of place from which these preferences arise, it is not necessarily the primary determinant of Internet adoption. In the final part of the chapter, we suggest how this particular instance of digital exclusion might be overcome.

Our analysis draws on two major research projects at the Swinburne Institute for Social Research. The first is the Australian component of the World Internet Project (WIP), an international study of the household adoption of the Internet and its social, political, and economic implications. WIP is a sample survey that has been administered in Australia on a biannual basis since 2007. The second is the Home Internet for Remote Indigenous Communities project, a qualitative longitudinal study into home Internet and computing in remote Aboriginal communities in central Australia, conducted in partnership with two Indigenous organizations (the Centre for Appropriate Technology and the Central Land Council), as well as the Australian Communications Consumer Action Network.

6.2 A Narrowing but Deepening Divide

Between 1998 and 2003, the percentage of Australian households with access to the Internet rose from 16 to 53 percent.[1] The first WIP survey in 2007 found that 68 percent of households were connected to the Internet, a figure that grew to

81 percent in 2009, 88 percent in 2011, and 90 percent in 2013.[2] The survey results show that income and age remain predictors of whether a particular household will have an Internet connection, although the significance of both has decreased over time as prices have fallen. The data also provide insight into current levels of use and nonuse, indicating how broadband inequality has been influenced by individual and household priorities, which differ across income and age groups. Looking just at broadband connectivity, in 2007, less than a quarter of those with household incomes of less than $30,000 had a connection, compared to 8 in 10 on household incomes of $100,000 or more. The difference considerably diminished by 2013, when 8 in 10 households earning less than $30,000 had a broadband connection compared to nearly all households earning $60,000 or more.

A more nuanced picture of the relationship between income and Internet adoption emerges when looking at the peripherals that facilitate access within the home. Home broadband access has been greatly improved through the advent of wireless networks and mobile devices that enable access anywhere in the house, untethered from the wired personal computer. The ecosystems of smartphones, tablets, e-readers, and other devices do not depend on home wireless networks, but substantially benefit from them. Nine in 10 of those households earning $100,000 or more had a wireless network in 2013. This figure steadily decreases as we move down the income scale. Eight in 10 households earning $60,000 to less than $100,000 had a wireless network, this fell to 7 in 10 for the next income group and to 55 percent for those on the lowest incomes. A similar pattern was observed for ownership of laptops, tablets, and e-readers. In the Australian context, household wireless networks offer lower cost connectivity and more bandwidth than cellular connections; it also connects multiple devices. This is a possible indicator of the variable *efficiency and intensity* of household Internet use across different social groups. It may follow that, if better-off families are typically using the Internet more intensively, they also will be deriving greater benefits from it.

Age continues to be a major factor shaping Internet use in Australia. By 2007, almost all those aged 18 to 24 used the Internet, while less than a third of those aged 65 and over and only two-thirds of the 50 to 64 group did. Older Australians' use of the Internet has increased, but is still appreciably less than that of younger people. In 2013, the entire sample aged less than 35 used the Internet, whereas more than a third of those aged 65 or over did not. Further, Internet adoption among those aged 65 and over slowed dramatically between 2011 and 2013. Between 2007 and 2009, older persons' participation rose by 34 percent and rose again between 2009 and 2011 by 42 percent. Between 2011 and 2013, this rate slowed to 11 percent. The difference between the proportion of men and women who use the Internet is small but persistent. In 2007 men's participation was 5 percent greater than women's, this fell to 3 percent in 2009, increased to 5 percent in 2011, and was at 4 percent in 2013.

While the proportion of Australian households—now 9 in 10—that are connected has grown, so have the disadvantages of living in a household without a broadband connection. Identifying the groups of people that are not online, therefore, remains a matter for social policy, more broadly in terms of the provision of government services as well as economic participation. However, it is also the case that nonusers do not necessarily view their lack of connectivity as a disadvantage. In terms of encouraging nonusers to embrace the Internet, our data demonstrates that many of those not using the Internet have little interest in embracing the new technology. Just under a half of nonusers cite "no interest" as their main reason for not using the Internet. Only a quarter agree that they would like to use the Internet in the future and just over a quarter feel that they miss out by not using the Internet. Only 14 percent say they could perform better in their daily tasks if they used the Internet.

6.3 Broadband Policy and the Geographic Divide

Australia is one of the most sparsely populated countries in the world, but also one of the most urbanized. Six in 10 of Australia's 23 million people live in the five largest cities. The Northern Territory, the least populous of Australia's mainland states and territories, is slightly larger than France, Germany, and Spain combined. While the three European countries have nearly 200 million inhabitants, the Northern Territory is home to 233,000 people. Australia, therefore, faces the particular challenge of providing Internet services to small populations across large geographical areas; the same difficulties it encounters with other public infrastructure and services. The task of providing a national communications system has been a key function of Australia's federal government since the creation of the Commonwealth at the turn of the twentieth century. As in other areas of communications policy, digital divide debates, therefore, have tended to focus especially on the disparity in access, and quality of access, between capital cities and the regions.[3] Here the WIP data shows a significant, although declining, difference in Internet connections between capital cities and regional and rural areas (excluding remote ones). In 2007, the difference was 12 percentage points, falling to 9 in 2009, 8 in 2011, and 6 in 2013. However, these figures tell us little about differences in the *quality* of access between urban and regional Australia—a major theme in the government's successive reviews of regional telecommunications, from 2002 onwards.[4]

Australia's first major federal program to address Internet access, Networking the Nation, was launched in December 1996 with a $250-million fund that was augmented in 1999 with a further $174 million.[5] From the start, the program was aimed at rural, remote, and regional Australia, and its objectives were set out following the second tranche of funds to

■ assist the economic and social development of rural Australia by funding projects, which
  - enhance telecommunications infrastructure and services
  - increase access to, and promote use of, services available through telecommunications networks
  - reduce disparities in access to such services and facilities[6]

Following the winding up of the initiative at the end of 2004, a number of programs were established to improve Internet access (and broader telecommunications access) in rural and remote Australia and to address the specific telecommunications needs of Indigenous Australians. As Notley and Forth explain:

> These initiatives were largely informed by ABS (Australian Bureau of Statistics) data and the Regional Telecommunications Inquiry (2002), which identified that, while overall access disparities appeared to be closing in many areas, access quality (broadband) remained highly stratified between urban and nonurban Australia and between Indigenous and non-Indigenous Australians.[7]

Although other aspects of the digital divide and digital exclusion were not completely absent from the policy discussion, until the coming of the Rudd Labor government in 2007, major initiatives aimed at Internet access were focused largely on access outside of the major population centers.

6.4 Big Country, Big Network

The next major phase of Australian Internet access policy was the development of the NBN. Despite the programs established from 1996 onward to "network the nation," the issue of lagging broadband take-up and relatively low broadband speeds became a focal point in the 2007 national election and the two subsequent elections. In 2007, the two major parties put forward distinct options for broadband infrastructure development. The incumbent Coalition government promised to spend AU$1.9 billion on further developing Australia's broadband infrastructure, delivering speeds of between 2 Mbps and 50 Mbps to 99 percent of Australians through a mix of wired and wireless technologies. The Labor opposition, on the other hand, wanted to develop a publicly funded high-speed broadband network, based on fiber to the node (FTTN) technology, which offers slower speeds, but is easier to implement than fiber to the premises (FTTP). Their objective was to provide a minimum 12 Mbps connection to 98 percent of the Australian population by 2012 (Australian National Audit Office, 2010) and they pledged to spend $4.7 billion on the new network, with a total cost of $15 billion.[8]

The initial rationale for the NBN was not the digital divide, but rather international economic competitiveness, and the question of whether Australia would be able to take advantage of future opportunities of a digital economy, especially in comparison with certain Asian and European countries with better-developed broadband infrastructure. In discussing the need for improved broadband in Australia, Stephen Conroy, who became the minister for Broadband, Communications, and the Digital Economy with Labor's election in 2007, relied heavily on the Organization of Economic Cooperation and Development (OECD) league tables of broadband penetration and costs, making a case that Australia was lagging the rest of the world and was on the wrong side of a digital divide. As far back as 2006, when still in opposition, a Conroy press release noted that "… the latest OECD broadband statistics show Australia's ranking in the use of broadband remains mired at 17th out of 30 surveyed countries."[9] The document that set out Labor's broadband policy for the 2007 election included reference to this figure, plus a number of other references to OECD data.[10] Minister Conroy, when responsible for implementing the NBN, continued to argue the need for it based on Australia's poor performance as measured by the OECD.[11]

Following its election in late 2007, Australia's new Labor government established a tender process to undertake the work on developing the FTTN network. Telstra, the privatized former government monopoly that still owned the majority of Australia's telecommunication infrastructure, submitted a nonconforming bid and the government was unconvinced by other proposals. The government now changed tack, deciding instead to develop a much more ambitious fiber to the premises broadband network (FTTP), which offers higher speeds for households, but is more expensive, with a total estimated cost of $43 billion. The new objective was to provide minimum speeds of 100 Mbps to 93 percent of Australian households by 2018, and next generation satellite and wireless Internet to the remaining 7 percent. According to the Australian government, the NBN is the largest infrastructure project undertaken in this country.[12]

In a speech not long after the announcement of the upgraded NBN, Minister Conroy told the National Press Club that broadband would "transform healthcare," "revolutionize education," underpin the nation's "future carbon constrained economy," ensure infrastructure investments, and "support applications and services in these and other sectors that today we cannot begin to imagine."[13] In April 2009, the Australian government created the National Broadband Network Company (NBN Co) as a government-owned corporation to design, build, and operate the new network. The press release announcing the creation of NBN Co set out the following objectives for the NBN: "It will fundamentally transform the competitive dynamics of the telecommunications sector, underpin future productivity growth and our international competitiveness." These remarks point to the dual interests of the then government. The NBN project aimed to address two closely related policy problems: (1) the failings in Australia's Internet infrastructure, and (2) the need for microeconomic reform in telecommunications. Competition had been introduced to the Australian telecommunications sector in 1991, and Telstra, subsequently, was privatized in stages between 1997 and 2006, but it remained both the dominant telecommunications wholesaler *and* retailer in the market. However, under the NBN, Telstra would relinquish its wholesale operations to a single broadband wholesaler who would sell bandwidth to retailers (to be known as retail service providers or RSPs) of which Telstra is one. After a protracted series of negotiations, Telstra agreed to be part of the NBN in June 2011. As part of this agreement,

Telstra agreed to decommission its copper phone network as the NBN was rolled out and to move those customers over to the NBN.

The 2010 federal election left neither of the two major parties with a parliamentary majority. The incumbent government's ambitious broadband plan was a major factor in the decision of the last two independents, both representing regional electorates, to support a minority Labor government.[14] Not surprisingly, given the large government investment, the NBN gave rise to a major debate about the potential benefits of such a network. Opposition leader Tony Abbott described the network as a "white elephant" and ordered his communications minister Malcolm Turnbull to "demolish" the government on what he saw as wasted spending.

While the opposition was critical from the announcement in April 2009, it took a number of months to begin a campaign for a cost benefit analysis.[15] They were joined in this effort by the Business Council of Australia.[16] Prominent Australian economist Henry Ergas undertook his own appraisal, and found that the project cost between $14 billion and $20 billion more than its benefits.[17] The Australian government resisted calls from the Opposition and other interested parties to subject the NBN proposal to a "full" cost-benefit analysis. Communications Minister Stephen Conroy argued that a cost-benefit analysis would not capture the "transformative" nature of the NBN and would be a waste of time and money.[18] In November 2010, a report released in the United States questioned the economic benefits of subsidizing broadband, quoting liberally from the then Prime Minister Rudd's speech, in which he announced the NBN.[19] In a report almost tit-for-tat, the Institute for a Broadband-Enabled Society released *Valuing Broadband Benefits: A Selective Report on Issues and Options*. This report made some attempt at cataloguing the benefits of the NBN, but concluded that conducting a social cost-benefit analysis would necessarily miss the benefits from applications that would only develop once a critical mass of users had access to superfast broadband.[20]

The report set out the following categories of benefit:

- Home entertainment and communication
- e-Health
- e-Education
- e-Government
- Smart grids
- Transport
- Teleworking
- Cloud computing

Alongside the debate about the relative merits of the NBN came a discussion about the speed of the rollout. The NBN commenced construction in Tasmania, the small island state off the southeast corner of mainland Australia in mid-2009 and the network was activated in three prerelease trial sites in July 2010.[21] Five first release sites on mainland Australia were announced in March 2010 and commercial services became available in these areas from October 2011. Not surprisingly, given the scale of the project and its highly politicized nature, it was subject to intense media scrutiny. There were two key issues: the speed of the rollout was slower than that forecast in the NBN Corporate Plan and the take-up of services by households who could access the network was less than forecast. Part of the problem with take-up was caused by the structural separation that lay at the center of the NBN as a government initiative. NBN Co was only responsible for building and operating the wholesale broadband network. It was retailers who would deal directly with households and businesses; they were the ones who had to convince customers to take up services. In June 2013, there were 234,799 premises that had access to the NBN, with 70,100 on the network. In the NBN's initial corporate plan, they estimated that they would have passed 1.7 million households with 572,000 connected to the network. The actual premises connected were just 12 percent of those predicted in the first corporate plan.

In 2013, for the third consecutive election, the NBN was a major electoral campaign issue, reflecting both its continuing popularity, practical complexity, and high cost. The conservative opposition had moved on from rejection of a government-funded national wholesale network to supporting a leaner, more efficient version. The opposition went to the election promising a full review of the NBN and a cost-benefit analysis. Their proposed NBN would be cheaper and quicker to build. This would be achieved largely through leaving the last mile for existing premises to be funded by property owners. Owners could choose to connect through the existing copper network to a node that would connect to the fiber network or pay for the fiber to continue from the node directly to their premises. New developments would continue to be connected directly to the fiber network. The opposition estimated that their strategy would cost $29.5 billion (compared to the NBN's then estimate of $37.4 billion) and shave two years off the rollout time. Households and businesses in hard-to-reach locations (approximately 7 percent of the population) would remain relatively unaffected, in that they would still be served by fixed wireless and satellite Internet services, as originally proposed under Labor's plan.

Following their election in September 2013, the new conservative Coalition government wasted little time in revamping the board of the NBN and establishing a review of the project. The entire board was asked by the minister to resign and was replaced by an interim three person board. The strategic review reported in December 2013, estimating that the previous government's NBN would have cost $73 billion to build and taken until the end of 2024 to complete. The review's favored option, a mix of FTTP, FTTN, and the use of the existing hybrid fiber coax (HFC) network was estimated to cost $41 billion and be completed by 2020. The estimate for the breakdown between the three fixed-line technologies for the preferred option was FTTP 26 percent, FTTN 44 percent, and HFC 30 percent. Presumably the 26 percent for FTTP does not include those premises where the owner chooses to pay for fiber optic connection directly to the premises.[22]

At the time of writing, in 2014, the NBN has grown from a relatively modest proposal in 2007 to a project that the once opposed Coalition is now building at a cost of $41 billion. This is around 10 times the amount that Labor first suggested in 2007. The project is not a digital divide initiative as such, rather it is a form of nation-building infrastructure designed to provide a common service for all Australians. While clearly aimed at improving Australians' access to high-speed Internet, the issue of access for disadvantaged groups has not been a central one in debates about the NBN. The NBN as a wholesaler does not have a direct relationship to consumers. To this stage, governments have resisted calls from bodies, such as the Australian Communications Consumers Action Network, for programs to ensure low cost to access the NBN, arguing that the competition benefits the NBN will bring will drive down prices.

The NBN was aimed at improving the access for mainstream consumers and business; its principal digital divide elements consisted of an aspiration to bring regional Australians into that digital mainstream. As commentators have observed, the model of a national monopoly infrastructure provider delivered a large benefit to those outside major population centers. Rather than enabling commercial providers to "cherry-pick" easy to reach households in densely populated areas and demanding a commercial return on infrastructure to all consumers, the NBN will be able to cross-subsidize those households that are more expensive to service. The Coalition's revamped NBN further benefits those in regional areas by continuing Labor's focus on rolling out the network earlier in these underserviced areas. The major advantage of the NBN for low-income consumers was a pricing model designed to ensure that entry level prices remained at pre-NBN levels.[23] The promise for these consumers was the prospect of a faster and more reliable service at the same price as the asymmetric digital subscriber line (ADSL).

The issue of access for remote Australians also was not a major part of the mainstream NBN debate. As discussed below, the model that has been implemented to serve remote Australia may offer affordable services, yet this alone will not necessarily lead to adoption for all.

6.5 Indigenous Australians and Access in Remote Australia

In 2011, 2.5 percent of Australia's population (548,370 people) were identified as being of Aboriginal and/or Torres Strait Islander origin.[24] The majority of Indigenous Australians live in cities and regional towns along the eastern seaboard.[25] Indigenous Australians, however, are more likely to live in remote areas than other Australians, making up 2.4 percent of the nonremote population and 27.6 percent of the remote population.

Australia's 1,187 discreet Indigenous communities are dispersed across the continent, with over half located in the Northern Territory. Almost three-quarters of all remote communities have a population of less than 50 people, and only 17 have a population of more than 1,000 people.[26] The smaller settlements were established from the 1980s, as families moved back to their traditional lands, assisted through policies of self-determination. Kinship systems and practices carried through from precolonial times continue to govern life in remote communities to varying degrees, and families in some regions speak one or more Indigenous languages at home. As anthropologists have observed, the contemporary Indigenous sociality of remote communities is an expression of both traditional and Western culture, including new capabilities "in languages, technology, practical knowledge, ritual, and ways of organizing social, political, and economic life."[27] Many remote settlements also have become places of extreme hardship, characterized by unemployment, high rates of alcohol abuse, and chronic illness.[28] In recent years, remote Indigenous communities have been subject to an increased level of state intervention, intended to overcome generational social disadvantage.

6.5.1 Internet Adoption and Indigenous Australians

Access to telecommunications has long been considered an area of policy failure in respect to remote Indigenous communities.[29] Although 77 percent of remote communities had access to some form of telecommunication service by 2007, for many this consisted of one public telephone. Only 20 percent of the population of remote communities had a fixed telephone line, and only 26 percent of communities had mobile telephone coverage.[30] The dispersed nature of remote communities and the proportionally small population has meant that market solutions to telecommunications have not emerged, and the provision of telecommunications infrastructure has fallen to various government programs to address. For instance, since 2009, the Indigenous Communications Program has provided satellite public phones to small communities, as well as limited funds to support digital literacy programs and shared Internet facilities in some larger communities.

Within the government's NBN planning, most remote Indigenous communities fall within the "final 3 percent" of the population receiving improved satellite broadband services rather than FTTN or fixed mobile. As the most recent census was conducted a month prior to the commencement of the NBN Interim Satellite Scheme (ISS), which began in June 2011, there is currently no comprehensive public data that capture the impact of this development. However, at the time of the census, households in remote communities were able to access subsidized satellite Internet services through an earlier program, the Australian Broadband Guarantee (ABG), which provided "metro comparable" prices, albeit with inferior speeds and limited download capacity.[31] Although this program ensured that satellite Internet was technically available to all Australian households no matter how remote, very few Indigenous households appear to have been accessing this service at the time.[32]

In the remainder of this chapter, we use the 2011 census statistics to discuss possible explanations for this divide, including socioeconomic status, infrastructure availability, and cultural factors. Where others have interpreted the divide as evidence of the relationship between socioeconomic status and Internet adoption, we present an alternative case, arguing that consumer preferences—stemming from a particular remote Indigenous sociality—are a more likely explanation.

6.5.2 Broadband and Indigenous Disadvantage

A number of scholars have explored the connection between social disadvantage and the digital divide, leading some to conclude that the digital divide is best understood as a symptom of social disadvantage rather than as a disadvantage in its own right.[33] In the case of Indigenous Australia, it is possible to draw a correlation between the digital divide and disadvantage. A series of studies by the Centre for Aboriginal Economic Policy Research has found that, overall, Indigenous people living in urban and town locations are better off than those living in remote areas. In all parts of the country (remote and nonremote, with a significant Indigenous population), Indigenous people also were found to be worse off than non-Indigenous Australians living nearby across a range of socioeconomic measures, including educational attainment, income, labor force participation, and housing.[34]

The 2011 census data clearly shows that there is a digital divide between Indigenous people living in urban areas and those living in remote areas, as well as between Indigenous people and non-Indigenous people living in the same area. For instance, in the Northern Territory (where 27 percent of the total population identify as being of Aboriginal and/or Torres Strait Islander origin), 31 percent of Indigenous people living in the capital city of Darwin reported that they did not have an Internet connection at home during the 2011 census, compared with 11 percent of non-Indigenous people. However, in the rest of the Northern Territory, 75 percent of Indigenous people did not have an Internet connection at home, compared with only 15 percent of non-Indigenous people. In an analysis of the 2006 census data, the Australian Bureau of Statistics suggested that "the lower rate of connectivity for Indigenous people might be attributed to a range of several socioeconomic factors.[35]

Although the socioeconomic argument makes sense when looking at differences between remote and nonremote Indigenous peoples, as well as between Indigenous and non-Indigenous populations, it does not explain significant differences in Internet adoption that occur *within* remote regions. Since 2010, the Swinburne Institute has been working with two Indigenous organizations, the Central Land Council and the Centre for Appropriate Technology, to investigate broadband adoption in the central desert region in the Northern Territory.[36] This qualitative research investigated one small community where no households had Internet connection at the commencement of the project (60 percent of adults had never used the Internet), yet observed significant Internet use in a nearby larger community with mobile coverage. The socioeconomic profile was the same in both communities, suggesting that disadvantage was not an adequate explanation for low take-up in the smaller community.

Instead, availability of mobile broadband was the major difference between the two communities. Case study research conducted in other remote regions has similarly observed that where mobile coverage exists, Indigenous people have been quick to adopt. For instance, in their 2009 study of mobile adoption in the Bloomfield River Valley in Queensland, Brady and Dyson found:

> In recent times, mobile telephones have become increasingly popular in remote communities. They provide both communication capabilities and Internet access, now that Internet-enabled (3G, or Third Generation) phones have become the norm in remote areas where mobile networks have been established.[37]

The 2011 census data provides some useful insights into the hypothesis that arises from the qualitative research—that the availability of mobile broadband is a significant factor in the digital divide between Indigenous households in remote Australia and other households. In 2011, only 11 locations in the southern half of the Northern Territory (south of 19 degrees South) had mobile phone coverage. These were the townships of Alice Springs and Tennant Creek (including town camps), the tourist resort of Yulara (near Uluru and Mutitjulu), three highway stops, and five remote Indigenous communities (Yuendumu, Hermannsburg, Ti Tree, Santa Teresa, and Ali Curung). A comparison of households in locations with mobile coverage to those in areas without mobile coverage shows that Indigenous households in areas with mobile reception are significantly more likely to have access to the Internet at home.

The towns, their town camps (Indigenous housing estates), and the five remote communities can be identified in the census data using the Indigenous Structure of the Australian Statistical Geography Standard, which enables analysis of discreet communities, or of a group of small communities in a given area. Where the boundaries correspond to a particular community or town with mobile reception, it can be assumed that most of the houses in that Indigenous location (ILOC) have coverage, or are within close enough proximity to mobile reception for it to be a viable option for broadband consumers. This is not the case with three ILOCs that cover large areas, and where there were likely to only be pockets of reception: "Julalikari Outstations" (40 Indigenous households, some of which may be in close proximity to Tennant Creek); "South MacDonnell Ranges" (72 Indigenous households, some of which may be in close proximity to Alice Springs); and "Tjuwanpa Outstations" (38 Indigenous households, some of which would be within range of Hermannsburg mobile reception).

Across all ILOCs known to have mobile reception in 2011, 40 percent of households had an Internet connection of some kind (13 percent were not stated and 47 percent reported they had no Internet connection). This compares with only 4 percent of households with an Internet connection in areas that did not have mobile reception. The number increases to 7 percent when the Julalikari, South MacDonnell Ranges, and Tjuwanpa Outstations are included.[38]

Although there may be some difference in socioeconomic status between households in major towns (Alice Springs and Tennant Creek) and those that are far from employment and services, the five communities with mobile reception are not significantly different from those without mobile reception in terms of socioeconomic measures. Moreover, affordability is not necessarily a direct determining factor in Internet use because mobile broadband was generally more expensive than basic satellite Internet plans at the time. A more likely explanation for the difference is that local systems and economies, as well as other community capacities, are influencing Internet adoption. For instance, research has found that in 2013, residents of Ali Curung were purchasing mobile broadband as prepaid, not as postpaid plans, despite the fact that postpaid plans are a more affordable option. As satellite services are only offered through more conventional billing mechanisms (not prepaid credit), the different retail offerings could be a significant factor behind the digital divide.[39]

The preference for prepaid services possibly relates to an alternative system of exchange that occurs in remote communities, known as *demand sharing* where individuals are obliged to share certain resources among family and close friends. The consequence of this system is that money is regularly distributed among community members rather than accumulated,[40] making the as-needed nature of prepaid credit appealing. Although, it is also the case that some everyday objects of contemporary Western culture (including communication technologies) are invested and treated differently to those that might fall within traditional systems (shelter, food), the sharing of mobile devices within family and friendship groups also is common. Therefore, one $30 phone or tablet credit can serve a number of people, albeit for a short period of time.

Some have suggested that temporary mobility—moving from one's home community into town or other communities for short or long periods—also may be a reason for mobile broadband adoption.[41] As the degree of mobility varies between communities, and is dependent on factors, such as distance to nearby towns, kinship relations, and local services, mobility is unlikely to explain the widespread preference for mobile broadband, yet may be a factor. Other explanations include the availability of mobile credit vouchers at community stores, or the lack of information on the relative costs and availability of prepaid mobile as opposed to satellite Internet under the ABG.[42] Such explanations add layers of complexity to the digital divide, where preferences are an expression of convenience, agency and group behaviors, as well as information sharing and social network effects. One possible conclusion from these statistics is that the digital divide is less about disadvantage, and more of an indication that consumer needs are not being served under current infrastructure, market and regulatory conditions.

6.5.3 *Implications of the Mobile Divide*

When taken at the nationwide level, the 2011 data suggest that the digital divide between Indigenous Australians and non-Indigenous Australians is closing.

Between 2006 and 2011, the percentage of Indigenous Australians with an Internet connection grew from 40 percent to 61 percent.[43] The corresponding figures for non-Indigenous households were 63 percent and 77 percent. However, as the (central desert) Northern Territory statistics demonstrate, the distribution of connectivity within the Indigenous population varies greatly across, and even within, statistical regions. How we understand the digital divide has significant implications for broadband and social policy more generally. If the digital divide is tied to socioeconomic status, then the question arising from this is whether the Internet can assist in overcoming disadvantage, or whether improvements in living standards are a necessary precursor to online participation.

However, if it is one of consumer preferences, then other policy solutions emerge. Although statistics show that Internet adoption is higher where there is mobile coverage, extending mobile coverage is just one of a number of possible responses. For instance, alternative billing options for satellite services may increase adoption in areas where mobile is not available. Another response could be the provision of public, or shared wi-fi networks, both in communities where mobile is not available, and to augment cellular services where they do exist. Research suggests that satellite broadband can be an alternative for areas without mobile coverage as households with satellite access do make use of the Internet on a regular basis. However, programs to increase adoption in these areas may need to include information and assistance, and possibly provide wireless networks that work across multiple dwellings in order to accommodate different household structures and movement between houses.

6.6 Conclusion

The story of the digital divide in Australia reflects, to some degree, the experiences of developed countries elsewhere. We see a comparatively small and diminishing group of nonusers, generally characterized as older and poorer than most, facing increasing relative disadvantage as mainstream government and business services shift their center of gravity toward online platforms. However, when we look beyond the comparatively simple matter of access and connection to the network, a more complex, distinctive, and persistent divide comes into focus; one shaped by geography and the specific challenges of providing a national communications infrastructure over large, thinly populated regional and remote territories. The recent history of Australia's information and communications policy responds to these challenges through a multiplicity of complex, and sometimes competing, objectives: the need to foster Australia's emerging digital economy, the need to untangle the conflicting interests of the country's dominant carrier in both wholesale and retail markets, and the need to provide services for regional Australia ("the bush," as it is colloquially known) that overcome some of the disadvantages created by long distances.

Of all the problems Australian communications policymakers and planners encounter, the problem of ensuring adequate services for those mainly Indigenous Australians who live in the most remote part of the continent, is the most difficult and intractable. The Australian government's NBN includes provision for improved satellite services for remote communities. These have the potential to make a significant difference, although the take-up to date of existing satellite Internet, for many reasons, has not been encouraging. In fact, the example of remote Indigenous communities suggests that policy priorities directed at mainstream consumers, focusing on pricing and speeds, can result in barriers to adoption for the minority. The uneven patterns of adoption across remote Indigenous communities suggest that consumer preferences, deeply embedded in the culture and economy of remote Indigenous society, are likely to be more critical determinants of adoption than disadvantage.

Endnotes

1. Australian Bureau of Statistics (1999). *Household use of information technology 1998*; Australian Bureau of Statistics (2004). *Household use of information technology 2002–2003*. Online at: http://www.abs.gov.au/AUSSTATS/abs@.nsf/Lookup/8146.0Main+Features12012-13?OpenDocument
2. The analysis that follows is based upon data collected as part of the World Internet Project. We have conducted sample surveys of 1,000 Australian households in 2007, 2009, 2011, and 2013. Given the sample size and the very small population that lives in remote Australia, this data provides no information on Internet use in remote Australia. Online at: http://www.cci.edu.au/projects/world-internet-project-australia
3. Holloway, D. (2005). The digital divide in Sydney. *Information, Communication & Society* 8 (2): 168–193. Online at: http://www.tandfonline.com/doi/abs/10.1080/13691180500146276#.VBEDXbFyETA
4. Australian Government (2011–12). R2011–12 Regional Telecommunications Review. Online at: http://www.rtirc.gov.au/files/2012/06/Regional_Communications-Empowering_digital_communities.pdf
5. Department of Communications, Information Technology, and the Arts (2005). Networking the nation: Evaluation of outcomes and impacts.
6. Networking the Nation Board (1998). *Annual Report*. Published as Appendix 9 to Department of Communications, Information, and Technology and the Arts, Annual Report 1997–1998.
7. Notley, T. M., and M. Foth (2008). Extending Australia's digital divide policy: An examination of the value of social inclusion and social capital policy frameworks. *Australian Social Policy* 7: 91. Online at: http://eprints.qut.edu.au/12021/1/12021b.pdf
8. Australian National Audit Office (2010). *The National Broadband Network request for proposal process*. Department of Broadband, Communications and the Digital Economy. Online at: http://www.anao.gov.au/Publications/Audit-Reports/2009-2010/The-National-Broadband-Network-Request-for-Proposal-Process

9. Fletcher, P. (2012). Way to go to reach Conroy's broadband nirvana. *The Australian*, March 27. Online at: http://www.theaustralian.com.au/business/opinion/way-to-go-to-reach-conroys-broadband-nirvana/story-e6frg9if-1226310713950

10. Rudd, K., S. Conroy, and L. Tanner (2007). *New directions for communications: A broadband future for Australia—Building a National Broadband Network*. Australian Labor Party. Online at: http://www.theaustralian.com.au/business/opinion/way-to-go-to-reach-conroys-broadband-nirvana/story-e6frg9if-1226310713950

11. Conroy, S. (2012). Latest OECD broadband rankings reinforce the need for the NBN.

12. Australian Government (2009). New National Broadband Network. April 7, Australian Government, Canberra. Online at: http://pmtranscripts.dpmc.gov.au/preview.php?did=16491

13. Ibid.

14. Wright, T. (2010). 17 days ... and 30 minutes later we have a winner. *The Age* 7 September. Online at: http://m.theage.com.au/federal-election/17-daysand-30-minutes-later-we-have-a-winner-20100907-14z6g.html

15. Turnbull, M. (2010). Cost-benefit analysis of broadband network is essential. *Sydney Morning Herald*, October 6. Online at: http://www.smh.com.au/federal-politics/political-opinion/costbenefit-analysis-of-broadband-network-is-essential-20101005-16631.html

16. Business Council of Australia (2009). *Groundwork for growth: Building the infrastructure that Australia needs*. BCA, Melbourne. Online at: http://www.bca.com.au/publications/groundwork-for-growth

17. Ergas, H. and A. Robson (2009). The social losses from inefficient infrastructure projects: Recent Australian experience. *Strengthening Evidence-based policy in the Australian Federation, Volume 1—Proceedings*, Productivity Commission, Canberra, pp. 127–167. Online at: http://www.aph.gov.au/~/media/wopapub/senate/committee/broadband_ctte/submissions_from_april_2009/sub99_pdf.ashx

18. AAP (2010). NBN cost-benefit just wastes time: Conroy. *Sydney Morning Herald*, October 24; Kerin, P. (2010). Stephen Conroy's excuses for avoiding scrutiny of the broadband plan don't stack up. *Australian*, November 15.

19. Kenny, R. and C. Kenny (2010). *Superfast: Is it really worth a subsidy?* Communications Chambers. Online at: http://charleskenny.blogs.com/files/overselling_fibre_1127.pdf

20. Hayes, R. (2010). *Valuing broadband benefits: A selective report on issues and options.* Melbourne: Melbourne Business School, University of Melbourne and Institute for a Broadband-Enabled Society. Online at: http://papers.ssrn.com/sol3/papers.cfm?abstract_id=1856378

21. NBN Co Limited (2010). Corporate Plan 2011–2013. Melbourne. Online at: info@nbnco.com.au

22. NBN Co Limited (2013). Strategic review. Melbourne. Online at: info@nbnco.com.au

23. Morsillo, R. (2012). Affordable broadband for all Australians. *Telecommunications Journal of Australia* 62 (5). Online at: http://researchbank.swinburne.edu.au/vital/access/manager/Repository/swin:30495

24. Australian Bureau of Statistics (ABS). Online at: http://www.abs.gov.au/ausstats/abs@.nsf/Lookup/2075.0main+features32011

25. Australian Bureau of Statistics (ABS) statistics in Biddle (2013). Paper 16, p. 1.

26. CHINS (2006). Online at: http://www.abs.gov.au/Ausstats/abs@.nsf/Latestproducts/4710.0Mainpercent20Features42006?opendocument&tabname=Summary&prodno=4710.0&issue=2006&num=&view=

27. Austin-Broos, D. (2011). *A different inequality: The politics of debate about remote Aboriginal Australia.* Crows Nest, Australia: Allen & Unwin.

28. Sutton, P. (2009). *The politics of suffering: Indigenous Australia and the end of the liberal consensus.* Melbourne: Melbourne University Press; Langton, M. (2010). The shock of the new: A postcolonialist dilemma for Australianist anthropology. In *Culture crisis: Anthropology and politics in Aboriginal Australia,* eds. J. Altman and M. Hinkson (pp. 91–115). Sydney: UNSW Press.

29. McElhinney, S. (2001). Telecommunications liberalisation and the quest for universal service in Australia. *Telecommunications Policy* 25 (4): 233–248. Online at: http://www.sciencedirect.com/science/article/pii/S0308596100000963

30. In 2013, Telstra (the sole carrier in remote Australia) extended mobile coverage to a number of regional and remote locations in the Northern Territory and Western Australia.

31. Defined as "any service that offered a minimum 512 kilobits per second download and 128 kilobits per second upload data speed, with three gigabytes per month data usage at a total cost of $2,500 GST inclusive over three years (including installation and connection fees)." Online at: http://www.archive.dbcde.gov.au/2012/september/australian_broadband_guarantee

32. Barriers to adoption are discussed in E. Rennie, A. Crouch, A. Wright, and J. Thomas (2013). At home on the outstation: Barriers to home Internet in remote Indigenous communities. *Telecommunications Policy* July–August: 583–593. Online at: http://researchbank.swinburne.edu.au/vital/access/manager/Repository/swin:30416

33. Norris, P. (2001). *Digital divide: Civic engagement, information poverty and the Internet worldwide.* Cambridge, U.K.: Cambridge University Press; Warschauer, M. (2003). *Technology and social inclusion: Rethinking the digital divide.* Cambridge, MA: MIT Press.

34. Biddle, N. (2013). Socioeconomic outcomes, CAEPR Indigenous Population Project, 2011 Census Papers, Paper 13. Online at: http://caepr.anu.edu.au/sites/default/files/cck_indigenous_outcomes/2013/10/2011CensusPaper_13_Socioeconomic%20Outcomes.pdf

35. ABS (2007) Patterns of internet access in Australia, 2006, Cat No 8146.0.55.001, p7. Online at: http://www.abs.gov.au/AUSSTATS/abs@.nsf/Lookup/8146.0.55.001Main+Features12006

36. The Home Internet in Remote Indigenous Communities project is funded by an Australian Research Council Linkage grant. The Australian Communications Consumer Action Network is also a partner in the project.

37. Brady, F. and L. E. Dyson (2009). Report to the Wujal Wujal Aboriginal Shire Council on mobile technology in the Bloomfield River Valley. (Unpublished report.)

38. Our analysis of the census data revealed some peculiarities that are likely to have been the result of the way in which the survey was administered. For instance, although the census asked residents what type of Internet connection was available at the dwelling, the options included "broadband," "dial-up," and "other," with an explanatory note that "other" includes "Internet access through mobile phones etc." However, in Santa Teresa, a community with mobile coverage, no dwellings were identified as having an "other" Internet connection while 30 houses chose "not stated." In Yuendumu, 27 houses stated that they had an "other" connection and only 3 were not stated. There are a number of possible explanations for these inconsistencies, including whether the question was adequately explained to the participant, as well as confusion as to whether

individual access to the Internet via a mobile device is considered to belong to a dwelling or not. Despite these discrepancies, when grouped into ILOCs with mobile coverage and those without, the differences in Internet adoption are significant.

39. See also Tangentyere Council Research Hub & Central Land Council. (2007). Ingerrekenhe Antirrkweme: Mobile phone use among low income Aboriginal people. Tangentyere Council & Central Land Council, Alice Springs. Online at: http://www. tangentyere.org.au/publications/research_reports/MobilePhone.pdf

40. Schwab, R. G. (1995). The calculus of reciprocity: Principles and Implications of Aboriginal sharing. Discussion paper, no. 100/1995. Canberra: Centre for Aboriginal Economic Policy Research, Australian National University. Online at: http://caepr. anu.edu.au/Publications/DP/1995DP100.php

41. Also that Internet access encourages temporary mobility. See Zander, K., A. Taylor, and D. Carson (2013). Technology adoption and temporary Indigenous mobility in the Northern Territory. Research Brief 201210. Darwin: The Northern Institute (Charles Darwin University). Online at: http://www.cdu.edu.au/sites/default/files/the-northern-institute/Tech%26TempIndigMob_FINAL.pdf

42. Rennie, E., A. Crouch, A. Wright, and J. Thomas (2011). *Home Internet for remote indigenous communities*. Ultimo, NSW: Australian Communications Consumer Action Network. Online at: https://accan.org.au/files/SWIN-CLC-CATHomeInternet.pdf

43. Australian Bureau of Statistics (ABS). Online at: http://www.abs.gov.au/ausstats/abs@. nsf/Lookup/2076.0main+features702011

Chapter 7

Digital Skills in Europe: Research and Policy

Ellen Johanna Helsper and
Alexander J. A. M. van Deursen

Contents

7.1 Introduction

Digital inclusion policies have been developed across Europe to improve Internet access and skills so that individuals can fully participate in all aspects of social life. At the same time, a great deal of academic work has been done that has led to a better understanding of who is and who is not digitally literate and, as an assumed consequence, more socially included. However, as the Internet becomes increasingly embedded in everyday life for many people in Europe, research on digital inclusion has been criticized for getting into an "intellectual rut." There are concerns about the lack of a strong theoretical development of the field and the measures typically used in this research have their limitations, particularly those concerning skills, engagement, and impact of use. In this chapter, we argue that this is reflected in the way European policy and impact evaluation is implemented.

We start with an exploration around how digital skills have been defined in research and policy. This is followed by a review of how researchers have measured digital skills and engagement and what we know about the status quo of digital literacy in Europe through this research. The chapter is derived from recent research and publications by the authors of this chapter, who used the Eurostat (Directorate-General of the European Commission), British World Internet Project, and Dutch national data. These form the basis for the empirical part of the review related to the unequal distribution of digital skills amongst different sociodemographic groups within different European countries. We also discuss how policy formulation and objectives are linked to this debate around definition and measurement and what the current policy landscape in Europe looks like.

7.2 Digital Inclusion in Europe: The Role of Skills

The concept of the digital divide describes the idea that information and communication technologies (ICTs) have bypassed disadvantaged communities. Recent theorization of Internet adoption recognizes that a binary classification around physical access does not reflect the complexity of what it means to be online and an increasing number of researchers argue that more attention should be paid to motivational and skills aspects of engagement with ICTs and how these relate to different types of social exclusion.[1] Consequently, the focus within digital inclusion debates has shifted from divides to gradations of inclusion.[2] Helper's conceptualization of the development of the debate is shown in Figure 7.1.

Access, skills, motivation, and engagement with different types of content make up most definitions of digital literacy as developed in Europe in both academia and policy making.[4] *Access* is understood broadly in terms of quality, ubiquity, and mobility; *skills* as having technical, social, critical, and creative elements; *motivation* and awareness of the benefits as determined by both individual and

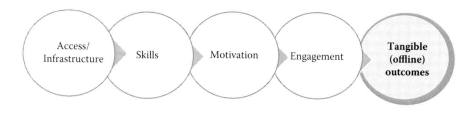

Figure 7.1 Thematical development in the focus of digital inclusion debates. (From Helsper, E. J. (2014). Digital inclusion in Europe: Evaluating policy and practice. European Commission expert peer review discussion paper.[3])

social circumstances; and *engagement* as driven by the everyday life needs of individuals through content created by and for them so that engagement with ICT is effective and sustainable.[5]

Within the theory around digital literacy and inclusion, digital skills, in particular, have gained prominence after decades of focusing on access. Unfortunately, our understanding of this is hampered because digital skills are often inferred from Internet use, and measures rely on self-reports of Internet activities that are context-dependent and positively biased.[6] Furthermore, digital skills are typically conceptualized as a single—often technical—dimension, which is problematic.[7] Several European researchers have tried to tackle this problem by creating more subtle classifications of skills.[8]

In the United Kingdom, for instance, Eynon and Helsper focused in particular on defining different levels of skills and came up with the classification of technical, social, critical, and creative skill types.[9] In the Netherlands, van Deursen and van Dijk came up with two broad skills categories of medium- and content-related skills and six subtypes.[10] They divide medium-related skills into operational (required to operate a digital medium or "button knowledge") and formal (handling the formal structures of the medium; here, browsing and navigating) skills. Content-related skills are subdivided into information (searching, selecting, and evaluating information in digital media), communication (mailing, contacting, creating online identities, drawing attention, and giving opinions), content creation (making contributions to the Internet with a particular plan or design), and strategic skills (using the digital medium as a means to achieve particular professional and personal goals).

To understand the importance of digital literacy in the broader sense of the word (i.e., including access, skills, motivation, and engagement), European theorists have argued that we need to refocus the debate around the tangible, "real" outcomes that digital inclusion policies and interventions can address.[11] It is necessary to determine categories in which benefits from online engagement can occur and link these to the particular skills and types of engagement needed to achieve these outcomes. Often, the classification of resources in economic, cultural, and social capital is used as a starting point for classifying benefits provided by the Internet. Economic capital refers to monetary assets, property, and other economic possessions, while social capital consists of resources drawn from relationships, networks, and social support. Cultural capital comprises the types of knowledge, skills, and education that increase one's social status. van Dijk elaborated on this idea of resources in his classification of participation in the different societal fields, adding spatial (the extent to which one is able to visit geographical locations and lead a mobile life), political (expressing and participating civically and politically in society), and institutional participation dimensions (engagement with public information and services).[12] Helsper added personal resources, such as an individual's psychological and physical health.[13]

As outlined above, there are several participatory fields in which the Internet matters. From digital divide research, we have learned that benefits from Internet use are not equally distributed in society. Access is being tackled through policy in most European countries with varying levels of success in regards to decreasing digital and socioeconomic inequalities. Digital skills are increasingly considered to be the key factor in determining whether individuals can participate in these fields through their engagement with ICTs and beyond the access they have to ICTs.[14] Unfortunately, the distribution of these skills is as, if not more, unequal as the distribution of access.[15]

7.2.1 Theory around Digital Literacy Policies

In European policy, there is a strong focus on supporting initiatives that ensure a workforce and citizenry capable of living in an information society. There is now sufficient research demonstrating the multivariate nature of digital literacy (i.e., access, skills, motivations, attitudes) that informs our understanding of the ways in which people use the Internet. Nevertheless, implementation of policy remains problematic because there is not enough theoretical clarity about how individuals' skills and types of engagement with services should be measured and defined. European policy research has proposed several ways in which digital literacy policies should be implemented and evaluated.[16] Helsper argues that "sustainable and successful digital inclusion initiatives start and end with tangible (offline) outcomes."[17] Policies incorporating digital access, skills, motivations, and engagement, therefore, should aim to "alleviate challenges encountered in the 'real' lives of disadvantaged groups" (p. 2). She suggests that after identifying the relevant social outcomes and groups vulnerable to exclusion and the organizations that are best positioned to engage with these, the next step is to identify the extent to which digital literacy, in terms of access, skills, motivation, and engagement, inhibit reaching the desired tangible offline social outcomes. van Dijk and van Deursen question the dominant focus on access provision in their critical theoretical framework for digital skills programs. They argue that digital literacy policy should:[18]

- *Take a social-contextual perspective.* Evidence shows that a techno-determinist approach, focusing on infrastructure provision, is not a sufficient solution for those lacking digital skills. Hardware provision programs that offer tax reductions and price discounts have not significantly improved diffusion of ICTs in disadvantaged populations, let alone improved digital skills.[19]
- *Combine technical and substantive views* and pay more attention to content-related digital skills. The techno-determinist view has created policies focusing on technical skills, ignoring the multiplexity of skills needed to engage with online content.
- *Adopt a clear target group strategy.* Current standardization and certification of digital skills in policy specifies clear learning goals, but is not adapted to the particular needs of disadvantaged groups.[20] Impact evaluation theories can suggest more effective ways in which groups that struggle with digital literacy, such as the elderly, the disabled, illiterate individuals, and migrants, can improve their skills.[21]
- *Accommodate individual needs and local cultures.* The design of digital media, courses, and training is more attractive for individuals when it is built around contents and assignments that are appealing to those concerned. Participatory design of courses and policy implementations, therefore, is best practice.

Besides the multiplicity of elements that make up digital literacy and the difficulties in identifying (vulnerable) target groups, the compound nature of digital exclusion is a complicating factor for European policy debates and implementation. Especially in countries with high levels of ICT diffusion, those most likely to have low levels of digital literacy tend to be simultaneously economically, socially, and personally disadvantaged. Identifying these individuals is difficult because they do not make up neatly, separate target groups as most policy impact evaluation frameworks stipulate. However, identification is fundamentally important for effective policy and interventions.

7.2.2 Stakeholders

Because digital inclusion is a cross-sectional issue in policymaking, policy implementation needs to take place across a range of stakeholders. van Dijk and van Deursen specify the roles that different stakeholders are expected to play in European digital skills and inclusion policy.[22] These roles can be largely identified as policy development, infrastructure and software provision, ICT-related training, and awareness raising about the benefits of digital inclusion (and the costs of exclusion). In their framework, national and local governments across different departments should engage with most of these aspects providing infrastructure, building a skills framework, raising awareness, organizing stakeholders, developing educational policy, supporting and motivating citizens to use online government services, and providing public access in public libraries, community centers, and other public buildings.

Three types of institutions are identified as involved in public access provision: schools, public libraries, and community access centers. In van Dijk and van Deursen's multisector stakeholder model, these also are ideally positioned to provide formal and informal ICT training within particular communities.[23] ICT training institutes can define the standards and certificates, and specialized skills training for particular professional groups. This is done in collaboration with publishers of learning tools; these provide skill assessments and training material.

In the category of awareness training and design, van Dijk and van Deursen identify the ICT industry and labor organizations as responsible for creating awareness about the social and economic costs of malfunctioning or badly designed ICT within businesses and organizations.[24] They also can push for and produce more user-friendly hardware and software. Helsper identified digital champions as another way in which European governments and third-sector organizations could try to promote awareness and motivate people to "get online."[25]

7.3 Status Quo in Europe

This section first overviews how digital literacy is distributed across European households and individuals from different sociodemographic backgrounds and then discusses European policy formulation and implementation in relation to the different elements of digital literacy, elaborating in particular on digital skills.

7.3.1 Digital Literacy

The potential impact of digital inclusion policies in Europe is best demonstrated by describing current inequalities in digital literacy levels. Comparative data are collected yearly by Eurostat, the European statistics office, using measures of Internet access, use and (indirect measures of) skills. The European Union (EU) Kids Online Survey has shown that similar inequalities in use, skills, and engagement also exist between European children of different age, gender, and sociodemographic groups, putting vulnerable children at risk of negative outcomes of Internet use.[26]

7.3.1.1 Access

Eurostat data show that in 2013 around 80 percent of households had Internet access at home. This comparatively high average diffusion rate masks significant differences between countries in Europe and, within individual countries, between different types of households.

Figure 7.2 shows that the difference in Internet access between households within the first income quartile (55 percent) and the fourth income quartile (79 percent) is

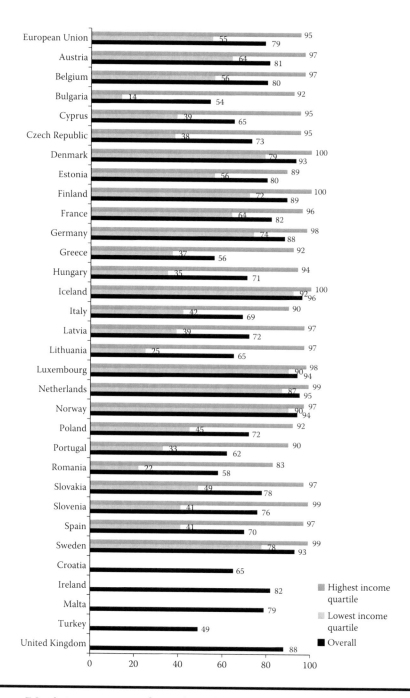

Figure 7.2 **Internet access at home in EU households (in percentages). Note: For Croatia, Ireland, Malta, Turkey, and the United Kingdom, no income level data were available. (From Eurostat, 2013.)**

40 percentage points,[27] almost all highest income quartile households are connected while only just over half of lower income households are. The Nordic countries have high household access rates of above 90 percent (96 percent in Iceland, 95 percent in the Netherlands), while the Southern and Eastern European countries (49 percent, Turkey; 54 percent, Bulgaria) have much lower rates. The smallest differences between households from the highest and lowest income quartiles (around Δ7 percent) can be found in the Nordic countries and the largest difference in the Eastern European countries (Bulgaria, 14 percent in the lowest, and 92 percent in the highest income quartile, i.e., Δ78 percent, Lithuania, Δ72 percent, Romania, Δ61 percent).

7.3.1.2 Individual Use

According to Eurostat, 77 percent of Europeans have used the Internet in the last year, but this again masks differences between groups. Overall in Europe the difference between men and women is small (Δ4 percent), but there are considerable differences related to age (Δ54 percent) and education levels (Δ42 percent).

Figure 7.3 shows that the size of these differences varies by country; there are significant differences between men and women, between older and younger persons, and between those with high and low levels of education, especially in southern and Eastern European countries.

The largest difference between men and women is around 21 percent (in Turkey), the largest difference between those under 35 and over 65 is 79 percent (in Croatia and Lithuania), and the largest difference between those with higher and lower levels of education is 70 percent (in Romania). Generally, in the Nordic countries over 90 percent of all the different sociodemographic groups are online. However, education remains a considerable barrier even there; only Iceland, Denmark, and Norway have over 90 percent of Internet users in both higher and lower educated groups. This pattern is different for age; in the "top" countries (Iceland and Sweden), only around 80 percent of 65- to 74-year-olds use the Internet.

7.3.1.3 "Skills" and Engagement

A problem with the current data for skills provided by Eurostat is that the indicators measure different types of use rather than skills and, thus, assume that someone who undertakes more activities is more skilled. Six different types of Internet use are measured to indicate Internet skill levels (see Figure 7.4 for overall percentages).

More detailed analysis by Helsper showed that there are considerable differences between age groups (32 percent to 67 percent differences between 25 to 34 and 65 to 74) and education groups (12 percent to 50 percent differences between those with no/low educational levels and those with higher education levels), and smaller, but not negligible, gender differences (4 percent to 8 percent between men and women) in the ways in which Europeans engage with the Internet.[29] These differences are larger for more common uses, such as search engine use.

	All	Age		Gender		Education	
		25–34	*65–74*	*M*	*F*	*None/Low*	*High*
European Union	77	93	39	79	75	54	96
Austria	82	97	35	85	78	58	95
Belgium	83	95	49	85	81	65	97
Bulgaria	56	78	10	58	55	22	89
Croatia	68	97	18	76	62	31	92
Cyprus	66	88	16	68	64	33	92
Czech Republic	76	90	29	77	75	64	91
Denmark	95	100	78	96	95	92	99
Estonia	82	99	33	83	81	69	93
Finland	92	100	67	93	92	84	99
France	84	96	48	85	82	66	97
Germany	86	98	51	88	83	74	95
Greece	61	86	10	65	58	26	92
Hungary	74	94	23	75	73	44	95
Iceland	97	100	80	98	96	94	100
Ireland	80	95	37	80	81	52	97
Italy	61	80	19	65	56	37	89
Latvia	76	98	26	77	76	58	93
Lithuania	69	94	15	69	69	49	94
Luxembourg	95	100	77	96	93	79	98
Malta	70	94	23	72	69	41	98
Netherlands	94	100	78	96	93	85	99
Norway	96	100	76	96	95	92	99
Poland	65	92	18	66	64	42	95
Portugal	65	94	20	69	61	46	96
Romania	55	73	12	57	53	26	96
Slovakia	81	97	30	81	81	59	98
Slovenia	74	97	26	75	72	41	97
Spain	74	94	23	76	71	51	96
Sweden	95	100	78	96	95	87	99
Turkey	46	63	5	57	36	29	95
United Kingdom	91	99	66	91	91	65	98

Figure 7.3 Internet use by individuals (in percentages) (From Eurostat, 2013; Helsper, E. J. (2014). Digital inclusion in Europe: Evaluating policy and practice. European Commission's expert peer review discussion paper.)

	Search Engine Use	Emailing Attachments	Chat	VOIP	File Sharing
European Union	75	65	37	33	14
Austria	81	71	35	33	7
Belgium	81	72	45	37	15
Bulgaria	56	42	30	35	19
Croatia	65	45	29	30	19
Cyprus	64	49	40	40	10
Czech Republic	76	70	29	40	8
Denmark	92	83	63	52	16
Estonia	78	65	39	55	24
Finland	90	78	56	45	14
France	81	72	31	40	12
Germany	83	69	28	24	4
Greece	62	47	39	34	12
Hungary	73	69	48	36	20
Iceland	93	84	47	75	37
Ireland	76	64	26	38	7
Italy	62	55	38	31	15
Latvia	75	59	37	53	25
Lithuania	71	57	57	58	34
Luxembourg	91	79	43	48	12
Malta	66	55	31	32	19
Netherlands	92	84	13	46	31
Norway	91	81	31	44	25
Poland	64	50	41	28	14
Portugal	65	53	39	29	17
Romania	50	43	27	15	6
Slovakia	81	73	37	52	15
Slovenia	74	58	36	34	20
Spain	73	60	41	25	25
Sweden	92	79	54	54	26
Turkey	47	29	20	9	10
United Kingdom	86	78	47	39	na

Figure 7.4 Individual Internet use in the last 12 months: Different "skills." (Adapted from Helsper, E. J. (2014). Digital inclusion in Europe: Evaluating policy and practice. European Commission's expert peer review discussion paper.[28])

Helsper's detailed examination of inequalities for the five types of Internet activities showed that the level of inequality within a country depends on the activity under review.[30] Generally, the Nordic countries showed smaller differences, and the southern and eastern countries showed larger differences between age, gender, and education groups. There were exceptions. For example, for *emailing attachments,* the largest gender differences observed across the European continent were in Turkey (Δ15 percent) and Luxembourg (Δ11 percent) and the smallest in Lithuania (Δ-2 percent) where women do this more than men. The largest and smallest age group differences in the use of *chat* rooms were found in Lithuania (Δ88 percent), Turkey (Δ38 percent), and the Netherlands (Δ8 percent). The largest gender differences for this activity were in Croatia (Δ13 percent). The largest and smallest gender differences in VOIP (voice-over Internet protocol) was also in Croatia (Δ8 percent) as well as Norway, while it was smallest in Iceland and Malta (Δ-2 percent). The largest gender differences in *file sharing* were observed in southern and northern European countries (Δ21 percent in Iceland) and the smallest in Malta (Δ1 percent). The largest differences between educational groups were in Bulgaria and Malta (Δ32 percent).

Considering the inadequacy of current measures, the European Commission's Media Literacy Unit attempted to define and test media literacy levels in Europe (2010).[31] Their initial evaluation of *basic use skills* (e.g., visit a specified web address or print a web page), *medium use skills* (e.g., use and compare search engines/websites to find information or download software), *advanced use skills* (e.g., creating a blog/web page or sharing text, games, images, films, or music to websites), *critical understanding* (e.g., trust of information that is presented by different media sources or awareness of information that is presented by different media sources), and *communicative* skills (e.g., engagement with public debate or social networking) showed that use skills' levels were highest (16 percent basic and 35 percent advanced level), followed by critical skills (28 percent basic and 31 percent advanced), and the lowest levels of competencies could be found for communicative skills (64 percent basic and 16 percent advanced).

So far, the core questions proposed by the Media Literacy Unit have not been implemented in representative national or European surveys. Therefore, it is not yet possible to draw conclusions about distributions of skills levels within and between countries.

7.3.2 Digital Skills Case Studies: The Netherlands and the United Kingdom

In order to paint a picture of digital literacy levels in Europe, two case studies are discussed here: The Netherlands and the United Kingdom. Recent skills research has been conducted in these high diffusion countries and the data can shed light on skills distribution and the factors explaining digital skills in Europe when physical access issues have been largely resolved.

van Deursen and van Dijk measured operational, formal, information, and strategic Internet skills in three large-scale performance tests in which subjects were asked to complete assignments on the Internet.[32] The main conclusion of these tests was that Dutch citizens show a fairly high level of operational and formal skills. On average, 80 percent of the operational skill assignments and 72 percent of the formal skill assignments were successfully completed. However, the levels of information skills and strategic Internet skills attained were much lower. Information skill assignments were completed on average by 62 percent and strategic skill assignments on average by only 25 percent of those subjected to these performance tests.

The second conclusion was that there are significant differences in performance depending on the resources of the individual. The most important explanatory factor for these differences was educational background. People with higher education performed better on all skills than people with a lower educational background. While no gender differences were observed in actual performance, men indicated having more confidence in their Internet skills than women. Age also directly contributed positively to the level of content-related skills, that is, older people performed better in information and strategic skills compared to younger people with the same levels of Internet use experience.[33] Nevertheless, older people were limited in applying these content-related skills because they lacked the medium-related Internet skills necessary to gain access to Internet content. The amount of Internet use and years of experience did not seem to affect content-related Internet skills.

In a recent survey conducted in the United Kingdom, Helsper and Eynon considered critical, social, creative, and technical skills.[34] These four types of digital skills are both operational (creative and technical) and strategic (social and critical) in nature, making them comparable to the skills used in the Dutch performance tests. They showed that different types of resources significantly predicted different types of skill. Education was related to all indicators of digital skills and self-efficacy; those with university education perceived themselves to be more skilled than those without, for all types of skill. Age also related to all skills. Older individuals were less confident and felt less skilled. Gender was similarly related to all skills. Men perceived themselves to be more skilled and had higher levels of digital self-efficacy. Social isolation was (negatively) related to all skills except for social skills and digital self-efficacy. Socially isolated people were less likely to indicate that they knew, for example, how to judge whether information online is reliable. In general, they argued that, when an exclusion indicator was related to one skill, it was related to other skills in the same manner, but that this did not always result in the same types of engagement for different groups, thus suggesting that different resources compound to form complex, multilayered explanations of digital inclusion.

7.3.3 *European Digital Literacy Policy*

In this section, we briefly review the current European policy landscape and its implementation and challenges in terms of the broad definition of digital literacy, including access, skills, motivation, and engagement.

The Digital Agenda for Europe (DAE) is the most important policy framework at the European level.[35] Three particular pillars are related to digital literacy: pillar 4 relates to access, pillar 6 relates to skills, and pillar 7 relates to engagement. The European Road Map for Digital Inclusion was established in 2011 after a DAE working group came together and established key priorities, mostly around infrastructure. The primary objective of infrastructure policy was

> ... to bring basic broadband to all Europeans by 2013 and seeks to ensure that, by 2020, (i) all Europeans have access to much higher Internet speeds of above 30 Mbps and (ii) 50 percent or more of European households subscribe to Internet connections above 100 Mbps (p. 19).

Besides infrastructure (as emphasized in pillar 4), the DAE stipulates the need for a common framework for understanding and evaluating digital skills levels (in pillar 6). According to the documents produced around the roadmap, this framework is required to design effective, contextualized formal education, and training and certification that can be used outside formal education systems. The skills needed to participate in the digital society are indirectly identified in the policy along the lines of technical, social, cultural, civic, and creative skills and related to a variety of different tangible outcomes, such as employability, health, and countering social isolation. The emphasis, however, is mostly on the skills needed to work in information technology (IT) industries. Gender issues are particularly stressed because women continue to be severely underrepresented in the IT sector. This focus on (high level) IT industry skills partly ignores the type of digital illiteracy that prevents many from doing everyday tasks and making it hard for them to participate fully in society. Elsewhere, the DAE identifies these groups at risk of digital exclusion as consisting of the elderly, low income, unemployed, and less educated.

In relation to engagement, there is an emphasis (in pillar 7) on the provision of universal cross-border national and European e-government services. Many of the other objectives under pillar 7 do not directly deal with digital inclusion; they identify a few additional important areas of personal and social well-being where ICT could help in overcoming disadvantages. In particular, "... ICT is becoming a critical element for delivering policy objectives like supporting an ageing society, ... empowering patients and ensuring the inclusion of persons with disabilities" (p. 27). The specific targets in the DAE under pillar 7 are mostly technological interventions, rather than user-driven design of technologies in areas such as e-health. User-driven or needs-driven policy is clearer in the area of cultural and creative content, but focuses on stimulating national cultural projects, such as cinema and language preservation rather than in the sense of cultural diversity and underrepresented groups.

Five targets and priority areas were identified in the Gdansk Roadmap with reference to grassroots sectors and linked to the e-skills policy for small- and medium-sized enterprises (SMEs) and disadvantaged groups.[36] The five areas reflect van Dijk and van Deursen's multistakeholder framework:[37] awareness raising about the costs of digital exclusion, accessible and stable funding for digital inclusion initiatives, digital literacy, supporting the creation of knowledge hubs for digital inclusion stakeholders, and developing and promoting common tools. The roadmap leaves open which target groups should be addressed, but mentions gender inequality, ageing, and disability in reference to digital inclusion issues.

7.3.3.1 Related European Policies

The DAE needs to be seen in the context of the wider Europe2020* framework of which the aim is to "… turn the EU into a smart, sustainable, and inclusive economy delivering high levels of employment, productivity, and social cohesion" (p. 5).[38] There are clear links between the specific target areas of Europe2020 and the digital inclusion objectives within the DAE. The access aspect of the DAE is explicitly mentioned as a flagship initiative (p. 14, Europe2020) with the objective "… to speed up the roll-out of high-speed Internet and reap the benefits of a digital single market for households and firms" (p. 6). This explicitly digital aspect of Europe2020 does not go farther than infrastructure policies, although the "circulation of content with high level of trust for consumers and companies on digital platforms as regulated by national legislation" (p. 21) is also mentioned.

In related policy documents, such as the Social Investment Package (SIP), two policy objectives regarding social innovation can be linked to digital literacy (p. 6):[39]

■ *"Preserving access to adequate social protection benefits, services, health, and long-term care."* Access and digital skills to use the Internet effectively and in a sustainable way should be a priority, especially among the most vulnerable in society (i.e., those in need of care or benefits).
■ *"Access to more personalized services ('one-stop shop')."* This relates to digital engagement, in particular to guarantee that content is available for particular vulnerable populations and targeted to the specific needs of those individuals.

7.3.3.2 Previous Policies

There was one round of policies related to digital literacy that preceded the DAE and Europe2020. The i2010 and its accompanying eEurope 2005–2009 action plan consisted of a strategic framework with broad policy guidelines for the information

---

* http://ec.europa.eu/europe2020/index_en.htm

society. i2020 was the first time that there was an "integrated policy, which aimed to encourage knowledge and innovation with a view to boosting growth and creating more, better-quality jobs."[40] Concerns were raised about the lack of digital R&D development in Europe and these were tackled partly through the DAE. Even though the i2010 was considered a success in creating a better infrastructure and increasing engagement in Europe, the current DAE incorporates many of the same objectives as the eEurope 2005–2009 action plan. It was clear that digital inclusion objectives had to be readjusted in a changing digital landscape. There was a strong need for a better understanding of the complexity of factors leading to digital and social exclusion. Particularly prominent was the concern about a lack of digital skills and the relative lack of policy understanding and impact assessment in this area.

7.3.4 Policy Classification in European Countries

There is no space in this chapter to describe all the national policy landscapes in detail. There is a wide variety of formulas across Europe and there are significant differences in where responsibility is located within countries. Often the involvement of different government departments and other sector actors is left unspecified. Helsper classified a number of European countries by whether or not publicly available policy documents mention digital inclusion in terms of access, skills, awareness, and engagement as objectives in their government policies.[41] She showed that they do not often specify how targets related to digital literacy are to be achieved, if they specify targets at all, as illustrated in Figure 7.5.

7.3.4.1 Access

Infrastructure provision (e.g., rural rollout, high-speed broadband, and accessibility) was part of almost all countries' national policies and many mention the establishment of a platform that joins up all government and public services to provide easy access. None of the policies mentioned setting up a cross-border service, with the exception of Norway. The main challenge for the access area is that these policies focus on geography (e.g., increasing connectivity in rural areas) rather than on targeted access provision or funding for organizations working with specific vulnerable groups. Monitoring of whether sites and platforms are used by individuals from groups with different sociodemographic backgrounds is not transparently done, in particular, in countries with lower levels of diffusion. This universal, as opposed to a contextualized, approach is likely to be one of the reasons why implementation is less effective than expected for these policies.

7.3.4.2 Skills

A number of countries have digital skills initiatives that focus on school or libraries/ Community Technology Centers (CTCs) training and, as indicated by van Dijk

Strategic Policy Areas	Operational Objectives	AT	CZ	DE	EE	EL	GB	HU	IT	NL	NO	PT	PL	RO
Infrastructure	Increasing speed	V	V	V		V	V	V	V		V		V	V
	Integrated platforms for services (e.g., G-Cloud)			V	V	V	V	V		V	V		V	V
Access	Ubiquitous access (CTCs, libraries, schools)		V			V	V	V	V		V	V	V	V
	Accessibility					V	V		V	V	V	V		
Skills	Formal education in schools	V		V	V	V	V	V		V	V	V	V	V
	Formal certification for adults (on-the-job training)	V		V			V			V	V	V	V	
	Stimulating informal learning	V		V			V			V	V		V	
Awareness	Digital champion	V					V			V			V	
	Public awareness campaigns about benefits of the Internet	V		V	V	V				V				V
	Public awareness of online risks			V	V	V	V		V	V	V	V		V
Engagement	Content for specific vulnerable/excluded groups	V			V		V			V	V			V
	eGov content	V		V	V	V	V	V	V	V	V	V	V	V
	Commercial content		V	V	V	V	V	V	V	V	V		V	V

Note: This overview refers to the reported focus in public policy documents and not to implementation.

Figure 7.5 Strategic digital inclusion policy foci of selected European countries. (Adapted from Helsper, E. J. (2014). Digital inclusion in Europe: Evaluating policy and practice. European Commission's expert peer review discussion paper.[42])

and van Deursen, assume that access provision in these locations is akin to increasing literacy in vulnerable groups.[43] Very few policies mention specific certifications for those who are not in education. The least prevalent are policies that refer to stimulating informal learning either through volunteer digital champion schemes or by encouraging public–private partnerships that set up learning through play programs or provide such training online. If anything is mentioned, the elderly are usually the focus and the European Computer Driver's License (ECDL) is the certification. Conspicuously absent from implementation and evaluation of digital skills initiatives are those from disadvantaged socioeconomic backgrounds, those with lower levels of education, and migrants and women from particular socioeconomic backgrounds identified in Europe2020 as at risk of social exclusion. Even when specific target groups are mentioned, national policies are not contextualized. That is, they do not discuss which types and levels of skills initiatives are needed for different groups and instead rely heavily on the decontextualized and universal ECDL.

7.3.4.3 Motivation

Digital champions are seen as a good way to create awareness and engagement about the benefits of digital literacy. Digital champions are either volunteers who help the disconnected online and increase their skills or national figureheads who raise awareness among industry and third-sector stakeholders. The European Safer Internet program has been successful in bringing together different stakeholders at the national and regional level in matters around making people aware of online risks. Most of these awareness-raising activities focus on children. At the moment, there is no equivalent for awareness raising around the benefits and there is no cross-European initiative nor is it connected to specific government departments in national policies. There is a notable absence of any awareness of benefits initiatives targeted at specific vulnerable groups with the exception of the elderly. In many countries, nongovernment organizations (NGOs) take on this role in a nationally uncoordinated manner. This slightly chaotic approach is partly due to the lack of integration in national policies that links digital literacy to traditional fields of social exclusion. The role of digital champions is not specified along those lines and there is no solid evidence for tangible positive social outcomes because most evaluations refer to individual, anecdotal success stories.

7.3.4.4 Engagement

Most policy initiatives around the provision of content for identified vulnerable groups are aimed at the elderly or at the disabled. For the former, this focuses on skills training and awareness of age-relevant digital services and, for the latter, on accessibility or care. Platforms with content for youth also are common. Policy rarely mentions guaranteeing or stimulating relevant content production for specific vulnerable groups that are underrepresented online. Conspicuously absent are the DAE target groups: women, ethnic minorities, low income, and the unemployed. Nor are other specific groups mentioned, which take prominence in the Europe2020 framework, such as disadvantaged youth (e.g., NEETs (not in education, employment, or training)). One challenge here is that those most likely to benefit from the full range of services offered online often have compound levels of social and digital exclusion. Content targeted at any one of these groups is likely to reach the most engaged within these groups and not those who are socially excluded.

Most country policies mention the creation of electronic government content without specifying (1) how this will affect particular groups at risk of social exclusion or (2) whether the content of these services is designed around the specific needs of these groups. The roadmap suggests participatory design, user-driven social innovation projects, and public–private partnerships, but the lack of definition of clear target groups means that NGOs and volunteer organizations are often on their own in figuring out what to do and with whom.

Policies that mention stimulating commercial content, for example, for SMEs, focus on safety and payment systems rather than on support for SMEs in creating content suitable to their needs. Worrying is that representation of target groups (e.g., women) in the creation of commercial online content is not part of national policies, reflecting the lack of these groups in IT industry and education.

7.4 Conclusion and Policy Recommendations

This chapter focused on digital literacy in European research and policy. We used a broad definition of digital literacy, seeing it as the sum of access, skills, and engagement. Most of the discussion focused on skills in particular because, increasingly, this is considered a key variable in inclusion theory. Furthermore, current European (and often national) policy development increasingly prioritizes digital skills. The good news, therefore, is that the emphasis is no longer primarily on access provision. Nevertheless, the measurement of digital skills is still contentious and lacks nuance, as evidenced by its lack of inclusion in large-scale European surveys. As a consequence, the evaluation of policy effectiveness beyond infrastructure provision, related to digital skills and engagement, is poor. This is problematic because individuals' skills and motivations seem more important than infrastructure, especially in northern and western European countries where diffusion rates are reaching saturation.

Policies dealing with inequalities in engagement with ICTs have focused on the supply rather than the demand side. Unfortunately, user-driven and participatory design is to a large extent absent in the provision of European e-government content and services for specific socially excluded groups. To support more effective and efficient policies, there is a need for a theoretical framework that not only links different digital skills to engagement with ICTs, but also explains how this relates to the needs of specific disadvantaged groups. This chapter showed that European researchers are making steps in this direction and that initiatives have started to go beyond seeing skills as the sum of merely operation of hard- and software. Thus, theory and practice are improving in regards to different skill levels and their antecedents and measurement adjustments are following, albeit slowly.

For this to be truly successful, cooperation between European countries is needed so that policymakers and digital inclusion stakeholders can learn from each other. Even at the national level, there is often a lack of interdepartmental and cross-sector collaboration. As a consequence, no real comparison is possible between and within European countries because integrated frameworks are underdeveloped and agreement on measurements is lacking. This is reflected in poor national policy development, implementation, and the absence of evaluations. A more valid and reliable universal definition of digital skill types would facilitate improved understanding and better monitoring of policy effectiveness at both national and international levels.

So, what do we know about the status quo of digital literacy in Europe? The research presented on the relationship between education, age, Internet experience, and Internet skills in Europe suggest that inequalities in digital skills will not automatically disappear in the future, even in countries with high Internet diffusion levels, unless clearly targeted interventions are implemented. One problem is that European policy emphasizes training (entrepreneurs) to work in IT industries, while there is still clearly a lack of knowledge of the basic skills needed for "everyday" jobs or for volunteer intermediaries helping others to get online.

Helsper showed that publicly available national policy documents rarely specify how targets related to digital literacy are to be achieved, if targets are specified at all.[44] Consequently, but not solely for that reason, evaluation of the effectiveness of the implementation of specific European policies in relation to improvements in access, skills, motivation, and engagement is extremely difficult. This review of national European policies also showed that the involvement of different government departments and actors in other sectors is often left unspecified. This is worrying especially in light of the multistakeholder framework set out by van Dijk and van Deursen that argues that digital skills policies only work if it has multisector support and is integrated across the work of a variety of actors.[45]

It is important to keep in mind that, in the end, it is not digital engagement or skills that matter, but the narrowing of inequality in relation to everyday social challenges like employability and general well-being. We have argued in this chapter that the current confusion around digital literacy and effective policies hinder thinking about how digital inclusion can help achieve tangible outcomes. A concerted European effort to create awareness about the benefits, targeted at specific disengaged populations and their everyday needs and a platform organizing public–private partnerships is desperately needed. European scholarly work on digital inclusion is moving toward the key areas of social exclusion and deprivation that need to be addressed and toward identifying the types of digital inclusion interventions and policies that are most effective in reaching these.[46] Encouragingly, this thinking seems to be filtering through in recent policy debates at the European level where digital inclusion is moving to education, business, and health departments instead of being located in isolated or separate policies.

Endnotes

1. For example, DiMaggio, P. and E. Hargittai (2001). From the 'digital divide' to 'digital inequality': Studying Internet use as penetration increases. Working paper series 15. Princeton, NJ: Princeton University Center for Arts and Cultural Policy Studies; Helsper, E. J. (2012). A corresponding fields model of digital inclusion. *Communication Theory* 22 (4): 403–426; Mossberger, K., C. J. Tolbert, and R. S. McNeal (2008). *Digital citizenship: The Internet, society, and participation.* Cambridge, MA: MIT Press; Van Dijk, J. (2005). *The deepening divide.* Thousand Oaks, CA: Sage Publications; Warschauer, M. (2003). *Technology and social inclusion. Rethinking the digital divide.* Cambridge, MA: MIT Press.
2. Livingstone, S., and E. J. Helsper (2007). Gradations in digital inclusion: Children, young people and the digital divide. *New Media & Society* 9 (4): 671–696; van Deursen, A. and J. van Dijk (2014). The digital divide shifts to differences in usage. *New Media & Society*, doi: 10.1177/1461444813487959; van Dijk, *The deepening divide*; Warschauer, *Technology and social inclusion.*
3. Helsper, E. J. (2014). Digital inclusion in Europe: Evaluating policy and practice. European Commission Expert Peer Review discussion paper.
4. Celot, P., and J. M. Pérez Tornero (2009). Study on the assessment criteria for media literacy levels. European Commission. Online at: http://ec.europa.eu/culture/media/media-literacy/studies_en.htm; Livingstone, S. (2004). Media literacy and the challenge of new information and communication technologies. *The Communication Review* 1 (7): 3–14; Ofcom (2010). Media literacy. Information about Ofcom's media literacy activities. Online at: http://stakeholders.ofcom.org.uk/market-data-esearch/media-literacy/
5. Helsper, Digital inclusion in Europe.
6. van Deursen, A., and J. van Dijk (2010). Measuring Internet skills. *International Journal of Human Computer Interaction* 26 (10): 891–916.
7. Ibid.
8. For example, Buckingham, D. (2005). The media literacy of children and young people. A review of the research literature. Ofcom. Online at: www.ofcom.org.uk; Livingstone, S. (2008). Engaging with media—A matter of literacy? *Communication, Culture & Critique* 1 (1): 51–62; van Deursen, A., and J. Van Dijk (2009). Using the Internet: Skill-related problems in users' online behavior. *Interacting with Computers* 21: 393–402; van Deursen and van Dijk, Measuring Internet skills; Warschauer, *Technology and social inclusion.*
9. Helsper, E. J., and R. Eynon (2013). Pathways to digital literacy and engagement. *European Journal of Communication* 28 (6).
10. van Deursen and van Dijk, Using the Internet; van Deursen and van Dijk, Measuring Internet skills; van Deursen and van Dijk, Internet skills and the digital divide; van Deursen and van Dijk, The digital divide shifts to differences in usage.

11. Helsper, A corresponding fields model of digital inclusion; van Dijk, *The deepening divide.*
12. van Dijk, *The deepening divide.*
13. Helsper, A corresponding fields model of digital inclusion.
14. van Deursen and van Dijk, Internet skills and the digital divide.
15. For example, Livingstone and Helsper, Gradations in digital inclusion; van Deursen and van Dijk, Internet skills and the digital divide.
16. Institute for Prospective Technological Studies (2011). Under the radar: The contribution of civil society and third sector organisations to e-Inclusion. European Commission, Joint Research Centre. Online at: http://ftp.jrc.es/EURdoc/JRC65414.pdf; Institute for Prospective Technological Studies (2012). Digital competence in practice: An analysis of frameworks. European Commission, Joint Research Centre. Online at: http://ftp.jrc.es/EURdoc/JRC68116.pdf
17. Helsper, Digital inclusion in Europe.
18. van Dijk, J., and A. van Deursen (2014). *Digital skills: Key to the information society.* London: Palgrave.
19. van Dijk, *The deepening divide.*
20. Helsper, Digital inclusion in Europe.
21. van Dijk and van Deursen, *Digital skills.*
22. Ibid.
23. Ibid.
24. Ibid.
25. Helsper, Digital inclusion in Europe.
26. Livingstone, S., L. Haddon, A. Görzig, and K. Ólafsson (2011). *Risks and safety on the Internet: The perspective of European children.* London: London School of Economics, EU Kids Online; Smahel, D., E. J. Helsper, L. Green, V. Kalmus, L. Blinka, and K. Olaffson (2013). *Excessive Internet use amongst European children.* EU Kids Online Short Report. London: London School of Economics.
27. Percent is used to indicate percentage point differences when comparisons between groups are made.
28. Helsper, Digital inclusion in Europe.
29. Ibid.
30. Ibid.
31. Online at: http://ec.europa.eu/culture/media/media-literacy/index_en.htm
32. van Deursen and van Dijk, Using the Internet; van Deursen and van Dijk, Measuring Internet skills; van Deursen and van Dijk, Internet skills and the digital divide.
33. van Deursen, A., J. van Dijk, and O. Peters (2011). Rethinking Internet skills. The contribution of gender, age, education, Internet experience, and hours online to medium- and content-related Internet skills. *Poetics* 39: 125–144.
34. Helsper and Eynon, Pathways to digital literacy and engagement.
35. Online at: http://eur-lex.europa.eu/LexUriServ/LexUriServ.do?uri=COM:2010:0245:FIN:EN:PDF
36. Online at: http://innodig.eu/download/Gdansk_Roadmap_Reworked_text_7.10.11.pdf
37. van Dijk and van Deursen, *Digital skills.*
38. Online at: http://eur-lex.europa.eu/LexUriServ/LexUriServ.do?uri=COM:2010:2020:FIN:EN:PDF)

39. Online at: http://ec.europa.eu/social/main.jsp?catId=1044&langId=en
40. Online at: http://europa.eu/legislation_summaries/information_society/strategies/c11328_en.htm
41. Helsper, Digital inclusion in Europe.
42. Ibid.
43. van Dijk and van Deursen, *Digital skills*.
44. Helsper, Digital inclusion in Europe.
45. van Dijk and van Deursen, *Digital skills*.
46. Helsper, Digital inclusion in Europe.

DIGITAL INCLUSION OPPORTUNITIES

Chapter 8

Digital Inclusion: The Singapore Perspective

Lim Swee Cheang and Guo Lei[1]

Contents

8.1 Introduction: The Singapore Journey

Singapore, an island country in Southeast Asia, is a highly developed digital economy. It has the third highest per capita gross domestic product (GDP) in the world, which was worth US$274.7 billion in 2013. Singapore embarked on the information and communications technology (ICT) journey in the early 1980s with a goal to transform the city–state into a world-class smart city and to be a leading innovator of digital technology. Its digitization agenda seeks to dramatically improve organizational efficiency, service quality, and workforce productivity, leading to national competitiveness. Some of the key strategies are to enhance the workforce skills; having the public sector take the lead to inspire other economic sectors to invest and deploy ICT; strengthening government, business, and workforce partnership; and maintaining social harmony.

After three decades, Singapore has been consistently ranked amongst the top in e-government, innovation index, education standard, best skilled, and most motivated workforce, labor/employer relations, most competitive city, most network-ready country, the best investment potential, most business conducive, and many other leading world-ranking reports.[2] For example, in the Networked Readiness Index 2013, Singapore remained in second place globally because of its extreme efficiency, business friendliness, strong intellectual protection, and high university enrollment rate. It also held the third position in terms of ICT usage with the world's highest mobile broadband penetration rate. In particular, Singapore has achieved the maximum possible score on the United Nations e-Government Online Service Index and ranked first on the indicator capturing the importance of ICTs for government.[3]

In this context, while it is difficult to imagine that anyone in a generally well-off digital economy, such as Singapore, is not positively affected by the ease of access to Internet and other ICT-enabled services, it remains true that not everyone is equally well-served. Singapore has a high degree of income inequality, which, together with the inequality in educational attainment, led to the digital divide between digital users and nondigital users. Accordingly, Singapore is ranked at 55th in the affordability of ICT, according to the World Economic Forum 2013. This chapter, based on extensive desk research, examines the history and current state of the digital divide in Singapore and highlights some key issues and challenges. We also provide a brief introduction on the digital inclusion programs initiated by the Singapore government, as well as the perspective and issues faced by the private sector and the involvement of community. Accordingly, this chapter concludes with a discussion of challenges and lessons learned.

8.2 Digital Inclusion

Digital inclusion is not an end goal, but rather a means to create a socially, economically, and politically harmonious society. Therefore, it is important to implement digital inclusion by not stopping at the digital space, but to work beyond it to also realize the end goals of bringing real benefits to individuals who are in disadvantageous positions in the society. The outcome is more important than an isolated view of digital inclusion.

It is widely presumed that access to ICT would bring about a society of better interaction, easy access to a wider body of knowledge, greater opportunity in obtaining learning, and higher productivity, resulting in higher standards of living, and intellectual enrichment. During the 1990s, researchers and policy experts also were aware of the existence of a "digital divide" between those who had access to ICT and those who had not.

There is an emerging body of evidence that those who suffer social exclusion, combinations of social disadvantages, such as poor skills, poor health, and low income, are likely as well to be excluded from the information society. Empirical research has revealed that annual income is the strongest predictor of individual Internet usage.[4]

More specifically, there are four major types of social disadvantages leading to an individual's inability to access and use of ICT services:[5]

1. People who are economically disadvantaged are particularly excluded from using resources on the Internet, such as government services and financial resources.
2. Those poorly educated encounter barriers when accessing education and learning resources on the Internet.
3. The elderly or retired have less likelihood of benefiting from social applications of the Internet.
4. Having a disability reduces the chances of accessing the Internet in general.

Moreover, Bradbrook and Fisher have proposed the "5 Cs" of digital inclusion: connectivity (the availability and reliability of Internet access), capability (digital capability at the individual and collective level), content (the substance and language), confidence (self-efficacy), and continuity.[6] The latter, continuity, is related to the idea that ICT technology has become an ingrained part of everyday life. Apparently, it is impossible to separate the "digital world" from the "real world." The social isolation can emerge as being particularly lacking in engagement with the ICT resources, which has the potential to help those disadvantaged become less isolated. Therefore, the link between digital and social exclusion has clearly increased the political spotlight on inequalities around the access and use of ICT.

While digital exclusion is a reflection of social exclusion or social inequality, improving digital inclusion might help reduce some gaps of inequality. However, implementing digital inclusion alone would not be sufficient to make a real difference in solving the inequality. The Singapore approach, therefore, has taken the task beyond the digital space.

8.2.1 Public Sector Initiatives in Singapore

The all-inclusive digital society in Singapore was made possible through careful planning and long-term strategies. The Infocomm Development Authority of

Singapore (IDA) has initiated a series of "Infocomm Bridging" programs and policies to ensure no individual will be left behind in the endeavor of an all-inclusive digital society.[7] In the celebration of 25 years of the Singapore National Infocomm Awards on October 10, 2006, Prime Minister Lee Hsien Long, announced the "Digital Opportunities for All" plan to "make the next-generation infocomm infrastructure readily accessible to all Singaporeans."[8] The new schemes would provide more targeted assistance to help needy Singaporeans make full use of infocomm, especially for the school-going children from low-income families, senior citizens, and the disabled community. With this plan, the economically disadvantaged would not be denied computer and Internet access due to financial destitution. People with disabilities could receive infocomm training, improved employability, and integration into mainstream society. The less tech-savvy seniors could be at ease with technology and stay connected in the digital age.

From 2003 to 2006, three programs were officially introduced to help disadvantaged groups of people cross the digital divide. They include:

- Equipping the Needy with NEU (new or refurbished used) PC Plus[9]
- Empowering the Disabled with Infocomm Accessibility Centre
- Engaging Senior Citizens with Silver Infocomm Initiative

Besides subsidizing access to ICTs and digital literacy trainings, task forces were formed to facilitate the development of multilingual and multicultural content for non-English literate citizens. IDA recruited hundreds of volunteers and worked with industry partners, community groups, institutions, and various media to implement these initiatives.

8.2.2 NEU PC Plus[10]

Although computers, broadband access, and mobile phones became necessities to many people in Singapore, they remained out of reach for 14 percent of households with school children in 2006, according to a speech by the Singapore prime minister in October 2006. The NEU PC Plus aimed to provide needy students equal access to ICTs and, as of March 2014, more than 17,000 low-income households with school children or disabled family members were beneficiaries of this program.

Evolved from a pilot "PC Reused Scheme," the NEU PC Program offered needy households either a subsidized, new PC or a free refurbished PC. NEU PC Plus provided free Internet connectivity, bundled with office applications, and antivirus software. The program achieved a wider reach to children homes, and other voluntary welfare organizations serving youths. More options on copayment schemes were made available to help needy students to own PCs, such as offering free PCs to students who would perform community service. Since its inception, the program has benefited students and disabled people from 17,000 low-income families with infocomm facilities, as of March 2014.

8.2.3 Infocomm Accessibility Center[11]

Access to Assistive Technology (AT) and ICT allows people with disabilities to achieve greater autonomy and independence, increase participation, and reduce psychosocial and physical stress, which may lead to an enhanced subjective quality of life and self-esteem. The Singapore Enabling Master Plan 2012–2016 seeks to build on the foundation laid by the earlier initiatives to strive toward an inclusive society.[12] It sets out to address the needs of people with disabilities as well as the needs of their caregivers. A master plan would be developed to scale up the adoption of AT and ICT in special schools and for the community, in general, with the purpose of enabling more independent living among the disabled people. The teachers and caregivers can use devices to provide creative solutions to help disabled people overcome challenges, such as difficulties in mobility and communication, and become more independent and productive.

While the use of AT and ICT can potentially enhance the quality of life of people with disabilities, many of them may not realize the benefits. A local survey suggested that AT was underutilized at the systemic level in Singapore. This was mainly due to low awareness of the devices and the lack of coordination of resources at the national level. There was also a shortage of trained AT specialists to support teachers and therapists, and to address parents' queries on AT. Under the master plan, the provision of AT and ICT is primarily targeted at helping people with disabilities in mainstream education or open employment by optimizing the use of devices in teaching, learning, and assistance in daily living activities. For example, an independent national-level resource center was set up to promote the adoption and use of AT and ICT. It aims to serve people with disabilities through the provision of consultancy support, knowledge transfer, and AT and ICT services.

Moreover, opened in July 2008, the Infocomm Accessibility Center (IAC) was conceptualized as part of the previous Enabling Master Plan 2007–2011 to provide accessible IT training to bridge the digital divide for people with disabilities, including those with physical, sensory, intellectual, and developmental disabilities.[13] IAC is managed by the Society for the Physically Disabled (SPD), which provides infocomm training to enhance employment opportunities of people with physical disabilities, sensory impairments, and developmental disabilities. The IAC successfully completed a five-year project by providing close to 5,800 training places from September 2007 to July 2012; it exceeded the planned target of delivering 5,244 training places by August 2012. In this five-year period, IAC has trained 1,500 individuals, enabling them to be more independent and helping them to achieve more with technology. With greater accessibility to AT and ICT, people with disabilities are empowered to live independently and productively, and lead their lives with greater dignity.

Along with this was the opening of the AT Loan Library and IT Apprenticeship Program (ITAP). The AT Loan Library was the first in Asia to cater to people with disabilities. It allows them to borrow computer accessibility tools and AT devices for trial before purchase, and for replacement use when their personal sets have been sent for repair or servicing. Meanwhile, the ITAP serves to bridge the gap between training and employment for people with disabilities by providing on-the-job training and structured courses to equip trainees with the necessary skills set for employment.

Another example is the job placement for the unemployed disabled people. The conventional wisdom was that the unemployed would first attend training and then look for a job. The SPD has tried it the other way around, namely, instead of train and place, they place and train. In 2012, SPD was accredited as an Approved Training Organization with the Workforce Development Agency that allows it to conduct Workforce Skills Qualifications courses. It has the Employment Support Program to provide job placement and job support services for trainees undergoing vocational training programs. The program assists people with disabilities who require direct job placement and support services by providing job matching and up to six months of job support. Upon successful placement, those who are placed would be able to adapt and sustain in open employment.

8.2.4 The Silver Infocomm Initiative[14]

Singapore is a fast-aging society and senior citizens tend to be reluctant to use ICTs and more likely to be marginalized from the digital economy. The Silver Infocomm Initiative (SII), launched in November 2007, aims to bridge the digital divide among senior citizens and help them get connected in the digital age and have richer lives. IDA has set up more than 100 Silver Infocomm Hotspots for senior citizens at convenient places, such as community centers, senior citizen connect areas, or at clan associations, and public libraries. The SII program employed a four-prong strategy to help senior citizens get connected in the digital world including raising awareness of infocomm and benefits, increasing adeptness of infocomm among seniors, enhancing availability of infocomm resources and access point, and promoting advocacy in infocomm usage.

Since 2007, more than 86,000 training places have been attained. First, senior-friendly infocomm workshops were conducted to help the senior citizens embrace the use of mobile services and web-based applications in their daily lives and forge closer ties with their loved ones. Secondly, the initiative promoted a digital lifestyle to seniors by enhancing their personal interests and recreational activities using infocomm. Thirdly, seniors who were tech-savvy would contribute actively as volunteers and help others acquire infocomm skills at their preferred pace and language. The three programs were implemented through the concerted efforts of partners from the industry and society.

Under the SII, the Intergenerational IT Boot Camp is a joint effort by the IDA and school partners, which was first introduced in early 2010. In this program, senior citizens learned IT skills with the help of their grandchildren guiding them along during the lessons, such as learning to surf the Internet, watch videos on YouTube, use handwriting devices to insert Chinese text on search engines, and make travel bookings online. It leveraged the resources of many neighborhood schools as the boot camps. Students conducted one-on-one tutorials for the senior citizens. They also were engaged in event planning and execution, and fostering relationships with the residents in the community. It offered a platform for students to impart practical computer skills to their grandparents who were drawn to participate by the "back-to-school" appeal and the opportunity to bond with their grandchildren. The Intergenerational IT Boot Camp program has gained international recognition, winning one of the top accolades at the Commonwealth Associate for Public Administration and Management International Innovation Award in 2012.

Another iconic annual event was the Silver Infocomm Day, which was organized by IDA and supported by Institutes of Higher Learning (IHLs), industry, and community partners. It was a three-in-one event consisting of seminars, exhibitions and hands-on IT workshops featuring the latest in infocomm lifestyle trends. Seniors can pick up infocomm tips and tricks to enhance their digital lifestyle. Specifically, these IT workshops were offered in all four national languages at participating IHLs. More than 25,000 senior citizens have attended the event since 2007.

8.2.5 ICT Support for the Social Sector[15]

Social sector organizations, such as voluntary welfare groups, nonprofit charities, grassroots organizations, and community groups can get help in making use of infocomm technologies to enhance their public outreach efforts as well as improve productivity and efficiency. The People Sector Infocomm Resource Center (PSIRC), for example, provides infocomm advisory services, gives social organizations access to information repository systems and provides them with networking platforms to interact and exchange ideas with other organizations. The PSIRC, which started its operations in October 2011, was officially launched by Chan Chun Sing, acting Minister for Community Development, Youth, and Sports, and Minister of State for Information, Communications, and the Arts, in April 2012. In his opening address, Chan said more funds would be invested in the center in its first two years, "so that Singapore's People sector, or 'heart' sector, which comprises voluntary welfare organizations, grassroots organizations, and community groups, can tap on infocomm to further reach out and increase participation in their activities".

Since its inception, the program has touched base with over 400 organizations, and is working on more than 30 projects at different stages of development. Completed projects include creating a Web 2.0 website for the Central Singapore Community Development Council, developing a video dictionary for the Singapore Association for the Deaf to compile signs for local words, such as durians and the esplanade, and revamping the website for the Bishan Home for the Intellectually Disabled. The PSIRC also is working with the YWCA on a siren mobile app to enhance the protection of women. The app triggers a siren or sends out an SMS (short message service) or e-mail to programmed recipients when a woman is in distress. The information relayed could even include the user's location for quicker assistance.

8.2.6 ICT Support for the Business Sector[16]

At present, there is a very big digital gap between local small- and medium-sized enterprises (SMEs) and the large local and multinational corporations. SMEs also are beneficial of the government's infocomm support. The Infocomm@SME program was one of the key initiatives to bridge the gap. Through the Infocomm@SME initiative, IDA provides comprehensive assistance that enable SMEs in Singapore to level up their business with the use of infocomm. The grant and resources for SMEs are designed to make infocomm adoption accessible and hassle free.

iSPRINT, for example, is an integrated grant scheme led by IDA in collaboration with SPRING Singapore, a government business development agency, and the Inland Revenue Authority of Singapore. With IDA as the one-stop gateway for grant applications, SMEs can get funding assistance for a wide scope of qualifying costs, ranging from basic, ready-to-use IT packages to large-scale, tailor-made enterprise systems.

The iSPRINT scheme makes it easy and convenient for SMEs to seek assistance in infocomm adoption by supporting them in the use of prequalified packaged solutions or customized solutions that will help them in their business. The packaged solutions consist of prequalified solutions that are available off-the-shelf or on a pay-per-use basis. Moreover, the SME Infocomm Resource Centers provide advisory and preproject consultancy services, as well as IT clinics and workshops for SMEs. There are currently two resource centers set up by IDA in collaboration with the Singapore Institute of Retail Studies and the Singapore Chinese Chamber of Commerce and Industry. In addition, a mass media campaign was used to promote the iSPRINT program, e.g., Project-I, a series of TV programs that featured how SMEs can adopt infocomm.

8.3 Civil Society: Beyond the Horizon

The Singapore Association of the Visually Handicapped serves to enhance the lives of people with vision impairment by promoting the use of assistive devices and technologies to help them get on in life in the area of education, recreation, or employment.[17] To achieve this objective, first, it carries a variety of white canes to meet the various mobility needs of the blind and visually impaired. Secondly, it has a comprehensive range of magnifiers and monoculars to cater to the varying eye conditions of people with vision impairment. Thirdly, the center offers a range of assistive lifestyle products, such as Braille watches, talking clocks, talking medical equipment, and games suitable for people with vision impairment. It also assists clients in purchasing electronic assistive devices and technologies, such as screen readers, screen magnifiers, and desktop or portable electronic magnifiers.

The Singapore Therapeutic, Assistive, and Rehabilitative Technologies Center is a social enterprise established with the vision to improve the quality of life for disabled people by promoting and offering medical equipment. The equipment is incorporated into a treatment plan, such as the alternative and augmentative communication devices that enables an individual with a significant communication impairment to obtain, maintain, or regain communication capabilities.

A website on inclusion of people with disabilities was set up by Senior Assistant Director Royson Poh, Society of Physically Disabled.[18] Royson is a senior nonprofit executive and independent news media journalist, advocating for the inclusion of people with disabilities into all aspects of society. The website provides stories on the challenges faced by individuals with disabilities, how they overcome them, and how we can all play a part in creating an inclusive society.

Research labs, such as the NUS Augmented Reality and Assistive Technology Lab, were launched to develop assistant technology for the elderly people and people with disabilities.[19] The augmented reality-based assistive technology devices and rehabilitation systems can be effectively employed to assist the handicapped and elderly individuals in their everyday life as well as rehabilitation needs.

In Microsoft's Digital Inclusion White Paper, *A Road Map Toward Digital Inclusion*, Karen Archer Perry (founder and principal consultant, Karacomm) explained how digital inclusion was not just a matter of being connected to the ICT:[20]

> The problem is not a binary one. It is not a question of being connected or disconnected. As such, the best initiatives address more than inclusion; they address digital empowerment, digital opportunity, digital equity, and digital excellence. These programs recognize that technology is a tool, but more and more it's a central tool for education, economic development, and social well-being. People may start as very basic users who simply need access to resources at a community technology center or a library. Digital empowerment refers to the ability to use the wealth of resources in computing and the Internet to learn, communicate, innovate, and enhance wealth—to move from being a digital novice to a digital professional or innovator. An effective digital inclusion strategy provides a path to full participation in a digital society. (p. 3)

The availability of physical access is arguably not enough, as it gave a passive connotation to using ICTs. Full participation and engagement should be a more appropriate indictor for "digital inclusion" or "social inclusion."

In 2006, Singapore started its sixth master plan, Intelligent Nation 2015 (iN2015), earmarking broadband network connectivity as a priority area to meet

Singapore's economic and social development needs.[21] This led to the development of the Next Generation Nationwide Broadband Network (Next-Gen NBN), a new all-fiber network delivering speeds of 1 gigabyte (GB) and beyond per second to homes, schools, government buildings, businesses, and hospitals.[22] To achieve this vision, IDA revised the Code of Practice for Infocomm Facilities in Buildings in May 2013, to require new residential homes to be preinstalled with optical fiber. Today, Next-Gen NBN has achieved over 95-percent deployment nationwide with new ultra high-speed services, such as interactive TV applications, cloud services, and learning resources.[23]

The ultra high-speed broadband network, as well as an enabling infrastructure, laid the foundation for Singapore to become a smart nation. Broadband-enabled innovative services now are being deployed to homes, schools, and businesses. Robust infocomm infrastructure and all-inclusive digital society could spur the development of new knowledge-based sectors, including R&D, business and social analytics, and creative industries. For example, IDA has established a High-Performance Analytic Center of Innovation, the first of its kind in Asia. Its role is to train professionals in data management and analytics, and to generate intellectual property through co-development with institutes of higher learning. Also, the Ministry of Manpower has developed an analytics solution that draws information from a variety of departmental sources to support its early detection of potential employment issues. This solution can provide information in a timely manner to give employers great visibility into skills availability, to identify and close skill gaps, and to offer a more targeted service to both employees and employers.

The Singapore approach, therefore, is to provide Next Gen NBN and at the same time establishing innovation centers to create an ecosystem for social inclusion and co-creation.

8.4 Our Singapore Conversation[24]

The Our Singapore Conversation (OSC) initiative was first announced by Prime Minister Lee Hsien Loong in his 2012 National Day Message.[25] The program was designed as an inclusive and iterative process. About 47,000 Singaporeans, from all walks of life, actively participated in dialogues with the government on key social issues, such as Singaporean hopes, dreams, and fears. In addition to dialogues, organized by the OSC Committee and Secretariat, the broader community took ownership of the process and organized dialogues to give their stakeholders a voice. Many dialogue sessions were attended and actively participated in by the government ministers, showing the sincerity and seriousness of the government for OSC.

The OSC process also provided an interactive Internet space for citizens to express and explain some of their ideas for Singapore's future, and these views and ideas had been conveyed to policymakers to consider. A public consultation website called REACH (reaching everyone for active citizenry @ home) was launched in October 2006 when the official Feedback Unit was restructured to move beyond gathering public feedback to become the lead agency for engaging and connecting with citizens. REACH was later appointed as the Singapore government's e-engagement platform in January 2009. It seeks citizen views on national issues and policies through the public consultations. The public consultations are posted by ministries and government agencies. Citizen feedback will go directly to the agencies concerned. The program reveals how diverse individuals and groups are in Singapore society and, yet, how much they share and value in common as Singaporeans.

A large scale survey of 4,000 Singaporeans was conducted as part of the OSC process. It ascertained Singaporeans aspiration by 2030 and their key priorities for today. The survey also asked Singaporeans about the values they felt were important for achieving the 2030 vision as well as the preferences they leaned toward on key issues. The survey was conducted via face-to-face interviews from December 1, 2012 to January 31, 2013. The sample was demographically representative of the national population in terms of age, gender, and ethnicity. The OSC has been a learning journey. The organizers listened and identified the action items. A few OSC reports, including the survey summary, were published and made available to the public.[26] For example, job security, healthcare, and housing emerged as the priorities of Singaporeans' concerns.

8.4.1 Cyber Wellness Education

Cyber wellness refers to the positive well-being of Internet users. It involves an understanding of online behavior and awareness of how to protect oneself in cyberspace. Parents play a key role in shaping students' behavior in cyberspace by anchoring values and managing their child's Internet exposure. Through the joint effort of parents and schools, the students can adopt the right attitude and behaviors when using technology.

The Ministry of Education (MOE) uses the Sense–Think–Act framework to develop the students' instinct to protect and empower them to take responsibility for their own well-being in cyberspace. The two principles, "Respect for Self and Others" and "Safe and Responsible Use," will anchor the students' well-being in cyberspace as they will then be able to make careful and well-considered decisions. Moreover, the cyber wellness framework guides schools in their planning and implementation of cyber wellness programs and schools can customize their cyber wellness activities based on students' profile and school environment.

Cyber wellness topics are integrated, where appropriate, into different subjects. For primary schools, cyber wellness also is being delivered through the Form Teachers' Guidance Periods. For secondary schools, each level will have four hours dedicated to the learning of cyber wellness in the curriculum. To support the schools, MOE provides various tools, such as an online resource portal for teachers, students, and parents. In addition, the TOUCH cyber wellness program has provided resources to help parents and educators better understand youth's cyber world and to equip them with up-to-date knowledge and tools to achieve cyber wellness.

8.5 Conclusion

Technology is changing rapidly and digital inclusion continues to evolve dynamically. The digital inclusion journey in Singapore has evolved through the "5 Cs": connectivity, capability, content, confidence, and continuity. Connectivity is expressed in the form of providing broadband access, mobile network, citywide wi-fi, affordable services, and free public access for disadvantaged groups. Capability is expressed in the form of the high degree of digital literacy among the majority of the citizens from young to senior, skills training for those who need it, and special assistant devices for the economically and socially disadvantaged groups. Content is expressed in the form of making availability of digital media content, e-services, e-applications, open government data, and tools for citizens to enable co-creation of mass development of new content. Confidence is expressed in the form of providing a secured digital environment, the ease of deploying ICT innovatively for economic development, workforce development, civic engagement, and special and mainstream education. Continuity is expressed in the form of realization by the citizens and organizations on the benefits gained through digital engagement for productivity gain, improved quality of life, and the enthusiasm in continuingly contributing to the success of digital Singapore.

This chapter shows Singapore's experience on digital inclusion, in particular, how its public, social, and private sectors help citizens use ICT in relevant ways that actually improve learning and foster the knowledge and skills necessary for meaningful participation in a digital economy.

In conclusion, some of the key challenges and lessons learned in Singapore are as follows:

First, there is a lack of longitudinal research in Singapore that can demonstrate changes in people's lives after the acquisition of more intense use of ICT. Previous research has confirmed that high-quality access, digital skills, and a positive disposition toward ICT would facilitate basic engagement with ICT among groups that are disadvantaged. Yet, the long-term impact of the Internet on addressing social isolation and economic disadvantage is largely untapped.

Secondly, many digital inclusion initiatives have been led by the government and public sector. Citizens' own initiatives are still relatively absent. Effort is needed to encourage and assist citizens to stand out by initiating or participating in more digital inclusion programs. There is a need to energize citizens' ability to give and contribute.

Thirdly, the design of digital inclusion programs may need to adopt a more systematic approach to ensure sustainability with compelling outcome. One such systemic approach is by developing digital inclusive programs along the lines of economic sectors, such as healthcare, construction industry, service sector, finance and banking, and tourism. Being economical sector focused, the private sector can take a lead in developing programs that are relevant to the specific characteristics of the disadvantaged workforce in that sector. Initiatives through collaboration, conversation, and consultation will be more cohesive and in meeting the needs.

Finally, digital services may consider applying user experience design and agile development approaches to improve user centric e-services, speed up delivery time, and make online channels more innovative and become a preferred channel by the citizens.

Endnotes

1. The authors would like to acknowledge the contributions of Shiow Pyng Wong (IDA), Keith See (IDA), James Kang (IDA), Amos Tan (IDA), and Leonard Lew (IDA).
2. Singapore Economic Development Board. Online at: http://www.edb.gov.sg/content/edb/en/why-singapore/about-singapore/facts-and-rankings/rankings.html
3. World Economic Forum (2013). The Network Readiness Index 2013. http://www3.weforum.org/docs/GITR/2013/GITR_OverallRankings_2013.pdf
4. Pew Internet & American Life Project (2003). http://www.pewinternet.org/2003/12/22/americas-online-pursuits/
5. Helsper, E. (2008). *Digital inclusion: An analysis of social disadvantage and the information society.* London: Department for Communities and Local Government.
6. Bradbrook, G. and J. Fisher (2004). Digital equality: Reviewing digital inclusion activity and mapping the way forward. CitizensOnline http://www.citizensonline.org.uk/digitalequality/
7. Infocomm Development Authority of Singapore. Online at: http://www.ida.gov.sg
8. Online at: http://www.egov.gov.sg/media-room/speeches/2006/speech-by-prime-minister-lee-hsien-loong-at-the-innovationation-gala-dinner-in-celebration-of-25-years-of-infocomm-and-the-national-infocomm-awards
9. The NEU PC program was introduced in 2003 to offer needy households with either a subsidized new PC or a free used PC. In 2006, the program was enhanced to NEU PC Plus and it stopped offering used PCs.
10. Online at: http://www.ida.gov.sg/neupc
11. Online at: http://www.iacentre.org.sg
12. Online at: http://app.msf.gov.sg/Portals/0/Topic/Issues/EDGD/Enabling%20Masterplan%202012-2016%20Report%20(8%20Mar).pdf
13. Online at: http://app.msf.gov.sg/ResearchRoom/ResearchStatistics/EnablingMasterplan.aspx
14. Online at: http://www.ida.gov.sg/Individuals-and-Community/Community-Development/Silver-Infocomm-Initiative
15. Online at: http://www.ida.gov.sg/Individuals-and-Community/Community-Development/People-Sector-Transformation
16. Online at: http://www.ida.gov.sg/Business-Sectors/Small-and-Medium-Enterprises
17. Online at: http://www.savh.org.sg
18. Online at: http://www.sharingthelioncity.com

19. Online at: http://serve.me.nus.edu.sg/ongsk/ARLab/
20. Online at: http://tlc-mn.org/sites/tlc-mn.org/files/presentations/Digital%20Inclusion%20White%20Paper%20by%20Microsoft.pdf
21. Online at: http://www.ida.gov.sg/Infocomm-Landscape/iN2015-Masterplan
22. Online at: http://www.ida.gov.sg/Infocomm-Landscape/Infrastructure/Wired
23. Online at: http://www.mci.gov.sg/content/mci_corp/web/mci/pressroom/categories/parliament_qanda/minister_s_responsetopqonngnbnrolloutcoverage.html
24. Online at: http://www.reach.gov.sg/Microsite/osc/index.html
25. Online at: http://www.pmo.gov.sg/content/pmosite/mediacentre/speechesninterviews/primeminister/2012/August/national_day_message2012english.html#.U0YN3PmSwn4
26. Online at: http://www.reach.gov.sg/Portals/0/Microsite/osc/OSC-Survey.pdf

Chapter 9

Leveraging Mobile Revolution for Turning Digital Divide into Digital Dividend: Examples from India, Bangladesh, and Sri Lanka

Vikas Kanungo

Contents

9.1 Introduction

The world has witnessed an unprecedented spread of information, communication, and new media technologies during the course of the last decade. It took radio technology 38 years to reach 50 million users; it took television 14 years, but the Internet accomplished the same feat in 4 years. As the information and communication technologies (ICTs) become increasingly affordable and penetrate all areas of economic and social life of people, their potential of bringing transformational changes in governments and societies (both in developed and developing countries) is more profound than ever. As the adoption of mobile devices (both feature phones and smartphones) soar in developing and underdeveloped countries and they become the first ever ICT tools used by billions of people for accessing information and connecting with each other, we are witnessing huge transformational changes in the way people and governments conduct themselves.

"With the advent of mobile technologies and increase in their affordability during the course of last decade coupled with availability of innovative livelihood applications, the question of whether poor people can afford to have a mobile phone has now changed to 'can the poor people now afford *not* to have a mobile phone,'" said R. Chandrashekhar, president of the National Association of Software and Services Companies in India recently. In many countries including India, this revolution has helped reallocation of power more equitably between the state and citizens.

However, the proliferation of technologies also have resulted in a divide between people who have access to all the opportunities of this revolution and those who have not been able to benefit from the full potential of these technological interventions; the traditional schism between the "haves" and the "have nots," has given way to a new dichotomy between the "connected" and the "disconnected." According to a recent Economic Intelligence Unit report, emerging markets, in particular, still struggle with achieving basic online access for a majority of their residents.[1] Mobile devices have helped to establish a new delivery channel, but divides remain in providing affordable access for everyone, and in extending third-generation (3G) network coverage and introducing high-speed fourth-generation (4G) access. While it might take some time for the entire world population to have smartphones and high-speed broadband access, the mobile revolution at present is impacting everyone's lives—rich and poor alike.

The focus of this chapter is on how the innovative use of mobile devices using the combination of short message service (SMS), Smart applications, and big data analytics techniques are enabling more inclusive participation in policymaking and access to service delivery in South Asia, a region home to 44 percent of the global poor. Selected projects from India, Sri Lanka, and Bangladesh will demonstrate how innovative thinking can help convert digital divide into digital dividend.[2] The examples demonstrate how government agencies and civil society organizations are innovatively using technological possibilities to address social realities, in the process effectively pursuing access to social justice, enhancing freedom of expression, enabling participation in policymaking, providing livelihood opportunities, and better access to public services. These developments have created new dimensions of economic, social, or political participation for individuals and groups through completely new ways of participating in governance and policymaking.

9.2 Mobile Seva Initiative: Enhanced Access to Public Services through Mobile Devices (Government of India)[3]

Mobile penetration in India has increased dramatically over the past decade with the country becoming one of the fastest growing markets of mobile subscribers in the world. Figure 9.1 provides the highlights of telephone and mobile subscription in India as of October 2013.

However, most of the mobile phone subscribers in rural India do not have smartphones with Internet access, thus being deprived of accessing mobile applications and government portals. The government of India recognized this divide and decided to use an innovative approach to turn the digital divide into a digital dividend by formulating a policy of mobile governance emphasized on identification and delivery of services/information that can be delivered through SMS.

Mobile Seva, the national mobile governance initiative launched by the Department of Electronics and Information Technology (DeitY), is a prime example of a nationwide comprehensive initiative that has been conceptualized and implemented

Particulars	Wireless	Wire Line	Total
Total Subscribers (Millions)	875.48	29.08	904.56
Urban Subscribers (Millions)	522.21	22.88	545.09
Rural Subscribers (Millions)	353.27	6.21	359.48
Urban Teledensity (%)	138.23	6.06	144.29
Rural Teledensity (%)	41.27[a]	0.73[a]	42.00[a]

[a] It is worthwhile to mention here that, in a majority of rural areas in India, it is still a norm where one mobile phone is shared by all members of a family. Thus, the number of citizens having access to mobile devices in rural India is much higher than the number of mobile subscribers mentioned in the table above.

Figure 9.1 Telephone and mobile subscriptions in India. (From Telecom Regulatory Authority of India (TRAI). Online at: http://www.trai.gov.in/Content/CopyRight.aspx)

effectively.[4] The initiative has brought the convenience of electronic public services to a wider section of the population by leveraging the much greater penetration of mobile phones in India as compared to access to computers and Internet, especially in rural areas. While more than 71 percent of the population owns mobile phones, access to Internet is limited to just over 12 percent of the population.[5] The decision to create a dedicated mobile service delivery gateway (MSDG) enabling government agencies at federal and state levels to deliver public services/information through SMS has proved to be especially beneficial to the poor, elderly, disabled, and women who otherwise have no realistic chance to access electronic public services.

The Framework for Mobile Governance was officially notified, in January 2012,[6] with the mission to leverage the penetration of mobile devices in the country in making the public services accessible to the citizens on a 24/7 basis.

In order to implement the supporting ecosystem to realize the policy goals of provisioning services for all sections of the society, the Mobile Seva initiative relies on a combination of MSDG for delivering services and information using SMS, mobile applications store for provisioning services for those who have access to Internet-enabled smartphones, and a helpdesk for central and state government agencies who wish to leverage on the government policy to use mobile phones and service delivery platform.

This initiative stemmed from the realization that millions of rural citizens in India without access to the Internet were on the wrong side of the digital divide having no means of accessing government/public services that were offered through the Internet under the National e-Governance Plan (NeGP). Given the fact that a majority of Indian citizens residing in rural areas have access to mobile devices, these are found suitable as alternative access and delivery channels for public services. Dr. Rajendra Kumar, additional secretary of e-Governance, government of India, commented:

> Mobile platform, especially the SMS-based services, were found to be best suited in present circumstances of low Internet penetration in rural areas to deliver government services.
>
> The impact of the Mobile Seva project was evaluated by a third party in 60 government departments and the results in terms of the contribution of the initiative in bridging digital divide has been significant. The requests to the government departments for information regarding various services have reduced drastically after the information services are made available through SMS resulting in enhancement of internal efficiency of the government departments. The citizens have reported enhanced satisfaction with the services provided.

Mobile Seva, through the MSDG, aims to provide a one-stop solution to all the central and state government departments and agencies across the nation for all their public services needs. Availability of government-wide shared infrastructure and services helps in realizing rapid deployment and reduced costs for the integrating departments. The integrating government departments and agencies can use Mobile Seva infrastructure to provide their services through various channels, such as SMS, Voice/IVR (interactive voice response), USSD (unstructured supplementary service data), and through mobile applications (m-apps). A long-term vision of the project is to offer all nonemergency public services to all citizens in the country through a single three-digit nationally available number. For this purpose, DeitY has already obtained the short code 166. DeitY also has obtained another short code 51969 for mobile governance.

9.2.1 Impact on Digital Divide

The availability of government services/information through SMS, IVR, and smart apps has enabled rural citizens to utilize government services as well as track the status of their service requests.[7] The innovative use of SMS by the government through the Mobile Seva program has been a game changer in bridging the digital divide and enabling the people on the wrong side of the digital divide to have access to public services.

With over 900 departments across the nation at central, state, and local levels having already adopted it, over 270 public services are available through pull (a service through which the end users can pull relevant information from a server such as tracking the status of a passport application by sending an SMS to a short code) SMS, an app store stocked with over 245 free-to-download and live and fully integrated mobile apps for a range of public services, and over 60 million SMS and mobile app-based transactions being delivered to citizens and businesses every month, Mobile Seva has enabled the country to realize the potential and power of mobiles to bring public services closer home to citizens. It is a truly centralized and cloud-based platform that any government department or agency in the country can integrate with immediately and start providing mobile-based services. Departments need not create their own infrastructure for mobile enablement, thus saving substantial cost, time, and effort in rolling out services. DeitY also builds capacity of the departments for developing mobile-based services and provides complete "handholding" support to other government agencies. All the telecom service providers in the country have been brought onboard to provide universal coverage of the population through these services.

Several very useful services and apps have been developed and made live for a number of citizen centric government organizations, such as Unique Identification Authority of India (UIDAI), Election Commission of India, High Courts, India Post, etc. Several state governments are using this platform for providing citizen centric services at the district and subdistrict levels. These include certificate services (birth, death, income, caste, etc.), land ownership details, pensions, etc., in states, such as Andhra Pradesh, Madhya Pradesh, Rajasthan, Himachal Pradesh, and Uttar Pradesh. In India, government departments and agencies at central and state levels touch over 1.2 billion citizens in their day-to-day lives. Implementation of Mobile Seva has brought all of these government departments and agencies at central, state, and local levels onto this common platform to reach over 860 million mobile subscribers in the country with public services.

9.3 SLB Connect: Citizen Engagement for Improving Public Services (Water and Sanitation Program India, The World Bank, India)[8]

In urban India, ICT applications are rapidly proliferating as a result of a tech savvy, affluent younger generation residing in the cities. Innovative use of their creativity in collecting feedback from less privileged citizens in urban slums can help in the provisioning of improved and inclusive services to all sections of society. In 2012, India's Ministry of Urban Development (MoUD) and the World Bank's Water and Sanitation Program (WSP) launched the initiative titled "SLB Connect," building on MoUD's Service Level Benchmarks (SLB) program, to both engage citizens in monitoring the performance of urban water suppliers and encourage them to demand better services. The pilot project implemented in one of the towns in Maharashtra (a province in the western part of India), clearly demonstrates that the slum dwellers in the city benefitted the most from the initiative by highlighting their grievance to the city administration through a mobile phone-based feedback collection exercise. Additionally, the city administration collects the mobile numbers of all the respondents during the exercise, which helps urban local bodies interact with the citizens on a regular basis through SMS messages.

The SLB program has been a flagship initiative of MoUD, government of India since 2009 to emphasize a shift in focus from infrastructure creation to the delivery of service outcomes.[9] The program covers water supply, wastewater, solid waste management, and stormwater drainage. Under the SLB program, the effort has been largely to collect data from the service provider. However, there was growing recognition of the need to engage citizens in setting service delivery standards and monitoring performance. Simultaneously, there was also a growing realization to exploit the opportunity for strengthening citizen engagement and accountability through the use of mobile phones that are available with entire population in urban India. With steady implementation of the government of India's NeGP, and the availability of new media, The World Bank recognized an opportunity to bring about a paradigm shift in the service delivery standards by using mobile technologies for citizen feedback and engagement.

Although SLB Connect aims to represent all urban citizens, one of its goals is to offer explicit tracking of service delivery in slums, including for facilities such as public stand posts and community toilets. In so doing, it seeks to address the prevalent service inequalities experienced by numerous people living in informal settlements in the nation's cities.

9.3.1 Project Details

The SLB Connect initiative aims at collecting and analyzing citizen feedback on service delivery using innovative mobile and ICT tools. It is aligned with the SLB framework, and provides feedback on SLB indicators that address customer service aspects. The analyzed outputs from SLB Connect help strengthen the SLB program by:

- providing a "reality check" on service levels from the citizens' standpoint
- providing city managers with more "granular" data at the subcity level (ward/zone) that could facilitate improved monitoring and problem solving
- providing inputs into project planning processes
- most importantly, it will provide a suitable platform to engage citizens in performance monitoring processes and encourage them to demand better service

Given that a large urban population is living in informal settlements in Indian cities, and the service inequities commonly prevalent in service provision, SLB Connect provides for explicit tracking of service delivery in slums including public facilities. The information systems and citizen engagement mechanisms developed during the implementation in PCMC (Pimpri-Chinchwad Municipal Corporation) as well as the knowledge gained from the deployment are being shared and made accessible to various stakeholder groups across India through a well-architected outreach and replication plan. The following three key ICT components were developed and tested during the implementation in PCMC:

1. **Mobile Application for Conducting Household Surveys:** A simple to use Android application in two languages (English and Marathi) containing the survey questions along with validations for quality control, provisions for automatically capturing the geo coordinates of the households surveyed, time stamping of the enumeration, and a provision to add a photograph to the survey form were developed. The application is usable on a wide range of Android-based mobile phones and tablets.

2. **Web-Based Survey Monitoring Tool:** The tool enables the authorized representatives from WSP, local government agencies, and the survey supervisors to monitor the data-captured progress of the survey and the performance of the enumerators on a real time basis. The tool is made available to the authorized users though the World Wide Web, enabling them to monitor the survey from any location in the world. It includes features to pass on instructions to on-field enumerators as well as accept or reject the records that are built into the tool.

3. **Dashboard-Based Analytical Tool to analyze the results of the survey:** A state-of-the-art web-based dashboard is developed to automatically analyze and graphically represent the results of the survey in real time based on predefined analytical formulae. Hence, the responses received graphically represents the number of households not happy with billing, and their distance between a standpost from the house etc. The access to various sections of the dashboard is rights based, thus providing control to the local government agencies in deciding the information that can be made public versus the information that remains accessible strictly to the policymakers for planning and budgeting.

To leverage what was learned from the pilot exercise, SLB Connect aims to replicate the citizen feedback exercise across multiple cities, as well as to integrate it into other World Bank projects and advocate for its integration with state and national investment programs in water supply and sanitation.

9.3.2 Impact on Digital Divide

The implementation of SLB Connect and associated innovative solutions was greatly appreciated by the local government agencies as well as the MoUD government of India. There is a great demand from many ULBs (urban local bodies) and also sector teams of The World Bank to have the tool enhanced and made available for collecting stakeholder feedback. The project team also has made a free mobile application available on the websites of municipalities that can be downloaded by citizens to provide regular feedback to the government agencies on the water and sanitation services. As a result of the project implementations in three states of India, the mobile phones in the hands of the citizens have become an effective engagement tool for them to be in constant touch with the government agencies for providing their inputs for enhancement of public services. In particular, the project has been successful in bridging the digital divide:

- There are more mobile phones than toilets in India, creating a unique opportunity for communicating social messages and for giving voice to the poorest in the policy making process. The tool developed during the pilot project helps improve governance mechanism, resulting in greater social benefits to the poorest. For example, feedback from slum dwellers is helping the city administration to respond faster to their grievances and track action taken, resulting in higher satisfaction among slum dwellers.
- ICT applications integrate information cost effectively through geo-tagging, uploading pictures and recording relevant data points.
- ICT reduces the transaction cost of doing business. For example, a mobile-based household survey can cover in few weeks a sample size that ordinarily took several months.
- Sharing and discussing findings with citizens at the local level increased transparency of government services.
- Incorporating the findings into departmental reviews and discussions encourages the service orientation of concerned agencies.
- Integration with supervisory control and data acquisition (SCADA) and operations enhances responsiveness and allows for demand-based planning.
- Finally, given that more than 30 percent of India's population lives in urban areas and for the first time the decadal population increase was higher in urban than rural areas, access to basic services, such as water supply and sanitation, is under pressure, in particular, the quality of access. Public providers, who account for more than 95 percent of service provision in urban areas, typically lack customer orientation and accountability for service delivery. The result is a growing disconnect between planning and service outcomes, and between providers and citizens.

The project has demonstrated that, through innovative use of new media technologies, many of these problems can be resolved.

9.4 Stakeholders' Engagement for Development through Action Accountability Probe (AAP): An Innovative SMS-Based System for NGOs to Provide Feedback on Development Issues[10]

Accountability of service delivery has the potential of improving governance and creating a society where equitable distribution of public wealth may be ensured, thus resulting in the bridging of the social divide. One of the major challenges in underdeveloped countries is the disconnect and distrust among the governments and citizens. While there are substantial investments in citizen services in Bangladesh, it has not resulted in proportionate improvement in quality of life for citizens. This calls for demand-driven feedback systems where the recipients of the services can raise their voice in a systematic manner and influence the policy decision by sharing their concern through the civil society group who is playing an enabling role in raising the voice of the grassroots communities in the country.

Historically, the failure of accountability is primarily because, in the existing manual system of governance, the government functionaries act as the repositories of knowledge regarding the development programs and formal links in framework of accountability from citizens to the government have never existed in a systematic manner. Moreover, there are very primitive country-wide ICT infrastructures that bar most of the citizens in accessing the information and services made available through the digital governance program in the country.

However, the humble SMS has proved to be a game changer and provided an opportunity for the civil society organizations to leapfrog directly to mobile governance, thus bypassing the entire e-governance cycle. Under a project called SE4D (Stakeholders' Engagement for Development), ANSA (Affiliated Network for Social Accountability), under BRAC (Bangladesh Rehabilitation Assistance Committee) University, developed an innovative tool called Action Accountability Probe (AAP), that utilizes SMS and voice messaging for collecting citizen feedback. The tool has created avenues to strengthen the critical links between government and citizens enabling citizens to provide their inputs for government services on a regular basis.

The mobile-based survey tool is used by the development organizations and individuals working on various development programs. AAP enables collection of citizen inputs through low end mobile phones that are available with most of the residents of the country. This application is designed to work on Android and J2Me-based mobile phone. Android is the emerging mobile platform with the latest rich functionalities. J2ME mobile application is supported in all mobile platform-support Java extension.

In addition to mobile application, the platform also is equipped with web-based content acquisition for the same form. The mobile tool is designed in a user-friendly manner so that this can be used by the citizen in possession of basic mobile handsets and knowledge of SMS usage.

9.4.1 Impact on Digital Divide

Bangladesh is one of the least developed countries with very low penetration of computers and smartphones. The project, therefore, focused on using the SMS-based feedback system with the features of integrated voice files so that citizens with no literacy also could provide their feedback on government services. The

Civil Society organizations were empowered to use the SMS-based tool and create their own forms for collecting feedback on government programs relating to health, agriculture, and education. The capacity building program for nongovernment organizations (NGOs) enabled them to use the mobile phone SMS-based application as well as install the application on a variety of feature phones for the citizens. Mobile devices proved to be powerful tools for raising awareness among citizens of their rights to access basic public services.

The projects demonstrated effectiveness of a SMS-based citizen connect system for measuring and improving performance in the delivery of basic services, community empowerment, and building trust between service providers and service users. The humble SMS available on most of the low-end phones proved to be a very powerful tool in mainstreaming the use of ICTs for helping Bangladesh leapfrog to use ICTs for citizen empowerment and the bypass online cycle.

9.5 Mobile Phones for Producing e-Citizen Report Cards under Local Economic Governance Project: The Asia Foundation, Sri Lanka[11]

Following three decades of civil war, Sri Lanka is currently reaping the benefits of a peace dividend as its economy is being rekindled, social trust rebuilt, and local governments are taking the reins of delivering public services to citizens, especially in the war-affected provinces of the north and east. Addressing regional disparities and ensuring access to public services remains top priority of the government. The Asia Foundation has been quite active in the local governance scene in Sri Lanka since 2006 through its Local Economic Governance (LEG) program supported by Australian Aid. The LEG program strives to make local governments financially strong, encourage business-friendly environments, and promote social accountability in 15 locations spread over 5 provinces in Sri Lanka.

In 2013, the Foundation, in partnership with the Batticaloa Municipal Council, embarked on a pioneering electronic citizen report card (eCRC) initiative under the LEG program. Batticaloa is a major commercial city in the eastern province of Sri Lanka, which was severely affected by the 26-year-long civil war conflict. The Municipal Council provides services to a population of 90,000 and is currently headed by a commissioner because the elected council is not yet in place. As part of the postwar reconstruction efforts, considerable infrastructure is being rebuilt to restore livelihoods and provide basic services to the residents of the city. However, no feedback mechanisms exist to elicit the extent to which the infrastructure provision has been found to be accessible and satisfactory by the residents. It was in this context that the eCRC was designed and executed as a pioneering example for the war-affected provinces. Built around the concept of user feedback, a citizen report card is a cost-effective way for a government to find out whether its services are reaching the people, especially the poor. Users of a public service can tell the government a lot about the quality and value of a service. The CRC represents an assessment of public services from the perspective of its citizens. A citizen report card on public services is not just one more opinion poll. The survey on which a report card is based covers only those individuals who have had experiences in the use of specific services, and interactions with the relevant public agencies. Citizen report cards have been used by local and national governments, civil society organizations, and development partners in over 20 countries as a tool for citizen engagement and service improvements. eCRC is a revolutionary concept that enables reliable collection of citizen feedback through an Android-based mobile application and analyzing and reporting the information collected in real time.

9.5.1 Project Details

The project commenced with a phase of sensitizing key decision makers, including political leaders on the concept and utility of eCRC. Following this, extensive consultations were held with various stakeholders to develop the survey instrument and reporting templates. The following processes were critical in the development of the eCRC:

1. *Conducting a mobile-based survey* of sample households on local infrastructure creation and delivery of public services using Android tablets. A simple Android application in three languages—Sinhala, Tamil, and English—was developed to survey residents on selected indicators of public service delivery. A GIS tracking system in the tablets indicated the location from where data was collected, thereby enhancing the reliability of data collection.
2. *A web-based survey management module* enabled survey managers to track the progress of the survey on a real-time basis. The module enabled remote monitoring and management of survey activities and, hence, ensured greater quality control.
3. *Online dashboard and data analysis tools* developed as a part of the eCRC address the information needs of various stakeholder groups (e.g., policymakers, administrators, political representatives, and citizens). The results of the survey were presented through easy-to-understand graphs, tables, and maps. Simple traffic signal color codes were used to facilitate easy inferences on performance levels.

A key and defining feature of the eCRC in Batticaloa was that the entire survey was carried out by the community development officers (CDOs) affiliated with the local government. This was perhaps the first time when government functionaries at the local level embarked on a large-scale survey of eliciting citizen feedback on local government services. From the pool of 20 CDOs trained as master trainers, 15 participated in the survey; 1,400 households were surveyed in four days.

9.5.2 Impact on Digital Divide

For the residents of a war-affected city, the eCRC provided a rare and powerful opportunity to provide feedback on a variety of parameters on the quality of services being delivered to them. After years of living in an environment of mistrust, a new social compact is being developed. The eCRC clearly highlighted the spatial inequalities in service delivery. A key finding of the exercise was that localities closer to the city center were served much better compared to those in the outskirts. The depiction of data collection points on a real-time Google map highly enhanced the credibility of the exercise.

However, the larger impact of the eCRC rests in the fact that there is a strong demand from other local governments to replicate this exercise in their locations. There is also a demand to use the ICT-led model for other sectors, such as business regulation and local infrastructure.

The potential of eCRC as an institutionalized practice can be summarized through the following:

- As an ***internal management and oversight tool***, when information provided can help identify performance gaps in service delivery and provide inputs for design of interventions.
- By ***identifying citizen priorities and needs***, eCRC can ensure that investments in provisioning public services are in alignment with the actual priorities and needs of the communities.
- Availability of real-time feedback data enables service providers to respond to emerging issues in a timely manner. Further, public disclosure of key performance indicators can foster an ***environment of improved transparency and accountability***.

More importantly, for local governments that missed the computer- and e-governance-led public sector reform window, the availability of cheap and ubiquitous mobile technologies offer a chance to leapfrog into the cutting edge state-of-the-art options. The Sri Lankan example is a case in point.

In addition to the above examples, there are numerous initiatives, such as SMS services for fishermen in Kerala, the m-interaction between the government of Bangladesh and sugarcane-producing farmers in Bangladesh, etc., that have unequivocally demonstrated the potential of mobile devices in not only bridging the digital divide, but also opening up new opportunities for the people who were earlier isolated and unable to benefit from the ICT revolution.

9.6 Converting Digital Divide into Digital Dividend: Opportunities and the Way Forward

It is evident from the examples cited above and from numerous case studies already available in public domain that there is an enormous potential for improving the state of governance and making public services available to each section of the society in an efficient and transparent manner if the focus of the efforts is not to overemphasize the prevalence of digital divide, but on finding out the innovative methods of utilizing the mobile penetration. Most developing countries are much better placed to benefit from mobile-based innovations as they have a real chance of bypassing the online era and leapfrog to mobile era directly.

In the cases described in this chapter, we have witnessed that innovations in mobile-based solutions for mainstreaming the marginalized are being championed by politicians, civil servants, NGOs, and technology leaders in isolated efforts. Though some of the efforts have been widely appreciated and benefitted the citizens, many of them have not been able to realize the true potential on a national or regional scale owing to lack of collaboration and want of capacity building.

In order to create a vibrant innovation ecosystem to leverage the full potential of mobile technologies for the benefit of citizens perceived to be on the wrong side of digital divide, policy and implementation frameworks to foster collaboration among various actors, including industry and academia, need to be developed. Enabling joined up workings of various government agencies and co-creation of innovative services will be the key to succeeding. The following sections discuss key challenges in accelerating the development and suggest some of the possible ways of speeding up the inclusion of disadvantaged communities to ensure their equitable participation in the next millennium digital societies.

9.6.1 Ensuring Collaboration among Government Agencies, Civil Society Organizations, Academia, and Industry Using Mobile and Cloud-Based Technologies as Key Enabler

Whether collaborating horizontally across state agencies, entering into a public–private partnership, or crossing organizational boundaries between central–state or state–local levels of government, all stakeholders must continuously work to connect silos to increase efficiency and outreach of the innovative initiatives. Mission convergence should be the motto. Technology has the power and the ability to converge hitherto compartmentalized functions of the state.

The concept of using technology as a facilitator for collaboration is inevitable for realizing the potential of new media technologies to ensure that the focus on leveraging the potential devices is already available with large sections of the population rather than waiting for the bridging of digital divide until everyone gets a smartphone. National governments can play a leading role in ensuring this by deploying effective, user-friendly, accessible, and innovative applications. Leveraged by investments in information technology, crossing organizational boundaries between levels of government can be used as a way to increase governmental effectiveness. Citizen aspirations (which will soon turn into demand) for streamlined, efficient government would drive agencies to seek out opportunities to deliver traditional services in nontraditional ways. For example, engaging in deployment of innovative mobile-based solutions for stakeholder engagement and delivery of services will result in following benefits for the deploying agencies:

- Cost reduction
- Establishing relationships between organizations
- Providing increased or better services to citizens/end users
- Streamlining processes and speeding transactions
- Improving information sharing and quality
- Leveraging enterprise solutions
- Sharing risk
- Addressing fiscal constraints and lower administrative costs by leveraging mutual resources
- Reducing response time and enhancing transparency in operations

While the advantages of collaboration can be applied universally, the approach and methodology of collaboration will vary depending on the initiative and the nature of service to be provisioned. When engaging in state–local collaboration, state agencies can provide services to citizens within the local communities in which they live and work. In turn, localities can take advantage of shared resources and deliver services that may not otherwise be possible. Local government institutions (LGIs) in each of the countries mentioned in the examples above provide an excellent opportunity to state and provincial governments in developing collaboration models with local jurisdictions for delivery of public services. However, the potential of LGIs in enabling the delivery of services at the doorsteps of citizens is largely unexplored and whatever little efforts are done are generally not collaborative in nature and were not crafted with a collaborative governance model.

9.6.2 Technology First Approach in Planning New Policy Initiatives

The argument that the development of new technologies is enhancing the digital and social divide is overstated. Also, the often cited statement that development cannot be driven by technology is not entirely true. The contextual use of technology depending upon the accessibility levels of various stakeholders is the key to innovation and impact. It is now an accepted fact that technology is going to be a critical part of the lives of all the inhabitants globally. The key stakeholders should avoid alienating groups of technology-related personnel and instead reformulate their policies and strategies based upon the new avenues of citizen engagement and services delivery opened up by technologies. The chief minister of government of Delhi, Arvind Kejriwal, in January 2014, asked the citizens to use their mobile devices to record any conversations with government officers who were asking for bribes and forward the same to a designated helpline number so that the recordings can be used as evidence by the anticorruption bureau of the state against such officers. This initiative resulted in enhanced services from the officers to the citizens. There are many such examples of innovative use of simple voice recordings, photo taking, and SMS capabilities on even the basic mobile phones available to most citizens in enhancing citizen participation in service improvement.

The technology personnel should be one of the key segmented audiences in the communication strategy. They should know that they are crucial in the program's success and expansion, and need to be precisely targeted, studied, and engaged. Communication programs should then be devised so that they are not alienated.

One possible issue relates to convincing high-level officials and politicians on the benefits of new media technologies in building political capital. Such messages might cause these officials/politicians to become keen to roll out services and citizen engagement initiatives using the technologies. The involvement of citizens in co-creation of public services through crowd sourcing methods also has been widely used globally both in developing as well as developed countries. Big apps competitions in the United States, Code for honor, Hackathon, etc., are some of the key examples of such initiatives.[12]

9.6.3 Enabling Co-creation of Public Services through Public, Private and People Participation (PPPP)

As digital connectivity reaches the hitherto unreached corners of the globe, new users are employing it to bring improvement in markets, systems, and governance structures. While the gaps in income equality and the unequal access to the Internet still persist and will always remain (by the time all rural citizens get smartphones globally, there will still be people who will have access to ultra smartphones, etc.), connectivity definitely has started solving issues like lack of economic opportunities. It is important to point out here that the developing countries are leading the innovations in mobile applications as opposed to developed countries. In the next decade, the developing countries will slowly migrate from being the beneficiaries of digital revolution to becoming the contributors to digital innovation. The resulting gain in equitable development, enhancement in productivity, and mainstreaming of marginalized communities truly can be defined as the digital dividend.

The process of converting digital divide into digital dividend, however, is not easy, and may require long-term and sustained efforts. The governments and industry will have to evolve new innovation ecosystems, including finding entry points for early adaptors, building innovation relay mechanisms where the innovators can collaborate with each other to evolve more matured solutions and market them, and capacity building (both development and absorption) of various stakeholders clearly demonstrating the enhancement in efficiency due to the improved communication opportunities.

9.7 Conclusion

The proliferation of mobile devices and new media technologies has advanced at an unprecedented speed even though the debate about the access levels of various users (known as digital divide) still remains a challenge. The number of people connected to the Internet has increased from 350 million at the beginning of the decade to more than 2 billion while the number of mobile subscribers increased from 750 million to well over 5 billion. It is predicted that by 2025, everyone will have some kind of access to communication and Internet.[13] At every level of society, connectivity is increasingly becoming more affordable and practical in substantial ways. The innovations in communications technology, including voice recognition systems and device manufacturing, is set to ensure online access to services, information, places, and people. The users are increasingly reaching out and relate to people far beyond their own borders and language groups, sharing ideas, doing business, and building genuine relationships. This boom in digital connectivity is resulting in productivity gains, innovative health services, inclusive and interactive education opportunities, and, above all, better quality of life for everyone including most advantaged users to those at the base of the accessibility pyramid. The focus should now shift to leveraging the benefits of digital dividend for creation of new-age inclusive information societies.

Endnotes

1. The Economist Intelligence Unit (2012). Smart policies to close the digital divide: Best practices from around the world. http://unpan1.un.org/intradoc/groups/public/documents/un-dpadm/unpan049753.pdf
2. Note: The author of the chapter has been personally involved in the design and implementation of most of the projects that are cited as case studies in the chapter.
3. Government of India. The National Mobile Governance Initiative: http://www.mgov.gov.in
4. Ibid.

5. Telecom Regulatory Authority of India. Online at: http://www.trai.gov.in

6. Ministry of Communications and Information Technology, Department of Information Technology (January 2012). Online at: http://deity.gov.in/content/framework-mobile-governance

7. Government of India (July 2013). The National Mobile Governance Initiative: Midterm evaluation report of Mobile Seva. Online at: https://mgov.gov.in/doc/Mid-Term_Impact-Assessment_MOBILE-SEVA—23082013-for-UPLOAD.pdf

8. Government of India, Ministry of Urban Development. Service Level Benchmarks (SLB). Online at: http://www.slbconnect.in

9. Government of India, Ministry of Urban Development: SLB Handbook. http://www.wsp.org/sites/wsp.org/files/publications/service_benchmarking_india.pdf

10. The Affiliated Network for Social Accountability (ANSA), Action Accountability Probe (AAP). Online at: http://www.se4d.org

11. The Asia Foundation: Sri Lanka. Online at: http://www.smartcity.lk

12. Online at: http://nycbigapps.com; https://www.codeKforhonor.com/Home/Index; http://www.sanitationhackathon.org

13. Schmidt, E., and C. Jared (2013). *The new digital age: Reshaping the future of people, nations and business.* New York: Knopf.

Chapter 10

e-Inclusion in Education: Lessons from Five Countries

Soobin Yim, Melissa Niiya, and Mark Warschauer

Contents

10.1 Introduction

The question of *why* to include citizens in an increasingly information-driven society has shifted toward a question of *how*. The abundance of new information and communication technologies (ICT) has transformed the global economy. From education and social inclusion to careers and politics, societies are increasingly networked; participation in an information-driven society necessitates access to technology, and the wherewithal and motivation to use it.[1] However, there are increasing concerns that differences in technology access and use have an impact on social inclusion, educational outcomes, and economic success. Boosting digital participation, or e-inclusion, has become the aim of policy decisions, but how best to accomplish this goal remains uncertain.

e-Inclusion has been conceptualized in many different ways. In the 1990s, the concept of a "digital divide" emerged, focusing on whether or not people had access to computers and the Internet. Attention later turned toward the quality of access to these technologies, such as the speed and stability of Internet access. For example, many low-socioeconomic status communities in the United States do not have broadband Internet available.[2] Internationally, a lack of Internet infrastructure contributes to significant gaps in technology use between regions.[3]

In addition to technology access, concerns also have shifted to include differences in how technology is used, particularly in schools. Having broadband Internet access or a computer does not necessarily mean that students use these technologies for their educational benefit, nor does it mean that they have the skills to use them. These differences may represent another level of the digital divide, one defined by unequal technology use.[4]

A number of strategies have been proposed to bridge the digital divide, one of which is to provide individual computers to children. These initiatives range in size and scope, from efforts to deploy computer labs and Internet connectivity in school districts to large-scale, nationwide programs that provide one computer for each student in some or all grade levels. Some programs, such as the One Laptop per Child (OLPC) initiative, give each child a computer to take home and rely on students and parents to teach themselves how to use the technology. Other programs specifically focus on providing in-school access. Some projects extend access beyond schools and attempt to build infrastructure for home connectivity. In addition to providing technology access, some efforts additionally attempt to address the issue of differential technology use. For example, initiatives might provide funding for supports, such as teacher development, community centers, computer repair, and training for parents.

Given the diversity of these endeavors, comparing them will enable policymakers to understand which designs and implementations—and in what socioeconomic and cultural contexts—are able to affect positive social inclusion and academic outcomes. To that end, this chapter broadly examines whether providing individual computers to students is effective in supporting e-inclusion.

This chapter examines five countries, all of which have implemented some kind of program providing individual computers to children: Romania, China, Peru, Uruguay, and the United States. An upper middle-income developing country of 21 million in central Europe, Romania continues to struggle with economic development and with digital literacy and computer use rates.[5] Although, also a developing country of upper middle income, China has a high rate of Internet and computer use.[6] However, China has a population more than 60 times that of Romania and, thus, faces different challenges when addressing the digital divide between urban, high-income students and their rural, low-income counterparts.[7] The chapter will then compare two Latin American countries, Peru and Uruguay, with similar problems of rural computer access and use, but with different political and sociocultural climates that led to very different outcomes. Lastly, computer distribution programs in the United States are examined. A high-income country, the United States nevertheless has large gaps in computer access and use. While the United States has used computers extensively for education, these computer initiatives have had inconsistent results.

These studies represent an array of countries that are geographically, developmentally, culturally, and economically diverse. These studies also examine a variety of individual computer deployments, from large-scale national distribution aimed at boosting basic access to evaluations of smaller distributions intended as part of targeted learning initiatives. By drawing from these studies, this chapter will discuss policy and program design choices, which of these were effective, and in what contexts.

10.2 Romania

Romania has attempted to narrow the widening gap in computer ownership among those of different races and socioeconomic status. As a nation with low computer literacy, Romania made it a priority to promote computer skills for young children, particularly those from low-income backgrounds. According to a recent Eurostat survey by the Statistical Office of the European Union (EU), Romania has one of the lowest ratios of computer use in the European Union, with only 50 percent of households having used a computer, while the average in the EU was 78 percent. The computer use ratio among Romanian young people is higher, with 81 percent of 16–24 year olds having used a computer; however, this ratio is also below the average of most EU states (above 95 percent). In terms of computer skills measured by a self-assessment approach, Romania also ranked below the EU average, reporting less frequent use of computer skills ranging from basic file management to computer programming as shown in Figure 10.1.

In 2008, Romania initiated the Euro 200 program to improve the nation's below-average computer literacy skills and increase computer use to foster greater national competitiveness. The government distributed approximately 35,000 vouchers, each worth 200 Euros (about $300), to low-income families for the purchase of a home computer; this voucher system was based on a ranking of family income.[9] The goal of the program was not only to increase ICT access and computing knowledge, but to also promote the educational use of computers among students. The Ministry of Education thus developed multimedia educational content in a number of subjects, including math, biology, physics, computer science, and encouraged computer retailers who participated in the program to install these lessons on the computers provided to voucher recipients.

Researchers looked for evidence on whether the Euro 200 program improved children's academic performance or behavior and examined whether the program

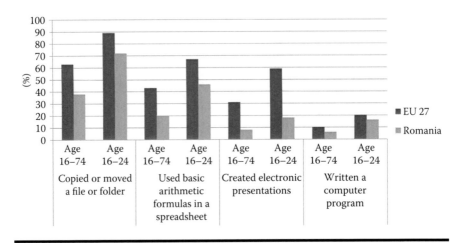

Figure 10.1 Comparison of level of computer skills in EU and Romania. (Based on data from Eurostat (2012). Computer skills in the EU27 in figures. News release. Online at: http://epp.eurostat.ec.europa.eu/cache/...26032012.../4-26032012-AP-EN.pdf.[8])

had an impact on children's computer ownership and use, academic achievement, cognitive assessments, computer skills, and various behavioral outcomes.[10] Analysis of various measures—parental and child questionnaires, interviews, cognitive ability tests, computer tests, and a battery of computer fluency questions—found mixed results.

Not surprisingly, the voucher program boosted the likelihood of household computer ownership by more than 50 percentage points and led to increased computer use. Children whose families won vouchers also scored significantly higher on tests of computer skills and cognitive ability than those who did not win vouchers. Yet, the students who received computers had significantly lower school grades in math, English, and Romanian than those without vouchers. The authors concluded that providing home computers to low-income children in Romania lowered academic achievement, despite the measurable gains in children's computer skills and cognitive ability.

A relatively small number of children reported using their computers for educational purposes or having educational software installed on their computers. The time voucher winners spent doing homework or reading decreased over the course of the program implementation. Instead, most computers had games installed, and children reported that most of their computer time was spent playing them. The researchers thus speculated that the lowered academic achievement was due to the increased time spent on computer games, which appeared to displace time on homework or reading. The study suggests that parental monitoring and supervision may be important mediating factors on the effects of computer ownership, as demonstrated in previous studies.[11]

The experience in Romania suggests that, without providing sufficient environmental support, efforts to merely increase computer access for disadvantaged children may have limited results or even be counterproductive. A child's own understanding of the purpose of using computers, as well as contextual factors, such as parental monitoring, teacher training, or classroom structure, may need to be addressed to ensure the effectiveness of the program.[12]

10.3 China

As one of the fastest developing countries in the world, China is experiencing a dramatic increase in the percentage of Internet usage each year. In the year 2000, only 1.7 percent of the Chinese population were Internet users, whereas the percentage increased to 42.1 percent by 2012.[13] While the frequent use of computers appears to have narrowed the digital divide between China and the rest of the world, there remains a greater divide between urban and rural areas of the country. With less than 5 percent of students in poor areas of rural China having access to Internet at home, computer ownership is 14 times higher for urban children than that of the rural children, which is indicated in Figure 10.2. Internet access rates are almost four times higher in urban areas than in rural areas. As for computer instruction and use, the rural–urban gap is smaller when comparing the most basic computer skills, but it remains large when examining the quality of computer instruction and access to learning software.[14]

Recognizing the detrimental consequences of this technological gap in employment, education, and income equality, the Chinese government is seeking to integrate computers into the nation's underserved schools. For example, in China's 12th Five-Year Plan, the government is planning to spend billions of dollars to provide computers for every classroom.[15] The Rural Education Action Program (REAP), a joint research initiative of Stanford University and prominent Chinese research centers, has carried out a number of studies investigating the impact of these initiatives. The studies use rigorous experimental methods and focus on the impact of computer use among China's rural and urban poor.

The first study investigated the effectiveness of a computer-assisted learning program (CAL, for short) for disadvantaged migrant children. This CAL program is intended to provide 20 million school-aged migrant children with computers and learning software. Researchers from REAP studied the effectiveness of the targeted intervention for closing the digital gap between rural and urban China. Located in the poorest rural areas in China, a typical migrant school may have a low level of instruction or low attendance rate, thus contributing to the school's inability to help students who fall behind. Specifically, the researchers investigated the impact of providing the migrant children with a package that included a home computer and game-based math or language tutorial software. This intervention involved two main activities: (1) the distribution of laptops installed with the

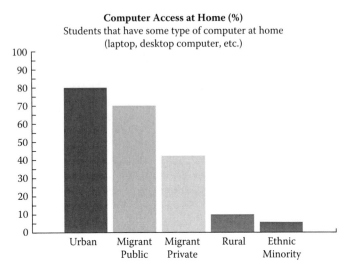

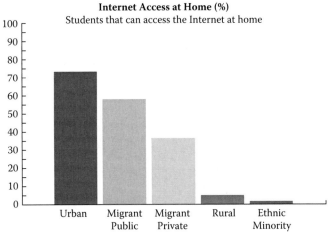

Figure 10.2 Chinese elementary students' computer and Internet access at home (From: Rural Education Action Program, 2013. With permission.)

remedial tutorial software and (2) a single training session for the children on how to use the computers and software.

To examine the effects for 300 third-grade students in 13 migrant schools in Beijing, half of the students were randomly assigned to the treatment group and the other half were assigned to the control group that did not receive the laptops, software, or training.[16] The results showed that after six months of intervention, the students' computer skills and standardized math scores improved significantly relative to the control group (0.33 and 0.17 standard deviation gains, respectively). One of the promising results of the study is the program's compensatory effect, in which less-skilled students (i.e., lower computer skills or no experience with computers) had greater gains in computer skills than students with higher skills. Moreover, the program also significantly increased student study time through computer software and, as a result, decreased the time students spent watching TV. Researchers also found an increase in students' self-esteem after the intervention.

The intervention examined in this study did not provide Internet access.[17] The authors suggest that having access to the Internet does not enhance students' math learning; instead they imply that having access to a computer and learning software may be effective for students with low or little prior access to a computer. As for the gains in math knowledge, the researchers attribute its success to the carefully designed materials and tutorial guides included in the intervention. The authors accentuated that the software provided remedial tutoring materials for math that was tailored to the regular school curriculum. The drills and exercises, as well as the animation/picture-based game interface, were both relevant to the classroom materials and engaging for students. These materials were developed by a team of expert elementary school math teachers in both public and migrant schools and graphic design majors of a volunteering university. Multimedia tutorials also were carefully designed to build the migrant students' low level of literacy by using simple directions, extensive graphic illustrations, and audio-enhanced explanations. It appears that the learning software and tutorials were much more closely tailored to students' needs than in the Romanian study above, and the Chinese students, unlike the Romanian students, were provided training on how to use them. These factors perhaps explain why the Chinese home computer intervention raised test scores while the Romanian program lowered them.

The above Chinese and Romanian studies both involved provisions of computers to be used at home. A second REAP study focused on a school intervention, in which Chinese schools in low-income migrant communities were randomly assigned to either a treatment group that would implement a computer-based instructional system, or a control group that would continue with previous practices. Two separate interventions were carried out. In the first, software-based remedial math tutoring was provided to schools located in migrant communities outside of Beijing and in poor rural mountainous regions in Shaanxi Province. The second intervention involved software-based Chinese language instruction in poor regions in Qinghai Province that are populated mostly by non-Han ethnic minorities who are not native speakers. Yang et al. conducted randomized field experiments of both these programs.[18] After the interventions, the treatment groups improved more in math (for Beijing migrant schools and Shaanxi rural public schools) and Chinese (for Qinghai rural public schools) test scores than did the respective control groups. Also importantly, the boys and girls in the study benefitted equally from the interventions. This demonstrates that, even though girls in China use computers far less than boys and have a lower skill level, they can still gain as much from computer-based interventions in schools.[19]

Taken together, the studies in China are very encouraging about the potential of providing computers to help ease educational gaps for the urban and rural poor, at least when combined with well-conceived instructional software and appropriate training for students and teachers.

10.4 Peru

In Peru, government officials have conceptualized technology inclusion as a way to modernize education and to boost student academic achievement. As part of a national education effort to bring ICT to schools, the government purchased and distributed hundreds of thousands of OLPC laptops to school children. Although some research has shown that access to OLPC laptops has improved student cognitive ability, inattention to infrastructural and cultural concerns has meant that the expensive initiative thus far has failed to achieve many of its goals.

A developing country of 30 million with a high percentage of its population in poverty, Peru seems suited to OLPC deployment; the OLPC laptop, the XO, was designed specifically to provide children in developing nations with the means to develop twenty-first century skills, access information, and promote human development.[20] While education in Peru is ostensibly free and compulsory through secondary school, parents often must shoulder some of the financial costs.[21] Academic achievement is very low, with a small minority of students meeting language (17 percent) and math (7 percent) standards; many students repeat grades.[22] Of the 30 percent of Peruvians who live in rural areas, many are from Indigenous backgrounds and are not literate in Spanish, the national language.[23]

Citing the need to "modernize" education and to enable "children and teachers to have ICT available and explore it in a nonthreatening way," Oscar Becerra, the general director for Educational Technology at the Peruvian Ministry of Education directed and designed the Peruvian laptop program, ULPN (Una Laptop por Niño, or One Laptop per Child).[24] In 2007, the government ordered and deployed its first laptops as part of a pilot study in the rural village of Arahuay.[25] An additional 40,000 XOs were distributed to students in 500 small schools; this distribution prioritized schools with electricity and Internet infrastructure.[26] Beginning in 2010, XOs were distributed to schools instead of to individual students.[27] This change was contrary to the namesake core value of OLPC and was made in order to extend distribution to more schools. Thus far, 902,000 OLPC laptops have been distributed in Peru. As part of ULPN, teachers are offered 40 hours of training.[28] Program evaluations conducted by the Inter-American Development Bank (IDB) examined the effects of ULPN on student achievement.[29] In addition, an ethnographic study evaluated the effects of ULPN on the communities in which laptops were deployed.

In one study, the IDB conducted a randomized control trial in order to examine the short-term effects of XO deployment in Peru by following 1,000 primary school children as they received XOs and were trained in their use.[30] The study collected student academic achievement and cognitive skills scores prior to XO use in Spring 2011 and a few months later in November 2011. As part of deployment, students were trained over three, two-hour sessions in August and September; however, only about 70 percent of the students attended at least one session.[31] In addition, these trainings did not take place during normal school hours, but instead on weekends. Students who received XOs did not see gains in their Windows' PC or Internet skills over their control group peers. While treatment students did see increased XO knowledge, they did not receive a boost in cognitive ability, which the authors suggest might have been due to the short timeframe. However, students who did not have computers prior to ULPN did see statistically significant gains in cognitive ability, suggesting that improved access might benefit those who most need the increased ICT access.

A similar randomized, controlled trial evaluated longer term effects of ULPN.[32] As ULPN gradually expanded the program to more and more schools in 2009, IDB was able to randomly assign treatment to similar schools ($N = 319$) in poor, rural regions. XOs were distributed to all students in treatment schools, and student achievement was measured using national standardized test scores in math and language. Providing an XO to each student improved basic computer access. The computer-to-student ratio in treatment schools was 1.18, whereas the control school ratio was 0.12. Additionally, 82 percent of treatment students reported using a computer in school in the previous week. Despite the increase in ICT access, the study found no statistically significant differences in math or language achievement between students in control and treatment groups. However, sixth grade students in laptop schools did see significant gains in math achievement, compared to younger students. This study also found no differences in school enrollment or attendance, suggesting that the promise of computer access alone was not enough to encourage students to go to school. Cristia and colleagues did find that providing individual laptops appeared to have positive effects on student cognitive skills, and students "displayed some useful skills in operating the laptop (p. 15)."[33] Despite some positive effects, the authors of this study conclude that, at $200 per laptop per child, the small positive effects on cognitive skills and math skills were not the best use of funds given the goals of the program, especially given that, on average, low- and middle-income countries spend $48 to $555 per primary student. In contrast, high-income countries spend on average $3,263 per primary student.[34] ULPN laptop purchases were a large proportion of a small education budget.

In addition to the lack of achievement results, the ULPN program faced challenges in meeting the needs of a diverse population. A study of elementary schools raised major concerns about the program's relevance to local communities.[35] The work suggests that the ULPN administrators undervalued the local knowledge and literacy of Indigenous peoples and had limited provisions for building XO use with teaching and learning materials for students and teachers. For example, teachers in one-teacher schools—schools in which one teacher is responsible for reaching all grade levels in that school—received one year of XO training. However, these teachers are typically only contracted for one year; they often left the target schools, meaning that students rarely had teachers experienced in teaching with the laptops. The program also ignored community needs. Whereas the program envisioned a "modern" education with increased technology use, teachers, parents, and students believed that schools should be centers for "the transmission of contextually significant knowledge" about "the life of their ancestors and the natural conditions, [and] to value the local culture and find an orientation for life in it (p. 88)."

While the Peruvian laptop program may have some positive effects, analyses suggest that it is not particularly successful in boosting academic achievement. Breitkopf's findings suggest that one of the reasons for this is perhaps due to its top-down approach.[36] Insensitive to the needs of its diverse Indigenous and indigent populations, perhaps ULPN cannot hope to incite these kinds of broad academic changes—and, as Breitkopf argues, cultural changes toward a restricted vision of an "educated person."[37]

ULPN failed to meet many of its educational goals at great expense to the government. A lack of infrastructure, as well as a top-down policy approach, may have contributed to this outcome. In contrast, empirical studies did find some positive associations with laptop distribution and cognitive score boosts. In light of these findings, the comparative success of a similar program in Uruguay may clarify how context, administrative decisions, and infrastructural design played a role in these outcomes.

10.5 Uruguay

A similarly large-scale deployment of one-to-one laptops, Uruguay's Plan Ceibal (*Conectividad Educativa de Informática Básica para el Aprendizaje en Línea*, or Educational Connectivity and Basic Computing for Online Learning) has been able to meet some of its e-inclusion goals. Like Peru, Uruguay administrators selected the OLPC XO laptop for distribution. However, Plan Ceibal differed from ULPN in several ways: (1) the current educational and political context, which included high literacy rates and strong political support for schools; (2) the project had goals focused on digital inclusion rather than academic achievement, and perhaps as a consequence; (3) the project included resources for building out the administrative, social, and technological infrastructure necessary to achieve these goals.

Uruguay is a small, primarily urban, Latin American country with more than 3.5 million people.[38] In comparison with neighboring countries, such as Argentina and Brazil, Uruguay has higher average math and reading scores on the Program for International Assessment (PISA) and a high adult literacy rate at 97.9 percent.[39] The public school system, the National Administration of Public Education (NAPE), oversees independent councils, one of which—the Primary and Initial Education Council—is devoted toward providing six years of compulsory primary education to all children. Although Uruguay is quite urban, half of its schools serve rural students; this comes at a great cost, with many schools serving fewer than 20 students, while being situated within the context of "a long history and considerable political support."[40] Within this political climate, an effort dubbed Plan Ceibal was developed in 2007 as part of a presidential mandate for e-inclusion.

Ceibal, like ULPN, selected the XOs (also known as *ceibalitas*) for deployment in schools. However, whereas the primary goals of Peru's ULPN program were to boost academic achievement, Plan Ceibal focused primarily on increasing Internet access and participation in information technology use. These goals included:

- Increasing IT access within families by providing a laptop to each student
- Providing citizens with the means for accessing information, boosting innovation through increased ICT use
- Increasing student digital literacies[41]

Multiple phases of deployment included priority distribution in rural schools as well as provisions for deploying infrastructure for wireless Internet connectivity, training teachers, and developing resources, such as digital textbooks and online assessments.[42] Among these resources included the development of educational centers where families could bring their XOs, use wireless Internet, and access technical and educational supports. Beginning in 2007 and completed in 2009, one XO was provided for each student in grades 1 through 6; this program has since begun to expand to secondary grades.[43] Additionally, Ceibal conducted regular evaluations of the program in order to assess the effectiveness of the program as well as the needs and attitudes of stakeholders.[44]

Internal and external evaluations of Plan Ceibal have found that—despite its large scale and the diverse needs of those it serves—the program has made some progress toward meeting its goals. A comparison of OLPC programs found that Uruguay, with nearly 400,000 laptops in use, had "put substantial effort into technical infrastructure and support and at least some effort into social support (p. 38)."[45] This included installation of Internet access in almost all schools, though the majority of teachers report substantial problems with the stability or speed of connection.[46] It also includes provisions for free or low-cost repairs of laptops, though the most recent reports suggest that only 74.3 percent of middle school students had functioning XOs in September 2013, with the remainder broken, under repair, stolen, or otherwise not available or functioning.[47]

Other evaluations have compared how access and use have affected access across income levels and communities. Plan Ceibal issued a report detailing the effects of the program on inequality in access and use. This report examines the effects of the program on students residing in Uruguay's provinces, outside of the country's urban center, Montevideo.[48] Although parents in rural areas were skeptical of the program initially and thought that the laptops were meant for urban children, attitudes did change after receiving the laptops. There also was evidence that the program increased Internet access not just for the children but for their families.

For example, one mother "learned to use the XO assisted by her children (p. 14)." Especially for low-SES (socioeconomic status) households, the XOs were the most frequently used computer by children's family members, compared with medium- and high-income households, whose access was most often via a home computer. When other family members used the XOs, the primary activities included entertainment, searching for general information, and searching for the purpose of studying (p. 23). Because these uses are primarily Internet-based activities, this finding suggests that the expanded wireless Internet connectivity played a role in this outcome.

In general, Plan Ceibal's evaluation found that communities, schools, and families that actively engaged in providing social support, supervision, guidance, and XO use enabled children to communicate via the Internet and boosted their motivation to work in class and on homework.[49] Within Plan Ceibal households, increased access and ICT participation by family members was observed as well. However, the authors also found that the XOs were frequently damaged and, thus, unusable; parents not monitoring children's use; and both children and families tended to use the XOs primarily for entertainment rather than to develop skills or to participate in media creation. Given these findings, Plan Ceibal developed a list of recommendations for family-oriented training and support, and training for older students in XO repair.

A later evaluation similarly found that familial and school supports were vital to children's outcomes. Based on interviews with stakeholders, including parents, school directors, and administrators, and data from Uruguay's annual household survey, researchers found that basic access to information and communications technology increased for all levels of income; in low-SES households, the XO almost always was the first and only computer in the household, with only 4 percent of low-SES families reporting that they had a computer other than an XO.[50] Similarly, another study found that while parents from rural areas used to feel like the XOs were just for children from cities, they now felt ICT was theirs to use, too.[51] As the primary users of the XOs, support from teachers and parents contributed to their computer activities: "… children who use this technology have proven to be those who have the support, guidance, and encouragement of adults."[52] Although Plan Ceibal has enabled some gains in home computer access and use, the program has not been successful in achieving school integration or educational effects. A recent national evaluation found that use of the laptops in schools has fallen substantially over the years.[53] The percentage of teachers reporting using the laptops daily in language classes fell from 41.5 percent in 2009 to 4.1 percent in 2012. In mathematics classes, the decrease was from 31.8 percent in 2009 to 6.1 percent in 2012. In both language and math instruction, more than 60 percent of teachers reported using the laptops less than once a week in 2012.

Perhaps not surprisingly, Plan Ceibal has had no effect on students' academic achievement. Using statistical methods that take into account test scores throughout the country from 2006 to 2012, as well as the dates that students received the laptops, a team of economists found no impact on students' mathematics or language arts test scores, neither in general nor by students of different socioeconomic status.[54]

In summary, Peru's ULPN and Uruguay's Plan Ceibal had both similarities and differences. Neither program was able to achieve much integration into schools or any measurable impact on academic achievement. Both were able to contribute to greater home access and use of computers. Yet, while Peru's program was ended, Plan Ceibal has continued and even expanded from primary to secondary grades. These differences are likely due in part to the different socioeconomic and educational contexts between the two countries. Whereas Peru has among the lowest PISA reading and math scores in the region and public education expenses too often rest in the hands of parents, Uruguay has relatively high PISA scores, a high literacy rate, and a long-standing political interest in rural education.[55] Secondly, the goals of Plan Ceibal—to increase ICT access and use—were more specific and perhaps more achievable within the context of Uruguay's smaller population. Conversely, ULPN aimed to improve Peru's low academic achievement rates, which was perhaps outside the scope of an OLPC-type program. Lastly, although both programs first targeted rural areas for deploying the XO laptop, the planning and execution of these programs differed. Plan Ceibal called for multiple phases, including the development of technical and social infrastructure; ULPN neglected to build wireless infrastructure, thus limiting XO use for one of its primary features.

10.6 United States

Although the United States has a long history of deploying computers in education, evidence is still unclear as to whether such efforts have helped overcome societal inequality. Many studies examining technology use in the United States indicate that simply placing computers and Internet connections in low-SES schools does little to address the serious educational challenges faced by these schools. Instead, such an emphasis on the provision of technological equipment may divert focus away from other important resources and interventions. Studies also have proved the existence of complex factors that moderate the link between technology use and academic gains, thus suggesting that technology may serve to either overcome or exacerbate educational inequalities depending on how it is used.

Whether home computers are academically beneficial or detrimental for American students also remains unclear. While a few studies report positive effects of home computers on test score outcomes or high school graduation rates, some suggest otherwise.[56] Several studies have indicated there are no academic effects at all. For example, one study of early childhood exposure to home computers demonstrated that simply having access to a home computer during kindergarten has no long-term effect on academic achievement.[57] The study also found that the amount of time spent on the computer for either educational purposes or games did not affect academic achievement in a positive or negative way. Similarly, a randomized control experiment with students in grades 6 to 10 attending 15 schools across California indicated that increasing access to home computers among students who do not already have access is unlikely to greatly improve educational outcomes, but also is unlikely to negatively affect outcomes.[58] One study of home computer and Internet access among 150,000 early secondary students in North Carolina even suggested that providing universal access could widen, rather than narrow, math and reading achievement gaps between students of high and low socioeconomic status.[59] Overall, these findings caution against a policy of simply distributing home computers to narrow achievement gaps.

The United States also has a long tradition of providing computer-enhanced instruction in schools. To assess its effects on academic achievement, one study used data from the National Assessment of Educational Progress to examine the relationship between computer use in schools and student test scores.[60] The results point to the fact that technology is a medium that facilitates teaching pedagogy and its effectiveness depends on how it is used. In math and science, when computers are used in a didactic fashion, they were either unassociated or negatively associated with student performance. Likewise, in reading, when students use computers for spell checking or reading stories, students performed worse. Notably, socioeconomic status had a moderating effect; students in high-income schools tended to get a small benefit from using computers, whereas students from low-income schools had a small negative effect. This also corresponded to differences in how computers were used, with high-income students being more likely to use them for more intellectually challenging purposes, such as simulations and data analysis, whereas low-income students used them more for mechanical drills. Similarly, and in contrast to the studies in China, another national study showed no positive impact from use of math or reading tutorial software among elementary students.[61] The study found a moderate correlation between several classroom characteristics (e.g., student–teacher ratios, time spent for the software) and effectiveness in reading; no such correlation was found for math.

The United States also has many one-to-one laptop programs, which, at least in principle, provide a more robust model of computer-assisted instruction, as students have access to the computers throughout the school day and, in many programs, at home. Most of these programs also put a good deal of effort and funding into professional development, curriculum development, and Internet infrastructure. A meta-analysis of 57 studies of these programs found that, overall, they had a moderate positive effect (.24 standard deviations) on math, science, reading, writing, and language arts test scores.[62] The analysis also showed some of the reasons behind these positive effects on test scores, as well as some other benefits. Students in laptop programs tended to engage in more project-based learning, write and revise more and in a wider variety of genres, and benefit from more individualized instruction.[63] Teacher–student and home-school relationships also were enhanced.[64]

Of course, not all of these programs are successful. What helps them succeed or fail is illustrated in a comparative case study of three laptop programs that provided small, inexpensive laptops equipped with open source software to all students in one or more grade levels as a way of raising academic achievement, especially for the disadvantaged.[65] While the three one-to-one laptop programs in Colorado, California, and Alabama had similar goals of narrowing achievement gaps between students of high and low socioeconomic status, the projects had different outcomes in terms of computer use patterns and sustainability, presumably due to their unique local contexts and approaches to technology integration. The programs in California and Colorado followed an integrative approach, in which provisions of hardware and software were balanced with infrastructural and social support (e.g., curricular reform, teacher training, technical support). These supports enabled the programs to achieve many of their aims in boosting technology use and academic performance, and the programs have continued to grow and expand over the years. In Alabama, the lack of these supports—and a lack of stakeholder buy-in—in the OLPC program meant that the initiative failed to achieve its similar academic and e-inclusion goals. Computers soon broke down and were seldom used for academic purposes at school or at home; with little benefits seen, the initiative was ended within a couple of years. The comparative study suggests that social, infrastructural, and administrative considerations are imperative for program effectiveness.

Other studies also address the potentials and challenges of implementing laptop programs for economically disadvantaged students. One study reported that after three years of participation in the laptop program, economically disadvantaged students in laptop schools grew in technology proficiency at a significantly faster rate than their more affluent peers and control group students.[66] Similarly, another report found that a laptop initiative was more effective with improving the low-achieving students' language and mathematics skills than those of high-achieving students.[67] However, these aspirations for at-risk learners in one-to-one laptop programs are met with challenges due to complex local factors, such as institutional support, the level of instruction, or the different types of assignments. It suggests that the differences in institutional support for technology use, homework assignment patterns, and emphases on preparation for testing all affected the potential to effectively use technology for academic preparation in low-income neighborhood schools.[68]

Similar to the findings from China, the studies in the United States suggests that laptop programs can serve disadvantaged students well when implemented as carefully tailored curricular interventions. With sufficient focus on the particular needs of at-risk learners, substantial curricular reform, and professional development, distributing laptops to individual students can help bridge technological and educational divides.

10.7 Conclusion

Many countries around the world are attempting to incorporate technology into schools in hopes of providing equal educational opportunities to students of diverse backgrounds. For educators and policymakers, the widespread use of technology in education and the disparity in both access and skills presents increasingly complex challenges. Though research on these issues always trails implementation, enough data have been gathered to begin to identify some trends. As seen in the cases of Romania and Peru, simply distributing computers to disadvantaged students may bridge divides in access and provide some cognitive benefit; however, the overall effect of these computers failed to produce significant academic gains. More tailored programs have achieved some gains. Though no academic benefits have been established in Uruguay's program, the combination of computer provision, funding for repairs, and increased Internet access are at least leveling differences in technology access in a sustainable way. In China, carefully targeted, software-based instruction brought up the math and language skills of low-income children in both rural and urban communities, whether or not the instruction was delivered at school or via home computers. Benefits were equally incurred by girls and boys. In the United States, the situation is more complex. As in Peru and Romania, simply handing out computers to students, whether in homes or schools, has not been clearly demonstrated as beneficial, though contradictory findings have emerged. In contrast to China, tutorial software has not yet been proved successful. However, well-designed one-to-one laptop programs in the United States have been very effective, raising test scores, improving students' broad learning skills, and lessening achievement gaps by race or income.

In many developing countries with low-income and isolated rural schools, technology has the potential to dramatically enhance students' learning resources. However, without proper environmental support and a pedagogical perspective, the expense of providing computers for individual students can be a low-return investment. Technology is costly and requires ongoing maintenance and support. Hard-headed, cost-benefit analysis is needed before making decisions about investing in a large-scale implementation of educational technology, especially in low income countries with pressing economic, social, and health challenges and little infrastructure to support computer programs.

For developed countries with widespread Internet and computer access, a more critical concern is how people utilize the Internet to build knowledge and what impact socioeconomic backgrounds have on the process. As access to digital devices and the Internet becomes widespread, the meaning of the digital divide is evolving.[69] In the past, digital divide research focused on accessibility to computers and the Internet and on consumption of information. However, as exemplified in the United States case, the digital divide in the field of education is shifting from a gap in access and connectivity to a second-level digital divide related to skills or a pedagogical divide related to teaching practices.[70]

These divides are much more challenging to address and require holistic approaches addressing not only the presence of technology, but, more importantly, its contexts of use. This represents a challenge to policymakers, who tend to favor technological solutions to complex social problems. More efforts are needed to move beyond a narrow notion of access and instead analyze the role of different forms of access to information as well as the specific conditions that nurture the effective integration of technology into communities, institutions, and societies (see Warschauer, 2003, for a comprehensive review).[71] While continuing the attempts to equip students with technology access, we need to ensure that students are able to make use of technologies to engage in meaningful social practice, integration of information, and production of knowledge.

Endnotes

1. Castells, M. (2010). *The rise of the network society: The information age: Economy, society, and culture*. Oxford, U.K.: Blackwell.
2. Prieger, J. E. (2007). The supply side of the digital divide: Is there equal availability in the broadband Internet access market? *Economic Inquiry*, 41(2), 346–363.
3. Chinn, M. D., and R. W. Fairlie (2007). The determinants of the global digital divide: A cross-country analysis of computer and Internet penetration. *Oxford Economic Papers*, 59(1), 16–44.
4. Hargittai, E. (2002). Second-level digital divide: Differences in people's online skills. *First Monday*, 7(4); International Data Corporation (2011). China's 12th five-year plan will benefit the PC market and create additional boost for rural markets. Online at: http://www.idc.com/getdoc.jsp?containerId¼prCN22776811
5. World Bank (2013). China: World development indicators database; Malamud, O., and C. Pop-Eleches (2011). Home computer use and the development of human capital. *Quarterly Journal of Economics,* 126, 987–1027. http://databank.worldbank.org/data/China---World-Development-Indicators/id/32bd0f0a
6. Chinese Internet Network Information Center (2010). 25th Statistical Survey Report on the Internet Development in China. http://prosperchina.com/netizens-jan2010.pdf
7. World Bank (2013). China: World development indicators database; Malamud, O., and C. Pop-Eleches (2011). Home computer use and the development of human capital. *Quarterly Journal of Economics*, 126, 987–1027. http://databank.worldbank.org/data/China---World-Development-Indicators/id/32bd0f0a
8. Eurostat (2012). Computer skills in the EU27 in figures. News release. Online at: http://epp.eurostat.ec.europa.eu/cache/.../26032012.../4-26032012-AP-EN.PDF
9. Ministry of Education, Romania (2007). Online at: http://portal.edu.ro/index.php/articles/5212
10. Malamud and Pop-Eleches, Home computer use and the development of human capital.
11. For example, Giacquinta, J. B., J. A. Bauer, and J. E. Levin (1993). *Beyond technology's promise: An examination of children's educational computing at home*. New York: Cambridge University Press.

12 Butler, D. (2007). The race to wire up the poor. *Nature*, 447, 6–7.

13. Chinese Internet Network Information Center (2013). Statistical report on Internet development in China. http://www1.cnnic.cn/IDR/ReportDownloads/201302/P020130312536825920279.pdf

14. Yang, Y., L. Zhang, X. Hu, Q. Qu, F. Lai, and Y. Shi (2013). The roots of tomorrow's digital divide: Documenting computer use and Internet access in China's elementary schools today. *China and World Economy*, 21(3), 61–79.

15. International Data Corporation (2011). China's 12th five-year plan will benefit the PC market and create additional boost for rural markets. Online at: http://www.idc.com/getdoc.jsp?containerId1/4prCN22776811

16. Mo, D., J. Swinnen, L. Zhang, H. Yi, Q. Qu, M. Boswell, and S. Rozelle (2013). Can one-to-one computing narrow the digital divide and the educational gap in China? The case of Beijing migrant schools. *World Development*, 46(2), 14–29.

17. Ibid.

18. Yang, Y., L. Zhang, J. Zeng, X. Pang, F. Lai, and S. Rozelle (2013). Computers and the academic performance of elementary school-aged girls in China's poor communities. *Computers & Education*, 60(1), 335–346.

19. For example, Li, N., and G. Kirkup (2007). Gender and cultural differences in Internet use: A study of China and the U.K. *Computers & Education*, 48(2), 301–317.

20. World Bank (2013). Peru: World development indicators database. http://databank.worldbank.org/data/Peru-World-Development-Indicators/id/3f822b80; One Laptop Per Child (n.d.). OLPC: Five principles. Online at: http://wiki.laptop.org/go/Core_principles

21. Cristia, J., P. Ibarrarán, S. Cueto, A. Santiago, and E. Severín (2012). Technology and child development: Evidence from the One Laptop per Child Program. Inter-American Development Bank. Online at: http://idbdocs.iadb.org/wsdocs/getdocument.aspx?docnum=36706954

22. Organization for Economic Co-operation and Development (2010). PISA 2009 at a Glance. Online at: http://dx.doi.org/10.1787/9789264095298-en

23. Wessendorf, K. (ed.) (2009). *The indigenous world 2009*. Kobenhavn, Denmark: The International Work Group for Indigenous Affairs (IWGIA).

24. Becerra, O. (2010). What is reasonable to expect from information and communication technologies in education? Online at: http://edutechdebate.org/computer-configurations-for-learning/what-is-reasonable-to-expect-from-information-and-communication-technologies-in-education/

25. Breitkopf, A. (2012). Cultural and educational implications of global media. The One Laptop per Child Initiative in rural Peruvian schools. Master's thesis. (p. 60) Online at: http://www.antje-breitkopf.com/wp-content/uploads/2013/01/OLPC_thesis2012.pdf

26. Cristia, Ibarrarán, Cueto, Santiago, and Severín, Technology and child development, p. 10.

27. Breitkopf, Cultural and educational implications of global media.

28. Cristia, Ibarrarán, Cueto, Santiago, and Severín, Technology and child development.

29. Ibid.; Beuermann, D. W., J. P. Cristia, Y. Cruz-Aguayo, S. Cueto, and O. Malamud (2013). *Home computers and child outcomes: Short-term impacts from a randomized experiment in Peru.* Cambridge, MA: National Bureau of Economic Research. (No. w18818)

30. Ibid.

31. Ibid.

32. Cristia, Ibarrarán, Cueto, Santiago, and Severín, Technology and child development.

33. Ibid.

34. Glewwe, P., and M. Kremer (2006). Schools, teachers, and education outcomes in developing countries. In *Handbook of the Economics of Education*, vol. 2, eds. E. Hanushek and F. Welch (pp. 945–1017). Amsterdam: Elsevier.

35. Breitkopf, Cultural and educational implications of global media.

36. Ibid.

37. Ibid.; Levinson, B. A., and D. Holland (1996). The cultural production of the educated person: An introduction. In *The cultural production of the educated person: Critical ethnographies of schooling and local practice*, eds. B. A. Levinson, D. E. Foely, and D. C. Holland (pp. 1–54). Albany: State University of New York Press.

38. Fullan, M., N. Watson, and S. Anderson (2013). Ceibal: Next steps. Final report. Online at: http://www.ceibal.org.uy/docs/FULLAN-Ceibal-English.pdf

39. Organization for Economic Co-operation and Development (2013). PISA 2012 results in focus: What 15-year-olds know and what they can do with what they know. Online at: http://www.oecd.org/pisa/keyfindings/pisa-2012-results-overview.pdf; Fullan, Watson, and Anderson, Ceibal: Next steps; Warschauer, M., and M. Ames (2010). Can one laptop per child save the world's poor? *Journal of International Affairs*, 64(1), 33–51.

40. Fullan, Watson, and Anderson, Ceibal: Next steps.

41. Martínez, A. L., D. Díaz, and S. Alonso (2009). First national monitoring and evaluation report on Plan Ceibal social impact, 2009. Online at: http://www.ceibal.org.uy/docs/Resumen-Ejecutivo_2009_English.pdf

42. Fullan, Watson, and Anderson, Ceibal: Next steps.

43. Pittaluga, L., and A. Rivoir (2012). One laptop per child and bridging the digital divide: The case of plan Ceibal in Uruguay. *Information Technologies & International Development*, 8(4), 145.

44. Martínez, Díaz, and Alonso, First national monitoring and evaluation report on Plan Ceibal social impact, 2009.

45. Warschauer and Ames, Can one laptop per child save the world's poor?

46. Plan Ceibal (2013a). *Evolución de la brecha de acceso a TIC en Uruguay (2008-2012) y la contribución del Plan Ceibal a disminuir dicha brecha.* Online at: http://www.ceibal.org.uy/docs/evolucion-de-la-brecha-de-acceso-a-TIC-y-contribucion-del-Plan-Ceibal-modificado.pdf

47. Plan Ceibal (2013b). *Resultados del monitoreo del estado del parque de laptops en Educación Media Básica.* Online at: ttp://www.ceibal.org.uy/docs/Resultados-Monitoreo-Estado-Parque-MEDIA_Setiembre_2013.pdf

48. Martínez, Díaz, and Alonso, First national monitoring and evaluation report on Plan Ceibal social impact, 2009.

49. Ibid.

50. Pittaluga and Rivoir, One laptop per child and bridging the digital divide.

51. Martínez, A. L., D. Díaz, and S. Alonso (2009). First national monitoring and evaluation report on Plan Ceibal social impact, 2009. Online at: http://www.ceibal.org.uy/docs/Resumen-Ejecutivo_2009_English.pdf

52. Pittaluga and Rivoir, One laptop per child and bridging the digital divide.

53. de Melo, G., A. Machado, S. Alfonso, and M. Viera (2013). *Profundizando en los efects del Plan Ceibal.* Online at: http://www.ceibal.org.uy/docs/investigacion/Informe_final_IECON.pdf

54. de Melo, Machado, Alfonso, and Viera, Profundizando en los efects del Plan Ceibal.

55. Organization for Economic Co-operation and Development, PISA 2012 results in focus.; Fullan, Watson, and Anderson, Ceibal: Next steps.

56. Beltran, D., K. Das, and R. Fairlie (2010). Home computers and educational outcomes: Evidence from the NLSY97 and CPS. *Economic Inquiry*, 48(3), 771–792; Attewell, P., and J. Battle (1999). Home computers and school performance. *Information Society*, 15(1), 1–10.

57. Johnson, E. (2012). Analyzing computer technology and achievement in early childhood. Poster presented at American Educational Research Association Annual Meeting, Vancouver, Canada, April.

58. Fairlie, R.W., and J. Robinson (2013). Experimental evidence on the effects of home computers on academic achievement among schoolchildren. IZA Discussion Paper No. 7211. Bonn, Germany: Institute for the Study of Labor. Online at: http://ftp.iza.org/dp7211.pdf

59. Vigdor, J. L., and H. F. Ladd (2010). *Scaling the digital divide: Home computer technology and student achievement.* Cambridge, MA: National Bureau of Economic Research.

60. Wenglinsky, H. (2005). *Using technology wisely: The keys to success in schools.* New York: Teachers College Press.

61. Dynarski, M., R. Agodini, S. Heaviside, T. Novak, N. Carey, L. Campuzano, et al. (2007). *Effectiveness of reading and mathematics software products: Findings from the first student cohort.* NCEE Rep. No. 2007-4005. Washington, D.C.: U.S. Department of Education, Institute of Education Sciences.

62. Zheng, B., and M. Warschauer (2013). Teaching and learning in one-to-one laptop environments: A research synthesis. Paper presented at the American Educational Research Association Annual Meeting, San Francisco, California, April.

63. Cavanaugh, C., K. Dawson, and A.D. Ritzhaupt (2011). An evaluation of the conditions, processes, and consequences of laptop computing in K-12 classrooms. *Journal of Educational Computing Research*, 45(3), 359–378; Corn, J. O., J. T. Tagsold, and R. K. Patel (2011). The tech-savvy teacher: Instruction in a 1:1 learning environment. *Journal of Educational Research and Practice*, 1(1), 1–22; Grimes, D., and M. Warschauer (2008). Learning with laptops: A multi-method case study. *Journal of Educational Computing Research*, 38(3), 305–332; Russell, M., D. Bebell, and J. Higgins (2004). Laptop learning: A comparison of teaching and learning in upper elementary classrooms equipped with shared carts of laptops and permanent 1:1 laptops, *Journal of Educational Computing Research*, 30(4), 313–330.

64. Lei, J., and Y. Zhao (2008). One-to-one computing: What does it bring to schools? *Journal of Educational Computing Research*, 39(2), 97–122.

65. Warschauer, M., B. Zheng, M. Niiya, S. Cotten, and G. Farkas (2014). Balancing the one-to-one equation: Equity and access in three laptop programs. *Equity & Excellence in Education*, 47(1), 1–17.

66. Shapley, K., D. Sheehan, C. Maloney, and F. Caranikas-Walker (2011). Effects of technology immersion on middle school students' learning opportunities and achievement. *The Journal of Educational Research*, 104(5), 299–315.

67. Bernard, R. M., E. C. Bethel, P.C. Abrami, and C. A. Wade (2007). Introducing laptops to children: An examination of ubiquitous computing in Grade 3 reading, language, and mathematics. *Canadian Journal of Learning and Technology*, 33(3).

68. Warschauer, M., M. Knobel, and L. Stone (2004). Technology and equity in schooling: Deconstructing the digital divide. *Educational Policy*, 18(4), 562–588.

69. Graham, M. (2011). Time machines and virtual portals: The spatialities of the digital divide. *Progress in Development Studies*, 11(3), 211–227.

70. Hargittai, E. (2002). Second-level digital divide: Differences in people's online skills. *First Monday*, 7(4); Cummins, J. (2008). Technology, literacy, and young second language learners: Designing educational futures. In *Technology-mediated learning environments for young English learners: Connections in and out of school*, ed. L. L. Parker (pp. 61–98). Mahway, NJ: Lawrence Erlbaum Associates.

71. Warschauer, M. (2003). *Technology and social inclusion: Rethinking the digital divide*. Cambridge, MA: MIT Press.

Chapter 11

e-Education at the Local Level: Challenges and Pitfalls of Public Policies in Rio de Janeiro

Bernardo Sorj and Denise Vaillant

Contents

11.1 Introduction

Virtually every Latin American country, including the poorest, has a computer distribution program for schools. However, the rationale behind them is not supported by previous assessments of how computers and the Internet might be used as tools to improve education. In most developing countries, assessment and monitoring studies are scarce and, in many cases, flawed. Surveys carried out in developed countries on the impact of new technologies in education are contradictory; in some, the outcomes are found to be positive; in others, neutral; and in some, negative.[1] Generally, when positive impact is found, it cannot be separated from the educational context in which the study was performed, such as schools with properly trained teachers and adequate support for school computer labs.

If computer access programs for school children do not imply an automatic positive consequence on education,[2] it does not mean that they are not useful as an e-inclusion policy, although this should then be recognized as their main purpose. However, e-education is more complex than digital inclusion. It implies a long chain of technical, pedagogical, and human resources, in which training teachers to work in a different environment is central and very difficult to achieve, in particular among the older generation. Changing the educational system to a computer-centered environment, even in the most favorable conditions, is going to be a long process. We still know little, very little, about how the cognitive abilities of current and future generations will be shaped by new information technologies, whose impact include, but greatly exceed, the school system.[3] There may be cognitive gains, but also losses, as happened when previous communication technologies revolutions (writing, printing, TV) changed the ways we use, store, and share knowledge. In the short term, new technologies pose great challenges to established education systems. This is compounded by a state of crisis that predates the Internet and involves the relation of authority between teachers and students, as well as the growing demand made by families that each student receive individualized attention—not to mention cultural transformations around values such as discipline or hard work.

The issue to consider, then, is not whether computers should or should not be distributed to schools; that decision has already been made. Politics must now be translated into responsible policies in both the use of resources and the educational goals they are meant to support, maximizing benefits and minimizing waste. We learn as much from mistakes as from success stories. Many cases that are presented in developing countries as benchmarks are related to exceptional conditions, including one-time outside funding that assures the success of the project for a limited time. The main challenge is to learn from mistakes and to understand why they tend to repeat.

This chapter provides a broad overview of educational public policies in Brazil, the largest country in Latin America, both in population (around 200 million) and in territory, with high levels of social inequality, including among different regions, and an overall Internet penetration rate of around 50 percent. It has a federal structure that transfers responsibility for basic education to the municipal level while "middle" education is the responsibility of each state, and higher education determined by the federal government, although, in practice, responsibilities are somewhat overlapping. To illustrate the challenge of implementing policies in this complex social and institutional environment, a case study on Rio de Janeiro, Brazil's second-largest city with about 12 million people, shows practical limitations toward greater e-inclusion in education at a local level. Combining this example and drawing broadly on lessons learned throughout Latin America, the conclusion discusses the implications for e-education moving forward.

11.2 Brazil's Complex Road toward e-Education[4]

Responsibility for the public education system in Brazil, a federal country, is divided between municipalities, which handle preschool and nine years of "fundamental" school, and the states, which provide for the following three years of "middle education." In practice, this rule is not always followed. Even the federal state itself is responsible for some schools and it has a decisive role in defining the curriculum in addition to its financial importance and permanent interventions with specific national programs.

In an e-education context, this institutional complexity means that any school will be simultaneously influenced by the policies of federal, state, and municipality programs. The consequence is a permanent overlap and lack of coherence, even at the most basic level. For instance, there are schools that received computers from the federal government using an operating system different from the computers received from the municipality. More common is the waste of resources related to the production and use of educational software. Each state and each municipality, in particular those related to big cities, has its own e-education policy and, in many cases, spend money to develop their own software (which, frequently, is in itself needless, given the availability of good, open source products).

Data regarding computer and Internet access in public schools in Brazil tend to be overoptimistic. Government data consider the number of computers it sends to the schools. However, this does not mean that they are currently functional, given the limited technical assistance available. If they are being used it does not mean that the school has Internet access or that they are being shared by teachers and children (in many cases, they are placed in the director's office or are kept in closed rooms with restricted access). Even surveys conducted by independent institutions are not completely reliable because generally the forms are filled in by the school directors who tend to present a rosier picture.[5]

This is not to say that there are not advances. Some municipalities and states have distributed laptops to teachers. The One Computer per Student, a federal government program, has distributed 150,000 computers to rural areas, according to official numbers. Similar programs were announced by some municipalities, but there is no available independent research on the effective implementation of those policies. Of greater impact is the government policy of lowering taxes and providing credit lines for individuals to buy basic and relatively inexpensive desktops and laptops. According to a 2012 CGI (Brazilian Internet Steering Committee) survey, almost 100 percent of teachers and 60 percent of public school students have access to computers at home.[6]

The number of schools with computer labs and Internet access also is growing each year. However, existing data are flawed and not very helpful to understand what happens in practice. For instance, the report indicates that the vast majority of public school desktops (the number of laptops is negligible) are located in technology labs or in the library. In other words, classes using computers can only be pursued in the labs, and with a number of computers almost always less than the number of children in a class. Furthermore, the CGI report claims that the labs are open daily; however, studies show that their use during class time is quite limited and, in most of cases, are only used by a few students during breaks, assuming the lab responsible (or librarian) is open during that time.

11.3 Local Realities: A Case Study of Rio de Janeiro

The practical realities are illuminated by field work in Rio de Janeiro in 2010/2011,[7] which included interviews with public schools' teachers, and visits to schools. Among the teachers surveyed, computer access was nearly universal: 98 percent of respondents stated that they owned a home computer, and 79 percent indicated that they had a broadband Internet connection. Only 16 percent used a dial-up connection, and only 5 percent did not access the Internet from home.[8] The survey findings imply that lack of computer knowledge can no longer be cited as a primary challenge for elementary school teachers.

Although the simple presence of a home computer does not guarantee its use, 93 percent of respondents were computer users, with widely varying levels of skill. Nearly all of those who described themselves as users were familiar with word processing software (99 percent). The second most familiar resource involved the creation of slide shows (with software such as PowerPoint'), used by 44.3 percent of respondents. About a third of the teachers also used image processing programs, such as Photoshop' (a surprising 33.9 percent), spreadsheets (31.4 percent), and image and sound editors (an even more surprising 30.3 percent). Skills, such as website creation and online editing, occurred in significantly smaller percentages (4.6 percent and 2.5 percent, respectively). Although the number of men in the sample was small, they were more likely than women to indicate proficiency in some of the tools just mentioned, such as PowerPoint (62 percent versus 42 percent) and spreadsheets (45 percent versus 30 percent).

Contrary to conventional thinking (given the varying age profile of the group and its overwhelmingly female majority), Rio's school teachers appear to be relatively familiar with the use of computers and the Internet, as illustrated in Figure 11.1. This trend is likely to continue as older teachers are phased out. The survey shows that younger teachers (21 to 30 years old) were proportionally more likely to be technologically proficient. The teaching profession shows the same tendency as the majority of the population, in which the youngest age group uses computer technology more skillfully and frequently.

On average, the younger a teacher, the greater their basic computing skills, and the more likely is that person to directly assist his/her students in computer-related activities. The age pattern is also reflected in the use of Internet for lesson planning, as shown in Figure 11.2.

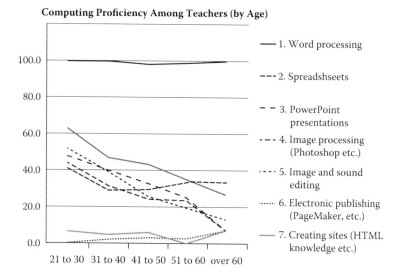

Figure 11.1 Computing proficiency among teachers (by age).

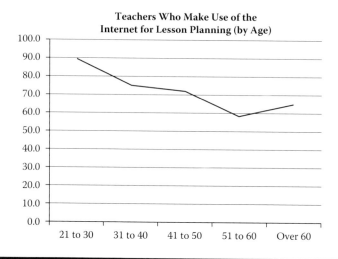

Figure 11.2 Teachers who make use of the Internet for lesson planning (by age).

This generational divide indicates that Brazil's school system faces a long period during which its teachers are likely to operate at two different levels: those generally younger who are interested and able to experiment with new technologies, and those generally older who feel threatened by them even to the point of resisting any form of innovation. This tendency suggests that, left to follow its "natural" course, the adoption of ICTs in education will occur in accordance with the pace—be it fast or slow—of the generational turnover of teachers. In the past two decades, Brazil has slowed down its demographic expansion and the number of children in primary schools has stabilized. As a consequence, the entering of new teachers will occur slowly.

Yet, a disposition to experiment with new technologies is not enough. Familiarity does not automatically translate into regular use and/or systematic adoption of computer use in schools. The "real" incorporation of information technology in teaching is dependent on access to computers and the Internet at the schools.

Among survey respondents, 59 percent indicated that they worked in schools with computer labs. The size of the school makes a difference in this regard. While 82 percent of teachers in large schools indicated that their institution had a computer lab, only 40 percent of teachers in small schools did so, as shown in Figure 11.3.

The number of available computers varies greatly (from 3 to 30), but the most frequently cited number was 10 (present in 58 percent of schools with labs). However, 27 percent of teachers indicated that they worked in schools whose labs had fewer than 10 computers. All available computers worked regularly in only half of the laboratories (51 percent); in another 30 percent, more than half of the equipment worked regularly; and in 19 percent, none or less than half of the computers worked adequately. Further, the mere presence of computers does not translate into Internet access: only 50 percent indicated full access, whereas 18 percent of teachers stated that their laboratories did not have access to the Internet at all, and 30 percent responded that access was limited.

Computer laboratory observation also reveals that maintenance conditions vary greatly from one school to another. In focus groups, comments were made that

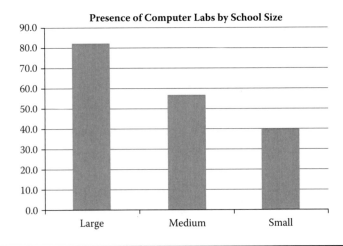

Figure 11.3   Presence of computer labs by school size.

machines are often cannibalized for spare parts, mainly due to the age of some of the equipment. Although the computers in the four laboratories that were visited were all in working order, the survey revealed that in 19 percent of schools, less than half of the computers worked consistently. One teacher responsible for the reading room at an Education for Work center stated that the center's laboratory used to be "hopping," but that, over time, the machines stopped working as their warranties expired. Currently, the center has only four working computers and no Internet access. She stated that this was "very discouraging," especially for science teachers who used the laboratory frequently to work on projects with their students.

In the group of administrators, the word "frustration" also was used several times when this topic came up. When describing the teachers who had received training but were not given the opportunity to apply what they had learned, one coordinator, who had also served as a training facilitator, put it this way: "They feel their knowledge is going to waste, because the school system invested in these training sessions, and they feel frustrated by not being able to apply things, whether because the computers don't work, or the Internet doesn't work, or because they can't teach what they learned in the courses because of the school."

Since 2000, the city of Rio has invested in programs to train its teachers in "educational computing." In the first two years, teachers received a bonus to participate in training courses, and training facilitators also were paid. In the teachers' focus group, the comment was made that "the majority" took the course just "for the money." After the attendance bonus was eliminated, the number of participants declined and, according to some, the quality of the course improved.[9] Another reason to explain the lack of interest in computer training is that many teachers took the courses because they expected to be made responsible for the computer labs that had begun to be installed in schools. When this failed to happen, interest fell off, and those who had enrolled in the courses hoping to be promoted were left frustrated.

One of the primary obstacles to integrate computers into the school system is the disparity in available resources between the training courses and the schools. The courses take place in comfortable classrooms, each with 10 functional computers, whereas this is not always the case at schools. A common complaint expressed by the teachers was that "I wasn't able to apply what I learned in the course." Once, this same teacher recalled, she had led a course with teachers from a variety of locations. The laboratory of the school where the course was being given used Windows', but some of the teachers worked at schools where Linux was used. "Their schools didn't have many of the programs I was trying to teach them, which made for a frustrating experience." To avoid this kind of situation, she argued that teachers should be trained at their own schools. This perspective was embraced by the entire group of teachers, who then manifested a preference for unpaid training held during work hours at the teachers' own schools.[10]

The study, like others that have been conducted in Brazil and elsewhere, suggests that there are tremendous gaps in ensuring that equipment is put to good use.[11] The technical support structure is still precarious, not to mention the lack of standardization in the systems being used. Teacher training, especially when carried out through online courses using outdated "distance learning" methods, leaves much to be desired because it does not take an individualized approach, something for which the Internet would provide ideal support and that these courses should exemplify. The commitment of school principals to introduce new technologies is uneven at best. Available teaching material is still limited and fragmentary.

There is certainly much to be learned from the experience of other countries, particularly those with similar characteristics. International research indicates that the effective use of new technologies requires increasing the time students spend at school, and some suggest, for example, that separate computer labs are not learning-conducive environments, leading to the creation of mobile laboratories that make it possible to transport equipment to regular classrooms where resources are scarce.

A central challenge involves those teachers, a considerable number, who see new technologies as a threat to their role as educators. Aside from conservatism and group interests (several of them claimed that working time did increase due to the use of Internet, both by the administration and by students), these teachers express a real concern: the redefinition of their role in a classroom where the computer (not to mention text messages sent by cell phones) "steal" students' attention. In this new technological environment, redefining the role of the teacher is a challenge that requires rethinking the role of formal education. A considerable number of refresher courses for teachers focus on technological issues, which, although important, miss the central point: the technical skills of many who were born in the digital world are ahead of those possessed by the majority of teachers.

11.4 Conclusion

In the 1990s, the first government programs for school computers in Latin America were aimed primarily, though not always explicitly, at digital inclusion, understood as "teaching children without home access how to use computers." The goal was to offer children access to computers at school where they could practice and develop the ability to use them.[12] In fact, "computers for all" become a popular political platform, as was the case during the latest elections in Uruguay, or currently in the use as a progovernment publicity in Argentina, where the *Conectar* (Connect) program has received great attention through a typically election-centered marketing campaign.

Although access to computers and the Internet has increased tremendously in recent years, a significant number of low-income children still do not have a computer at home. Despite the growth of LAN (local area network) houses, which are also present in low-income neighborhoods, and despite the current generation's ability to develop digital literacy, the argument that a percentage of low-income youth have little or no access to the Internet continues to be valid. Certainly a project like Uruguay's Plan Ceibal, is the best way to achieve the goal of universal inclusion. However, if "digital inclusion" is the objective, we should think carefully about the best way to achieve it without confusing it with e-education.

The focus of computer distribution in public schools is beginning to shift in Uruguay and other Latin American countries from digital inclusion to improved instruction with the support of new technologies.[13] The assumption is that these programs will boost school system quality, making it possible to overcome the problems faced by public education; however, as the Rio de Janeiro case study shows, this is not necessarily the outcome. Therefore, such developments should be properly monitored so that the necessary measures can be adopted to achieve the desired results.

Today, teachers in Latin American schools face students that are different from preceding generations[14] in terms of how they learn, live, and work with widespread access to digital technologies. In fact, most children in the OECD (Organization for Economic Cooperation and Development) countries, and more recently, those of Latin America and the Caribbean countries have grown up with some kind of digital device.[15]

Several expressions have been used to describe this generation, among which the most popular is that of "digital natives."[16] Digital natives are thought to fluently handle the language and logic of digital technology. This is in contrast to "digital immigrants," i.e., previous generations who speak the language of technology with an "accent." As such, e-education confronts two problems: (1) the generational gap between digital natives and their teachers, usually digital immigrants, is so broad that it becomes difficult to produce a meaningful teaching-learning process; and (2) the traditional teaching systems do not meet the needs of the new generation. Both problems have a negative impact on learning outcomes and the commitment of the students.[17]

Advances in information and communications technology (ICT) infrastructure and access in schools are a precondition for e-education, although it does not ensure its effective implementation. Access to digital devices has been increasing steadily in Latin America, but there are many teachers in the region who lack basic knowledge as how to work with them meaningfully. Each country has enormous social gaps, both among students and teachers, and also between different generations of teachers.

A recent study by UNESCO (UN Educational, Scientific, and Cultural Organization) analyzes the ICT integration processes in Latin America and the Caribbean and it examines, in particular, the digital skills of teachers.[18] The paper reports about the percentage of teachers per country trained and qualified to teach basic computer skills at basic education levels. The study's findings are worrisome, bearing in mind that less than 10 percent of primary and secondary teachers belonging to 14 of the 27 countries under scrutiny prove to be competent in ICT.

Some studies highlight the low impact of ICTs in the teaching practice and that their use is often limited to class preparation and management.[19] Teacher performance in incorporating ICT into education is linked to three sets of factors: their basic competence, attitude, and the educational use. Familiarity with ICTs is a prerequisite for their effective integration in the classroom, but this single factor is not enough; success depends heavily on the positive attitude of teachers toward them. And even when teachers are competent in ICTs and have a positive attitude toward ICTs, it is common that teachers fail to integrate them in their pedagogical activities. The explanation of this situation lies in the processes of both initial and continuing teacher training.

One study, which evaluated the ICT skills of teachers in OECD countries, found that, even when teachers have a high degree of familiarity with technology and feel comfortable with its use, they fail to integrate it in their everyday teaching practices.[20] Even in highly developed countries like South Korea, where the presence of electronic devices is widespread and Internet penetration is nearly universal, teachers still need a great deal of support, specifically on how to use technology to enhance the learning process of their students. In other words, the challenges and difficulties of introducing new technologies in education is a global problem. In Latin America each country has its own difficulties, but we are confronting a global phenomena.

Digital inclusion through school computer programs can actually serve five different functions that are interrelated to a certain extent:

1. As a means of improving the administrative structure of the school system, facilitating contact among superintendents, principals, and teachers
2. As a tool for teachers to complete in-service training and continuing education programs
3. As a way for schools, teachers, and parents to communicate, as well as a means of enrollment
4. As a way for teachers and students to communicate
5. As a teaching and learning tool both inside and outside the classroom

Each of these five facets calls for constant assessment, although the handful of existing impact studies has focused only on the last one. However, the introduction of computers is simply one element in the e-education chain as the Rio de Janeiro case study shows, and usually the least difficult to implement. This chain includes:

1. A system of technical support to ensure that computers are properly maintained, constantly updated, and supplied with peripheral material, such as paper and ink for printers (and the money needed to make such purchases).
2. Ongoing teacher training in the use of educational programs and software. The quality of training received by teachers affects their attitudes toward educational technologies.[21] Mastery of basic ICT skills is a necessary, but not sufficient condition, as adequate training is required in order to ensure the incorporation of the educational technology into teaching practices. Websites

with constantly updated material, educational programs, and online support for teachers and students.

3. Adequate communication among superintendents, principals, and teachers.

If one of these aspects malfunction, as in any production line, it will define the pace of the operation as a whole. For the most optimistic observers, the use of new technologies has enabled new forms of teaching that value the skills and individual learning pace of each student, as well as innovative forms of collaborative work that can bring colleagues together across space and time. However, as demonstrated by a recent World Bank study in Colombia,[22] disappointing outcomes in school computer programs may be the result, in large part, of failures in the earlier links in the chain rather than in the classroom itself.

The role of the teacher also needs to be expanded. e-Education is not only a matter of educating students about the dangers lurking on the web, such as cyberbullying and privacy issues (with an understanding of the ways in which information about one's personal life, and that of one's acquaintances, may be used in the future). These are central concerns, but they are often presented as the only issues about which students should receive guidance, reducing the role of teachers and parents to one of repression, rather than offering a broader perspective in terms of ethics[23] and citizenship[24] for the responsible use of the web. Maintaining a personal relationship with students will remain central during early schooling and it should include the ability of guiding students in the critical use of the Internet, helping them communicate ideas (verbally or visually), interpret information, and develop autonomous thinking. These challenges include finding one's way in a world of information overload, not blindly accepting the first hits that appear on Google or Wikipedia, problematizing and critically analyzing information, knowing how to ask questions and managing virtual relations.

These issues will redefine the role of the teacher as a Socratic figure who teaches students how to reflect and question. Until that promise comes to full fruition, the road ahead will certainly be a long one, at least for those responsible for administering the school system.

Endnotes

1. Learning Point Associates provides a number of studies online: http://www2.learningpt.org/catalog/. For a good summary of evaluations carried out through 2005, see Critical Issue: Using Technology to Improve Student Achievement. Online at: http://www.ncrel.org/sdrs/areas/issues/methods/technlgy/te800.htm; http://www2.learningpt.org/catalog/; http://www.ncrel.org/sdrs/areas/issues/methods/technlgy/te800.htm. The major studies carried out in the 1990s were summarized by John Schacter in The Impact of Education Technology on Student Achievement: What the Most Current Research Has to Say. Online at: http://www.waynecountyschools.org/150820127152538360/lib/150820127152538360/impact_on_student_achievement.pdf; http://www.

waynecountyschools.org/150820127152538360/lib/150820127152538360/impact_on_student_achievement.pdf. The argument that new technologies require a radical change in teaching methods in order to be effective is proposed by Clayton Christensen, Curtis W. Johnson, and Michael B. Horn. *Disrupting Class: How Disruptive Innovation Will Change the Way the World Learns* (New York: McGraw-Hill, 2008). Online at: http://www.amazon.com/s/ref=ntt_athr_dp_sr_1?_encoding=UTF8&sort=relevancerank&search-alias=books&field-author=ClaytonChristensen; http://www.amazon.com/Curtis-W.-Johnson/e/B001JRXAN2/ref=ntt_athr_dp_pel_2; http://www.amazon.com/Curtis-W.-Johnson/e/B001JRXAN2/ref=ntt_athr_dp_pel_pop_2; http://www.amazon.com/s/ref=ntt_athr_dp_sr_pop_2?_encoding=UTF8&sort=relevancerank&search-alias=books&field-author=CurtisW.Johnson; http://authorcentral.amazon.com/gp/landing/ref=ntt_atc_dp_pel_2

2. See, for instance, the Inter American Development Bank report on the impact of laptop distribution in Peruvian schools. Online at: http://www.iadb.org/es/investigacion-y-datos/detalles-de-publicacion,3169.html?pub_id=IDB-WP-304

3. There are countless studies on the impact of the Internet on young people. See, for example, John Palfrey and Urs Gasser. *Born Digital: Understanding the First Generation of Digital Natives* (New York: Basic Books, 2008); for Latin America, see Fundación Telefónica. *La Generación Interactiva en Iberoamérica—Niños y adolescentes ante las pantallas* (Editora Ariel, 2008). Regarding the broader impact of the Internet on society, opposing perspectives can be found in equal number. See, for example, from the "optimists'" camp, Manuel Castells. *Communication Power* (Oxford, U.K.: Oxford University Press, 2011); and also, Yochai Benkler. *The Wealth of Networks*. (New Haven, CT: Yale University Press, 2007). Online at: http://cyber.law.harvard.edu/wealth_of_networks/Download_PDFs_of_the_book. A more critical perspective can be found in David Singh Grewal. *Network Power* (New Haven, CT: Yale University Press, 2008); Jonathan Zittrain. *The Future of the Internet and How to Stop It.* (New Haven, CT: Yale University Press, 2009); and Nicholas Carr. *The Shallows: What the Internet Is Doing to Our Brains* (New York: W. W. Norton, 2010).

4. This chapter uses the results of the research we did in 2010 in Rio de Janeiro public schools; see Bernardo Sorj and Mauricio Lissovsky. "Internet nas escolas públicas: políticas além da política" (working paper no. 6, Centro Edelstein de Pesquisas Sociais, 2011).

5. Ibid.

6. TIC Educação—2102. CGI—Brasil, 2013. Online at: http://www.cetic.br/publicacoes/2012/tic-educacao-2012.pdf

7. Research made by Sorj and Lissovsky in Rio de Janeiro in 2010/2011 with public schools teachers, including focus groups and visits to schools. Online at: http://www.cetic.br/educacao/2012/escolas/

8. It is possible that part of the explanation for the widespread dissemination of computers may be attributed to the Municipal Secretariat of Education's 2008 laptop distribution program for all teachers in the school system. At the same time, according to some research participants, the program was not fully able to meet its goals; some teachers chose not to claim their computer, whether because they feared it would be stolen or because they thought it would be used as a form of control.

9. It was said that the system had been modified at the request of the teacher trainers themselves, since those who were there "just for the money" hindered class performance.

10. They are currently held on Saturdays and during "alternative" time slots.

11. This conclusion is echoed by one of the few systematic studies on the topic, focused on Colombia and carried out by the World Bank. Felipe Barrera-Osorio and Leigh Linden (February 2009). The Use and Misuse of Computers in Education: Evidence from a Randomized Experiment in Colombia. Online at: http://siteresources. worldbank.org/EDUCATION/Resources/278200-1099079877269/547664-1099079934475/547667-1145313958806/WPS4836_Computers_Edu_Colombia. pdf; also see CGI op. cit. report, which presents data on other Brazilian cities with similar results.

12. For instance, this was judged to be the initial impact, for example, of the Enlaces (Links) program of the Chilean Education Ministry (personal interview by the coauthor [BS] with team members). According to the interviewees, even in 2006, 60 percent of students had Internet access only at school.

13. In many Latin American countries, not only government, but also private foundations, most of them related to corporations, are investing in the use of the digital teaching materials to improve mathematics and science teaching.

14. M. Cabrol and M. Székely (eds.) *Educación para la transformación.* (Washington, D.C.: Banco Interamericano de Desarrollo, 2012).

15. OECD. '1-to-1', en Education: Current Practice, International Comparative Research Evidence and Policy Implications (working paper no. 44, 2010).

16. M. Prensky. "Digital Natives, Digital Immigrants," *On the Horizon en MCB University Press* 9 (5) (2001).

17. A. Piscitelli. *Nativos Digitales. Dieta cognitiva, inteligencia colectiva y arquitecturas de la participación* (Miami: Santillana, 2009).

18. UNESCO. Uso de TIC en educación en América Latina y el Caribe. Análisis regional de la integración de las TIC en la educación y de la aptitud digital (e-readiness) (Madrid: Instituto de Estadística, 2013). Online at: http://www.uis.unesco.org/Communication/Documents/ict-regional-survey-lac-2012-sp.pdf

19. Mario Brun "Las tecnologías de la información y de las comunicaciones en la formación inicial docente de América Latina," Serie Políticas Sociales, No. 172, CEPAL, 2011.

20. K. Ananiadou and C. Rizza. ICT in Initial Teacher Training: First Findings and Conclusions of an OECD Study (2010). Online at: http://library.iated.org/view/ANANIADOU2010ICT

21. P. Kirschner and M. Selinger. "The state of affairs of teacher education with respect to information and communications technology," *Technology, Pedagogy and Education*, 12 (1) (2003): 5–17.

22. Felipe Barrera-Osorio and Leigh L. Linden. *The Use and Misuse of Computers, in Education Evidence from a Randomized Experiment in Colombia* (The World Bank, 2009). Online at: http://siteresources.worldbank.org/EDUCATION/Resources/278200-1099079877269/547664-1099079934475/547667-1145313958806/WPS4836_Computers_Edu_Colombia.pdf

23. See, for example, Charles Ess. *Digital Media Ethics* (Cambridge, U.K.: Polity Publishers, 2009).

24. See, for example, Mike Ribble and Gerald Bailey's handbook, which addresses the United States: *Digital Citizenship in Schools* (Washington, D.C.: ISTE, 2007).

Chapter 12

Local + Digital + Scale: A Mass Movement for Digital Inclusion

Helen Milner

Contents

12.1 Introduction

The network of U.K. online centers, supported by Tinder Foundation, has helped millions of people to develop basic online skills. This ambitious program, primarily funded by the U.K. government, aims to tackle the inequalities that separate the people who use the Internet on a daily basis and those who don't or can't use the web.

The Tinder Foundation mass movement for digital inclusion helps people gain basic online skills that benefit their lives in transformative ways. In turn, that has led to wider benefits for society, transforming how millions of people connect to family and their community, to jobs, information, opportunities, and, in particular, how they engage with both commercial and public services.

What distinguishes Tinder Foundation from other digital inclusion initiatives is not just *what* products and services are provided, but *how* the model is delivered. This mass movement coordinates thousands of local delivery partners and leads them as well. It is both highly targeted and delivered at scale; a powerful network with ambitious delivery credentials and an independent group of people with a shared vision.

The Tinder Foundation model that delivers this mass movement for digital inclusion has three core strands:

1. *Local*: Working with 5,000 local partners and 25,000 volunteers, so that excluded offline people get the support they need in a local, familiar, and trusted environment.
2. *Digital*: The model not only helps people to learn to use the Internet, but also uses digital technology to deliver, through mass online learning, digital management systems, shared data, and the use of email, webinars, and social media to lead and inspire local partners.
3. *Scale*: Scaling up successful local practice, and amplifying it with clear focus, exceptional products, and collective vision; and delivering economies of scale. Thousands of local partners work with Tinder Foundation to impact millions of lives.

Tinder Foundation takes large, complex ideas and works out clear, practical ways to translate them into effective programs that create social impact. A focus on robust data collection means this impact can be clearly demonstrated, with more than 1.2 million people successfully supported since April 2010, representing £232.4 million worth of savings to government due to more than 50 percent of them moved contacts with public services from face-to-face or telephone to digital channels.

With eight years of consistent leadership—and of constant agile development and improvement—it is clear that striving for excellence and adapting to change are key in keeping a mass movement of any kind on the move. It is important to think of Tinder Foundation and the thousands of local partners as an ecosystem, working together, evolving together, and talking and listening to each other to make big change happen. "Whilst we are a very small operation, it's nice to feel part of something big," says Tracy Richardson at Planet Skills, a U.K. online center.[1]

This chapter provides a background on the efforts of Tinder Foundation, shows how it has accomplished its goals, and provides blueprints for success in the hopes that other organizations around the world can learn from this approach.

12.2 History

Tinder Foundation is a not-for-profit, staff-owned mutual, which was formed in December 2011 by the team that led an independent business unit within Ufi Ltd. (the original custodian of U.K. online centers, which also ran learndirect). In July 2013, the team took on the new name of Tinder Foundation, which was previously known as Online Centers Foundation. The organization is best known for its leadership and support of the U.K. online centers network and historically has been referred to as "U.K. online centers." For ease, throughout this chapter the team that leads and manages the U.K. online center's network from 2003 to the present are referred to as Tinder Foundation.

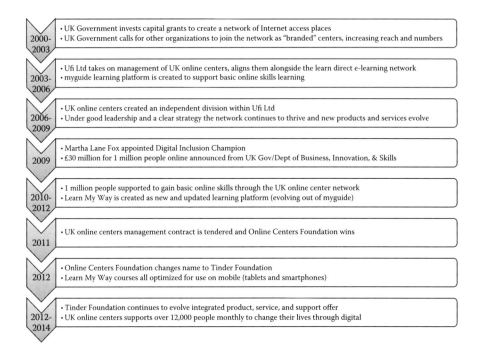

2000-2003
- UK Government invests capital grants to create a network of Internet access places
- UK Government calls for other organizations to join the network as "branded" centers, increasing reach and numbers

2003-2006
- Ufi Ltd takes on management of UK online centers, aligns them alongside the learn direct e-learning network
- myguide learning platform is created to support basic online skills learning

2006-2009
- UK online centers created an independent division within Ufi Ltd
- Under good leadership and a clear strategy the network continues to thrive and new products and services evolve

2009
- Martha Lane Fox appointed Digital Inclusion Champion
- £30 million for 1 million people online announced from UK Gov/Dept of Business, Innovation, & Skills

2010-2012
- 1 million people supported to gain basic online skills through the UK online center network
- Learn My Way is created as new and updated learning platform (evolving out of myguide)

2011
- UK online centers management contract is tendered and Online Centers Foundation wins

2012
- Online Centers Foundation changes name to Tinder Foundation
- Learn My Way courses all optimized for use on mobile (tablets and smartphones)

2012-2014
- Tinder Foundation continues to evolve integrated product, service, and support offer
- UK online centers supports over 12,000 people monthly to change their lives through digital

Figure 12.1   Tinder Foundation and U.K. online centers' timeline.

With over a decade of investment and evolution, there are many important milestones in the history of the U.K. online centers. Figure 12.1 illustrates the Tinder Foundation and the U.K. online centers' timeline.

In 2000, the U.K. government launched a network of U.K. online centers to ensure the two-thirds of the population without the Internet at home had access to it somewhere. Although many people used the services of U.K. online centers and became confident Internet users during the following decade, it became clear that for many others the biggest barrier to taking up and using the web was not a lack of access, but rather a lack of support to develop the basic skills needed to use it confidently.

In 2003, the management of the U.K. online centers network moved from the government department (which led on skills policy and had allocated grant monies for capital development) to Ufi Ltd., and, in 2006, the team heading the network moved into an independent business unit. It was under this focused leadership that the Tinder Foundation model began to take shape, as delivery models were tried and tested, new products and services were developed and improved, and the lessons for maximum impact were learned.

From 2008, it became clear that the Tinder Foundation model could support very high numbers of people to obtain basic online skills, and that additional grants administered by Tinder could substantially increase these numbers further. In 2009, a grant of £30 million from the Department for Business, Innovation, and Skills (BIS) to Tinder Foundation to support 1 million people was announced and delivery began in April 2010.

Between April 2010 and January 2014, the network of U.K. online centers—supported by Tinder Foundation—helped 1.2 million people in the United Kingdom to develop basic online skills. This ambitious program was funded by the U.K. government to tackle the inequalities that separate the people who use the Internet on a daily basis and those who don't.

In 2008 and 2009, Tinder Foundation worked with the government to develop a digital inclusion strategy, which led to the creation of the new government-appointed role of Digital Inclusion Champion. In June 2009, Martha Lane Fox took up this mantle, taking on the broader role of U.K. Digital Champion after the general election in May 2010. Her commitment and connections brought together powerful partners and accelerated the pace of change for digital inclusion across the public, private, and community sectors. Fox's work also inspired the European Commission to require all Member States to appoint Digital Champions, and, in 2012, she set up the Go ON U.K. charity that she still chairs, and which is still supporting the U.K.'s digital inclusion agenda.

In 2003, the government funded the creation of a simple-to-use web interface (including very basic email and search), plus a suite of learning materials. This tool was called Myguide. Over the subsequent seven years, commercial Internet tools (such as Google and Outlook) improved significantly, so Myguide was redeveloped to remove email and search, and the new Learn My Way platform was launched in 2010 to deliver high-quality, basic online learning materials. Learn My Way is now used by the U.K. online centers network, and other partners, to support digitally excluded people to learn how to use the Internet.

12.3 U.K. Online Centers

The U.K. online centers network is a unique collective of 5,000 independent organizations that are committed to helping people gain the essential digital skills they need to live and thrive in the twenty-first century. There are 11 million people in the United Kingdom who need help and support to gain these skills.[2] The majority live in poorer communities and, therefore, most U.K. online centers' work is focused on them.

All of the 5,000 centers are different from one another. There is no formula; it is not a franchise. Each one is separate from Tinder Foundation; they are all independently owned, managed, and funded. The common bond is a shared vision of a 100-percent digitally skilled nation, and a commitment to provide free or low-cost support to help people learn how to use the web.

All U.K. online centers do something else as well as digital skills support, such as run a community venue, host a youth club or older people's club, offer other informal or formal learning, or loan books. Each local partner who runs a U.K. online center has decided that their existing clients, or the people living in their community, need help to bridge the digital skills divide and that is why they have joined the U.K. online centers network. Local organizations join (and leave) all the time, and this organic growth and shrinkage maintains the number around 5,000; for example, between April 2013 and January 2014, 406 organizations left the network and 407 joined. Recruitment is primarily through recommendations from existing U.K. online centers. There is no cost to join the network, and most U.K. online centers will not receive any funding or financial support from Tinder Foundation.

U.K. online centers are often found in community centers and public libraries, but they also can often be found in village halls, places of worship (churches, mosques, synagogues, and temples), cafes, social housing, old people's homes, on mobile buses, and in pubs, clubs, and bingo halls. Many are local community organizations who also support people through other learning, for example, learning to speak English as a second language, or learning other computer skills. The vast majority are open to the public, although some aren't; for example, those based in prisons, factories, or women's hostels. The definition of a center is not fixed. It could be a computer in a village hall, four laptops or tablets taken into a pub on a Friday morning, or 50 computers in a school lab being used in the evening. Each center is based on the needs of the individual community it serves.

Most U.K. online centers are staffed by both paid staff and volunteers, with 10 percent surviving solely with the support of volunteers. Centers usually offer both fixed sessions that are more like a class, and are run at the same time each week, alongside informal drop-in sessions for one-to-one support or to practice the skills they have learned. Volunteers are vital to the successful operation of the U.K. online center network with more than 25,000 in place today.

Taking laptops and tablets out to where people live and socialize is a very important part of what U.K. online centers do. This approach is called *outreach* and it is particularly successful for helping older people learn basic online skills, for example, in the comfort of their own home, or inspiring them to get started alongside friends at a social club they attend. In rural areas, outreach is the only cost-effective method of delivery as the number of people who need help is small, and they are often isolated; centers run rural outreach sessions in places like village halls, schools, and pub.

The majority of U.K. online centers are in England, as funding for skills and digital inclusion tends to be devolved to each U.K. nation (England, Scotland, Wales, and Northern Ireland) with Tinder Foundation historically funded by the English government. In early 2014, there are around 600 centers in Scotland, Wales, and Northern Ireland, although this will change as a fuller picture of delivery in these nations is built.

In the United Kingdom, as in many other countries, there are several national organizations who help people to gain basic online skills. The U.K. online centers model empowers local organizations, or national organizations with multiple locations, to join and become part of a bigger partnership. National organizations with local delivery partners within the U.K. online centers network include Age U.K., Unionlearn, Citizens Online, the Salvation Army, Crisis (a homeless charity), Pertemps (a work program provider), and more than 90 percent of public libraries in England.

12.4 Thousands of Centers, One Network

Typically, digital inclusion initiatives choose either a very tailored approach supporting small numbers of people, or a homogenous approach supporting high numbers. The success of the Tinder Foundation model lies in doing both—achieving mass impact at a national scale through deep local engagement supported by a national single network. This is possible because of an "inverted pyramid" delivery model: the wider network delivers mass impact at a national scale; grant-funding and dedicated support helps specialist subnetworks and social housing providers deliver mass targeted support; and grant-funded, ultra-targeted projects, such as Community Hubs and Health Flagships (described in detail below), help smaller numbers of very hard-to-reach groups and drive significant, lasting social change. The "inverted pyramid" model is shown in Figure 12.2, and each level is then described in detail.

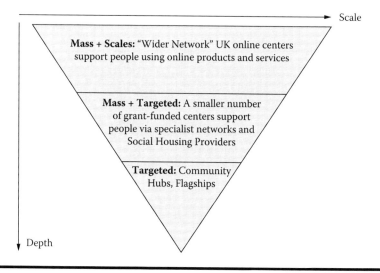

Figure 12.2   The Tinder Foundation inverted pyramid.

The three strands of delivery include:

- Strand one: mass + scale
- Strand two: mass + targeted
- Strand three: targeted

Each of these are explained further in the following sections.

12.4.1 Strand One: Mass + Scale—the Wider Network

Over half of Tinder Foundation's overall delivery is achieved through the wider network, represented by the widest part of the pyramid model—centers that have access to all of the resources that are made available for free to every U.K. online center, but who do not receive any grant funding. The fact that this unfunded part of the network has helped more than 600,000 learners to develop basic online skills between 2010 and 2014 is a testament to the strength of the shared vision that binds the network together, and to the effectiveness of the tools that Tinder Foundation shares with the network.

Even though this part of Tinder's delivery model involves the high-volume delivery of skills at scale, this does not mean that the wider network provides a "one size fits all" service. It successfully engages with many learners, from different backgrounds, with different learning styles, and additional support needs. Because centers in the wider network are located in the heart of communities with high levels of social and digital exclusion, and have unique knowledge of the needs of their local communities, they are able to determine the most appropriate model of engagement and delivery for learners. If the right partnerships are built at a local level, "mass" does not have to mean "impersonal."

12.4.2 Strand Two: Mass + Targeted

The middle section of Tinder Foundation's delivery pyramid is made up of centers that receive additional support and, in many cases, grant funding in return for achieving a certain number of learning outputs. Although there are far fewer of these centers than in the wider network (approximately 250, as opposed to approximately 2,500 wider network centers and 2,500 wider network access points), collectively they account for around half of all delivery. At the time of writing, this section includes social housing providers and several specialist subnetworks.

12.4.2.1 Social Housing Providers

Social housing tenants experience higher than average rates of social exclusion and deprivation, and 36 percent don't have Internet access.[3] Tinder Foundation has worked hard to build partnerships with social housing providers that will help get their tenants digitally included:

- facilitating partnerships between social housing providers and local U.K. online centers
- supporting U.K. online centers to run outreach sessions for social housing tenants, for example, in lounges in sheltered housing schemes for older people, or clubs run by tenants' associations
- supporting housing providers' boards, chief executives, and senior teams to develop digital strategies and digital inclusion plans, with targeted support from senior Tinder staff, and from the Social Housing Providers Digital Inclusion Strategy Group, which Tinder Foundation chairs
- creating and moderating the Digital Housing Hub,[4] which provides an open, online forum where people working in social housing can discuss ideas and challenges, and ask and answer questions peer-to-peer
- administering the Digital Deal Challenge Fund: a £400,000 fund launched in 2013 by two government departments—the Department for Work and Pensions, and the Department for Communities and Local Government—to support 12 social housing providers to deliver local innovations, such as large area free wi-fi networks, partnerships with credit unions, mobile wi-fi hotspots, and "gadget shows." The Digital Deal projects aim to teach basic online skills to 15,000 people by mid-2014.

12.4.2.2 Specialist Subnetworks

In the United Kingdom, as in most other developed nations, digital exclusion predominantly affects:

- People over 65 years of age
- People on low incomes
- People with low or no qualifications
- Disabled people[5]

For this reason, almost all grant-funded centers are organized into four specialist subnetworks to which Tinder Foundation commits both staff time and resources. The specialist subnetworks are Older People, Disabled People and their careers, and Into Work (for employed and unemployed people looking for jobs). The support these centers provide to learners, and the support they in turn receive from Tinder Foundation, is tailored to the specialized needs of the users. Together, these specialist networks have a mass impact.

Tinder is developing new affiliation of these and other potential specialist subnetworks by centers from the wider network, for example, to include centers working in rural areas with poor connectivity and bad transport links. Recruiting and retaining unfunded members to these subnetworks will be based on a clearly articulated offer to centers and the learners they work with, with an emphasis on peer-to-peer support, such as sharing good practice, hosting development seminars,

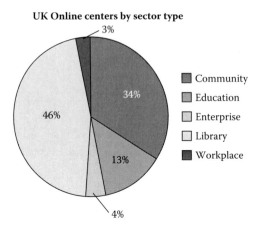

Figure 12.3 **U.K. online centers by sector type.**

and involving centers and learners in the co-creation of bespoke online learning materials.

Figure 12.3 shows the spread of the U.K. online centers network across various sectors, with libraries making up almost half of the network and community organizations making up one-third.

Figure 12.4 shows how delivery breaks down across sectors, based on registrations on Tinder's "Learn My Way" online learning portal (see section 12.5.1). Almost three-fifths of all delivery comes from community organizations, with a much smaller fraction from libraries.

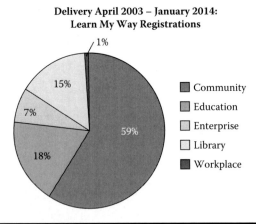

Figure 12.4 **Delivery April 2013–January 2014: Learn My Way registrations.**

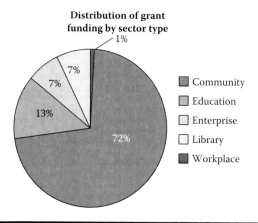

Figure 12.5   Distribution of grant funding by sector type.

Figure 12.5 indicates the significant percentage of grant funding allocated to community organizations, with their unique reach into disadvantaged communities and experience of overcoming social exclusion at a local level.

Figure 12.6 breaks down into almost identical percentages to Figure 12.3, reinforcing the fact that it is a shared sense of purpose, rather than grant funding, which unifies the U.K. online centers network.

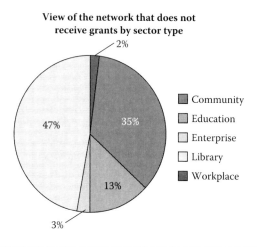

Figure 12.6   View of the network that does not receive grants by sector type.

12.4.3 Strand Three: Targeted

Over the many years that Tinder Foundation and the U.K. online centers network have worked together, the challenge of how to reach the most excluded people in society has required significant development. Tinder Foundation has developed partnerships with a smaller number of U.K. online centers who bring with them a range of highly specialist skills, thus being able to offer deep-dive support to extremely hard-to-reach groups of socially and digitally excluded learners, building digital inclusion capacity and partnerships across local communities, or supporting local community development using digital technology to bring about social change. The numbers of people helped in these ultraspecialist partnerships is relatively small, making up the tip of the pyramid model, but the depth of support provided has helped to reach severely excluded demographics who would not have been reached by other activities.

Since 2009, a range of specialist grant-funding relationships have developed and evolved; for example, Community Champions, Community Capacity Builders, and Community Hubs.

In 2009, 60 Community Champion centers were selected as hubs in the U.K. online center network. Their main role was to recruit and support local organizations that were new to delivering basic online skills support, as well as engaging people who wanted to volunteer in the network. These Champions involved into Community Capacity Builders in 2011.

In 2011, 54 U.K. online centers received Community Capacity Builders (CCBs) funding, and undertook capacity-building work with local organizations to recruit, train, and support volunteer tutors to help people gain basic online skills. This local capacity-building proved very successful, particularly for network development and outreach, and resulted in network growth across the United Kingdom. Evaluation of this program led to the development of the Community Hubs model in 2012. Community Hubs were grant funded to consolidate CCBs' capacity building activities by helping local organizations use digital technology to bring about social change. The project was aimed more at tackling community issues using technology as an enabler. For example, one Community Hub created a multiagency virtual hub to engage young people at risk of getting involved in knife crime. One outcome of the Community Hubs project was Tinder's development of the Community How To website, a curated collection of free digital tools to help local and community organizations deliver more, covering topics like marketing, evaluation, and project planning. Community How To has more than 3,000 registered users and more than 2,000 unique visitors per month, as of January 2014.

In autumn 2013, National Health Service (NHS) England contracted with Tinder Foundation to create a Digital Health Information (DHI) network aimed at reducing health inequalities and reducing the strain on acute care services by teaching learners how to use online health management tools including the NHS Choices website. Most of the DHI network were already funded as members of one of the four specialist subnetworks described above, with a new remit to pro-vide targeted, large-scale digital health inclusion support. In addition, 15 DHI Flagships received grant funding to pioneer Tinder's engagement with severely excluded groups including homeless people and asylum seekers, developing innova-tive partnerships with health professionals, testing new engagement techniques, such as social prescribing (GP surgeries referring patients to U.K. online centers), and co-developing learning content, which brings together wider health informa-tion with local specialist support services.

For example, Southampton Central Library, a U.K. online center and a flagship recipient, together with their partner Macmillan Cancer Support, is developing new online content aimed at people with cancer or mild mental health issues so they can access health information and support services online. Cancer Support Volunteers have been recruited to work in the recently revamped Cancer Information Centre at Southampton Hospital, where they support patients to access health information online using a computer in the library area. Southampton Libraries is using the Learn My Way course creator to build an online course—Coping with Cancer—that can be shared with other U.K. online centers who work with people experienc-ing similar challenges with this disease.

12.4.4 Network Strategy and the Tinder Foundation "Effect"

Tinder Foundation's principal priority is to strengthen, develop, and grow the U.K. online centers network, focused around four key themes:

1. *Network Innovation*: Driving innovation by continually improving and evolv-ing Tinder's offer to the network, in close collaboration with local partners.
2. *Network Retention*: Driving responsiveness by strengthening, consolidating, engaging, and segmenting network membership.
3. *Network Recruitment*: Growing coverage and reach by recruiting new centers who target socially and digitally excluded groups.
4. *Network Focus*: Reducing inequalities by targeting the existing network's activities to support the people most in need of support.

Tinder Foundation's inverted pyramid model allows for a range of impacts from mass to highly specialized "deep" impact, but at all levels the support offered to individuals reflects their specific needs.

An additional strength of the model is the "Tinder Foundation Effect"—the dissemination of innovation and best practice between and across levels of the pyra-mid. Ideas worth replicating are identified by Tinder Foundation staff through evaluation of funded activities and regular surveys of the wider network, studied in detail, and then shared widely across the network through various means, including online training products for centers, marketing materials, and new online courses for learners. For example, an innovative social prescribing partnership delivered by an unfunded center was recently identified through online survey data within six months of the center joining the network. This was quickly followed up with two in-depth telephone interviews with center managers; and a plan for centers wishing to replicate the model has been written into a handbook of resources designed to sustain and expand the Digital Health Information network. The Tinder Foundation Effect adds further capacity to the U.K. online centers network and provides better value to national funders.

12.5 Integrated Products, Services, and Support

As the U.K. online centers network of local partners is an independent collective, bound together only by a shared vision, it is the support of Tinder Foundation that brings these diverse organizations together, providing the glue that supports and reaches the maximum amount of people.

Tinder Foundation achieves this through a suite of products, services, and other support that allows grassroots organizations within the network to standardize their learning offer, measure their impact, market themselves effectively, and grow their capacity in the local community and become sustainable. On top of this, the Tinder Foundation team offers support, coaching, and mentoring to help organizations within the network to do more, and ensure they feel part of something bigger. The products and services provided, together with the personalized support, binds the U.K. online centers network together and amplifies the impact that the organizations would achieve alone.

The products and services that allow the U.K. online centers network to do this are detailed later in this section. Figure 12.7 illustrates the broad range of products, services, and support that Tinder Foundation provides to the U.K. online centers network.

12.5.1 Learn My Way: A Learning Platform

In 2009, Baroness Estelle Morris was asked by the U.K. government to carry out a review of the basic information and communication technology (ICT) skills needed by adults in the United Kingdom. Her report, "Independent Review of ICT User Skills," was published in June 2009, and in the foreword Baroness Morris said:

> We've always known the consequences for adults who lack basic literacy and numeracy skills; we need to better understand the impact on those who lack basic ICT skills.[6]
>
> It's hard to imagine that, in little more than a decade, knowledge that used to be restricted to a small group of enthusiasts should have become an essential life skill. Yet ICT is fast becoming exactly that and we need to be certain that we are doing as much as we can to make sure everyone has the chance to develop the skills they need.[7]

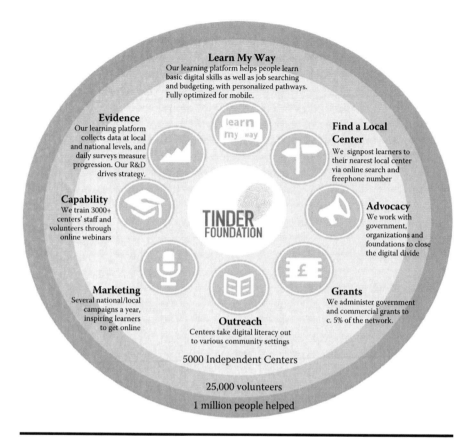

Learn My Way
Our learning platform helps people learn basic digital skills as well as job searching and budgeting, with personalized pathways. Fully optimized for mobile.

Evidence
Our learning platform collects data at local and national levels, and daily surveys measure progression. Our R&D drives strategy.

Find a Local Center
We signpost learners to their nearest local center via online search and freephone number

Capability
We train 3000+ centers' staff and volunteers through online webinars

TINDER FOUNDATION

Advocacy
We work with government, organizations and foundations to close the digital divide

Marketing
Several national/local campaigns a year, inspiring learners to get online

Outreach
Centers take digital literacy out to various community settings

Grants
We administer government and commercial grants to c. 5% of the network.

5000 Independent Centers

25,000 volunteers

1 million people helped

Figure 12.7   An overview of the Tinder Foundation.

The "Independent Review of ICT Skills" recommended an "entitlement" for any adult without digital life skills to get support to learn the basics for using ICT and the Internet, specified as: Use a mouse and keyboard, use email, use the Internet, and keep safe online. This led to Tinder Foundation creating a core online learning package (Online Basics), which in 2014 remains at the core of Learn My Way. Courses on using online public services online, and using a touch screen online, have since been added to support demand from learners, as well as government plans to move more services online.

Learn My Way has grown over the years, with a broad range of new courses added to help with job seeking, financial management and budgeting, as well as slightly more advanced digital skills, including online banking, online shopping, and using social media. In 2013, a new contract with NHS England led to a new portal being developed to help learners to use the NHS Choices website, alongside a new course: "Staying Healthy with NHS Choices."[8]

As the website's user base tends to have no or few qualifications, online courses use very simple language, and courses have an audio track for those with low literacy or where English isn't the first language. The website and courses are all optimized to work on computers, tablets, and smartphones.

e-Learning is also complemented with an optional Online Basics e-assessment and City & Guilds qualification. Accredited U.K. online centers can choose to offer this to learners so they can gain formal recognition for their basic online skills, which as of February 2014 has been awarded to 2,800 people. It is important that the e-learning remains informal and nonfrightening, and only when someone is ready can they then move on to a more formal qualification.

All the online courses are free and have been developed using open source software. Where it is good and relevant, free online courses or products from other developers are linked to from the site. In May 2014, Tinder Foundation launched the Learn My Way Course Creator tool that allows local U.K. online centers to build their own online learning content using a very simple tool, enabling them to create content relevant to their specific target audience, while continuing to take advantage of learner and learning data collected on the platform.

Learn My Way also supports government departments as they roll out online services. An online course has been created to support NHS Choices as well as to support the Department of Work and Pensions' Universal Jobmatch.

12.5.2 Measurement of Success: Evidence Collecting and Data

One of the most vital elements of the Learn My Way site is the data it collects about learners and their activities. Tinder Foundation uses this on a national level to prove its impact, and local centers can manage learners' progression, as well as having an overview of activity across the center, helping to prove this impact.

Tinder Foundation has always put a strong emphasis on measuring its impact, and uses a variety of mechanisms for assessment including the following data capture and research methods:

■ Learning data through Learn My Way, where individual activity is linked to a center, that can view progress, courses and modules taken, and completion rates. These data are automated and viewed at a center and a national level.

■ Impact data and learner demographics are measured through two surveys (the first online, and a follow-up progression survey by telephone). Surveys are in the field 52 weeks a year, providing Tinder Foundation with details of learner demographics, information around progression to learning and employment, use of government websites, information around confidence and well-being. This is supplemented with regular surveys with the U.K. online centers network.

■ Further impact evidence allows Tinder Foundation to apply volumetrics to economic impact for government, so they can show the financial benefit to government for each offline person who gets online and switches at least one government contact per month to online. Tinder Foundation undertakes regular research to measure social impact.

Tinder Foundation's strong emphasis on measuring impact has been extremely valuable to the network, to funders, and to the organization itself. In addition to this data collection, Tinder Foundation holds a great deal of information about the centers within the network, such as the target groups they work with, which campaigns they take part in, and the volumes of learners they engage.

12.5.3 Capability Development

To ensure the long-term sustainability and capability of the U.K. online centers network, Tinder Foundation identifies the training needs of staff and volunteers within the centers, creating relevant programs to support them via online webinars, online courses, and occasional face-to-face events, as well as a large annual conference. Content for courses and webinars includes applying for funding and recruiting volunteers. Tinder Foundation also has developed its own Level 3 Award in Community Development, delivered both on- and offline, to develop the capability of the leadership and management of the local organizations.

12.5.4 National and Local Marketing

To help more people use the Internet, we need to motivate and inspire them, helping them to understand the relevance of the Internet to their lives. 82 percent of people in the United Kingdom who do not subscribe to broadband say it is because they have no interest in the Internet, and so inspiring them is a vital part of the work Tinder Foundation does.[9]

Tinder Foundation supports the U.K. online centers network with nationally coordinated marketing and awareness raising campaigns. An overarching theme, national promotion, and profession collateral supports local events and local marketing run by U.K. online centers. In 2006, Tinder Foundation launched an annual campaign—Get online week—that has now run for seven consecutive years.

In 2011, Get online week was supported by the U.K.'s Digital Champion, Martha Lane Fox, and her campaigning organization Race Online 2012. This partnership enabled above-the-line public relations (PR) and marketing activity to be provided on an in-kind basis, with an advertising value equivalent of £16,118,000 at no cost to Tinder Foundation and the U.K. online centers. Many blue chip corporate partners lent their support, including Three Mobile, the BBC, Post Office, BT, Google, Marks and Spencer, Wetherspoons, Mecca Bingo, and TalkTalk.

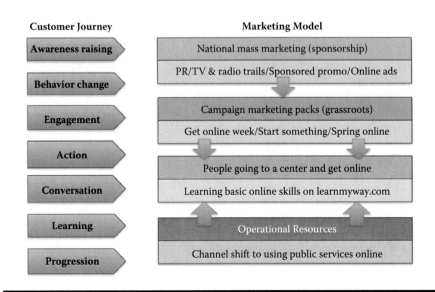

Figure 12.8 Customer journey and marketing model.

This partnership marketing allowed Tinder Foundation to mirror the national activity of traditional campaigns, driving awareness raising and behavioral change, creating noise and establishing credibility on a national level ... for free. Underneath this umbrella, targeted marketing activity took place at a local level, driving engagement and footfall. Between April and December 2011, U.K. online centers helped 426,155 new people gain basic online skills of which 32 percent (136,370) were as a direct result of the operational resources and campaign packs. This shows that high-profile, above-the-line activity is essential for awareness raising and behavioral change, but must be supported by local marketing to ensure engagement and conversion. Figure 12.8 shows the Tinder Foundation customer journey and marketing model.

Tinder Foundation also promotes "get online" messages throughout the year with press and media work plus social media promotions targeting friends and family who are online.

The U.K. online centers brand is not important to consumers. It is the local brand, for example, Southampton Library or Heeley Development Trust, that matters to local people. Use of the U.K. online centers brand is incorporated into campaigns to add credibility to the local branding, not to compete with it.

12.5.5 Helpline and Center Database

Awareness-raising campaigns need to have a clear call to action, and Tinder Foundation uses a free helpline to direct prospective learners to a local center, provided pro bono by the National Careers Service. Helpline staff use the publicly searchable database available at www.ukonlinecentres.com/centresearch, which also

Figure 12.9 An example center profile from Starting Point in Stockport.

allows friends and family to search for a local center for someone they know. Local centers can personalize their own page on the center search, add photographs and a center profile to attract local people. Figure 12.9 provides an example of a center profile from Starting Point in Stockport:

The center database is provided to key partners via an API (application program interface); for example, the U.K. government feeds this center search through their Gov.UK site, and Post Offices use it to signpost customers to their nearest U.K. online center.

12.5.6 Grants

As seen in the Tinder Foundation Inverted Pyramid model (in Section 12.4) there is a relationship between mass delivery (via a broad network of local partners who do not receive grants) and the mass + targeted activity that is achieved through incentivizing with grants.

Tinder Foundation allocates grants to local partners (U.K. online centers) to support them to help people gain basic online skills. Centers also are supported to find and apply for grants from other foundations and trusts. The average size of grant from Tinder Foundation to a U.K. online center is around £6,000 per center per year, and they range from £500 to £30,000. In 2013, 14,429 local partners were awarded with a grant (from an annual grant pot of £1.7m).

Each year, there is an online, automated grant process, with the awarding criteria changing depending on context, target groups, or the policy outcomes the grant is associated with. Local center partners in the most disadvantaged communities are positively weighted when applications are scored.

A key success of the U.K. online centers model is centers supported by grants sitting alongside those who don't receive any funding. This allows us to provide both scale and targeting.

Centers who do not receive grant funding will deliver for free on an ad-hoc basis, delivering activity according to the needs of their community. Grants are essential to ensure that centers support people through an end-to-end journey and provide the robust evidence vital for funders and partners.

The hardest to reach, most socially excluded people are by nature the most expensive to reach, but need the greatest support. Grants provide centers with the resource required to not only reach and engage, but then retain and support people with complex needs, ensuring resources are targeted on the areas that need them most.

12.6 The Glue That Binds the Products: Support and Dialogue

The products and services listed above, combined with the high quality, personalized support listed below, creates a holistic offer that binds together the U.K. online centers network and allows Tinder Foundation to operate on such a large scale.

12.6.1 Network Support

A small, dedicated support team at Tinder Foundation ensure there is frequent, personal contact between Tinder Foundation and each U.K. online center, both proactively and reactively. All centers in the network have a proactive contact made with them at least three times a year, and network coordinators are available to answer questions during office hours.

12.6.2 Network Communications

On top of proactive personalized contact from network coordinators, Tinder Foundation sends a weekly e-newsletter to keep local centers up-to-date with news and developments. There are a broad range of other network communications channels, including social media (Facebook, Twitter, Youtube) and the U.K. online centers website.

12.6.3 Advocacy

Tinder Foundation gives a voice to thousands of very small and very local organizations, ensuring even the smallest community organizations can make their views heard at a national level.

The senior team at Tinder Foundation works closely with key stakeholders inside government, and with trusted partners who also work to help influence and deliver government objectives. Those relationships have been key in giving the network a collective voice, but also in creating bigger, stronger national partnerships and national projects.

For government, the U.K. online center network represents a ready-made, ready-to-go delivery framework allowing them to tap directly into communities, and for small community centers being part of the network creates new large-scale project and funding opportunities they might otherwise not have been able to access, and, indeed, might not otherwise have existed.

The very nature of the network model meant it was clear Tinder Foundation could support very high numbers of people to obtain basic online skills, and that this could be quickly scaled with additional grants. Such as the grant of £30 million to support 1 million people Tinder Foundation secured in 2009, and, in 2012, the £1 million (per annum) contract from NHS England to support digital inclusion combined with digital health awareness.

12.6.4 Partnerships That Add Value

However, it's not just within government or the public sector that advocacy plays its part. Tinder Foundation also works to influence other public, community, and commercial partners, resulting in successful projects with partners including Nominet Trust, TalkTalk, and EE, and the national supermarket chain, Asda Stores, Ltd.

Partnerships are key in helping Tinder Foundation create maximum impact. Commercial partners with large reach are able to spread the word to customers and staff about the benefits of being online, provide funding for specific programs or even offer staff volunteering time that can add significantly to the sustainability of local U.K. online centers.

For example, Hamilton Davies Trust supports small communities near Manchester. Based near a large TalkTalk office, the Trust set up a U.K. online center to run special "iTea and Biscuit" sessions for older people scared of technology. TalkTalk has worked with the Trust to deliver these sessions for the past 18 months providing more than 100 volunteers.

The volunteers (part of an ongoing corporate social responsibility (CSR) initiative from TalkTalk) have been trained as Digital Champions by Tinder Foundation. They spend the first 15 or 20 minutes running a group session or presentation around a particular subject of interest, such as emailing or Internet safety. They then provide one-to-one support to enable learners to put things into practice, on laptops also donated to the center by TalkTalk. For David Taylor, the iTea and Biscuits manager, organizing the TalkTalk volunteers to support eight-week courses means he can deliver to more people, and provide them with the individual support they often need. The program also means that TalkTalk employees can fit their volunteering around their work week. The model is being replicated elsewhere, partnering TalkTalk offices with local U.K. online centers across England.

12.6.5 Dialogue and Evaluation

The Tinder Foundation approach is distinctive and unique due to the culture of dialogue. All staff, regardless of rank or role, are not only responsive to center needs, but actively seek the views and opinions of local organizations operating at a grassroots level.

Tinder Foundation aims to evolve and improve its services through regular feedback, including quarterly network surveys that provide quantitative analysis, and more detailed qualitative discussions at focus groups and user testing groups. As well as talking to U.K. online centers, Tinder also works with learner groups that can provide feedback on things like marketing materials and online content as part of the development process.

All staff make it their mission to visit at least one center each quarter. With a small team and a large network, not all centers will get a visit, but the learning brought back continues to help the central team to create, grow, and adapt its products, services, and support. As a result, the U.K. online centers' satisfaction rate with Tinder is a consistent 86 percent, showing the importance they place on being part of the network.

12.7 Impact

The work of Tinder Foundation and the U.K. online centers has a positive impact on people's lives and it focuses on the needs of the individual person that drives this mass movement model. Ninety-five percent of learners report that U.K. online centers have helped them to learn about the Internet.

What's more, learners say they have good experiences at their centers, with 88 percent rating the service of U.K. online centers as very good or excellent. Interestingly, positive opinions are most likely to be expressed by the most socially excluded learners, especially those over 65 years of age, disabled learners, and learners from black and minority ethnic communities.[10]

The impact however, goes beyond an improvement in digital skills; learners also report an increased enthusiasm for wider learning (91 percent) and improved self-confidence (88 percent), and many feel more engaged with community activities (70 percent), and even better equipped to make decisions about their future in terms of career, training, or learning (81 percent).

The very high opinion of U.K. online centers' services among learners is reflected in a high rate of learner advocacy, with 59 percent of learners recommending U.K. online center services to at least one other person.[11]

Since the beginning of the large scale £30 million program in April 2010 and present day 2014, Tinder Foundation has helped 1.2 million people to get online at an average cost of £30.25 per person. Of these, 960,000 (80 percent) were socially excluded, 598,000 (55 percent) were educated below level 2.[12] Meanwhile, 770,560 (64 percent) have progressed on to employment-related activities, including a new or better job. Further demographics of social exclusion and Tinder Foundation learners is shown in Figure 12.10.

Tinder Foundation works with an independent market research agency to carry out survey work with learners on an ongoing basis. One aspect to these surveys is to measure the progression people make after learning at a U.K. online center.

The impact for someone getting a job is significant for that individual and will have a positive impact on their family and community. However, it is important to see the compound impact for all of the people moving from unemployed to

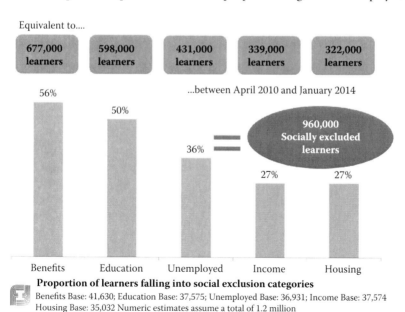

Equivalent to....

| 677,000 learners | 598,000 learners | 431,000 learners | 339,000 learners | 322,000 learners |

56%

...between April 2010 and January 2014

50%

960,000 Socially excluded learners

36%

27%   27%

Benefits   Education   Unemployed   Income   Housing

Proportion of learners falling into social exclusion categories
Benefits Base: 41,630; Education Base: 37,575; Unemployed Base: 36,931; Income Base: 37,574
Housing Base: 35,032 Numeric estimates assume a total of 1.2 million
Learners were helped during the period

Figure 12.10   Tinder Foundation learners and social exclusion.

employed in a mass movement, such as the Tinder Foundation model, and how that aggregates as a policy impact for the government.

For example, of the people supported, 7 percent of them moved from unemployment to employment, totaling 84,280 workers. Bristol University has calculated that each person who gains employment saves the U.K. treasury £8,000 each, and that totals a saving to government of £678 million.[13]

Looking at the 1.2 million people Tinder has helped and at volunteering, further informal and formal learning:

- 132,440 (11 percent) have engaged in volunteering activity, adding value to the U.K. economy of more than £137 million.[14]
- 818,720 (68 percent) have gone on to further learning, which has a total value for them as individuals estimated in excess of £626 million.[15]
- 156,520 (13 percent) are in work, of whom 13 percent went on to study for a qualification, resulting in wage increases totaling £8.6 million.[16]

The United Kingdom, like most governments in the developed world, is driving to digitize public transactions. The U.K. government Digital Strategy sets out clear actions for delivery, two of which are relevant to the work of Tinder Foundation, U.K. online centers, and others interested in digital inclusion:[17]

- Action 9 says, "There will be a cross-government approach to assisted digital. This means that people who have rarely or never been online will be able to access services offline, and we will provide additional ways for them to use the digital services."
- And Action 15 says, "Collaborate with partners across public, private, and voluntary sectors to help people go online."[18]

The work of Tinder Foundation has evidenced the close link between helping people "go online" or to gain basic online skills, and helping people see the relevance of their newly acquired online skills and their ability and desire to use online government websites and transactional services. In summary, Tinder Foundation has discovered:

- that, with the exception of looking for work, gaining government information, contacting or transacting with government is not a motivator for someone to go online
- that, by gaining basic online skills and being shown relevant and useful government websites, people do change their behavior and move contacts with government from face-to-face and phone to web

Socitm, the operating name of the Society of Information Technology Management, has calculated that every time someone shifts his/her method of contact with government from a face-to-face transaction to an online transaction, the government saves £8.47, and from telephone to online, they save £2.68.[19] Between 46 and 51 percent (46 percent from April 2010–March 2012, and 51 percent from April 2012 to 2014) of Tinder Foundation learners make that channel shift, and, on average, move 3.8 contacts per month online with government as a result. These transactions accumulate, as those who got online last month begin moving their transactions online, and those who got online in April 2010 are continuing to transact online with government month-in, month-out. This results in a saving to government from contacts being moved online since April 1, 2010 of some £232.4 million.

12.8 Innovation and the Future

With a network that has existed in some form since 2000, it would be easy to think that there has been no evolution or innovation over these years. The past eight years of continuous leadership have been a period of constant, agile development and improvement. Dialogue with the people who run the U.K. online centers enables Tinder Foundation staff to discover new ideas and excellent practice. These ideas are then piloted and seeded with other centers, and, when ready, they are scaled across the network.

Although the impact to date is remarkable, the Tinder Foundation team continues to develop and innovate. There is still a great deal to achieve, some of which is included below.

12.8.1 *Affordable Broadband and Devices Are a Barrier for Some People*

Of those people in the United Kingdom who do not use the Internet, 20 percent cite the cost of broadband and computer or Internet devices as their main barrier.[20]

In response to this, Tinder Foundation has created a new subnetwork of 60 U.K. online centers in a pilot Home Access network, all of which have staff or volunteers who have been trained by Tinder Foundation as Home Access Advisors. Twenty of these centers also have received small grants to buy equipment for learners to try in a safe, unpressured, and impartial environment. This nonsales approach is proving very popular with those on low incomes and with older people.

Tinder Foundation has developed "The Essential Guide to Getting Online at Home," hosted on Learn My Way, that provides information on understanding the commonly used jargon and advice on the most suitable equipment, based on user needs and requirements.

Refurbished computers provided by businesses free of charge have been included in the pilot. However, they have proved to be an unattractive option for some learners who often do not have space for a desktop computer in their home.

12.8.2 More Online Measurement of Centers' Activity and Engagement

Tinder Foundation is building a bespoke CRM (customer relationship management) database to build on the success over the past eight years of using an off-the-shelf software that holds all center details and contacts made with them. The new CRM will be created using open source software and will more easily allow the integration of Learn My Way (learning) data into the centers' database. It also will enable Tinder Foundation staff to target communications to different people working in the centers, for example, center managers, tutors, volunteers, etc.

With thousands of local partners and only around 35 members of staff, it is difficult to maintain contact and knowledge on how engaged a local partner is. The regular contact with local partners via telephone and email is good for dialogue and feedback and it also builds the trusted relationship mentioned in earlier sections. However, it also is time-consuming and relies on human resource. Tinder Foundation is currently building an online mechanism for measuring the engagement of a local partner that will complement, not replace, human contact. This dashboard will measure engagement against four criteria, all of which can be automatically monitored via Learn My Way or the Tinder Foundation's center database and CRM. The criteria include:

- A completed pen portrait on the center database, which has been recently updated by the local partner
- Use of the free, online training modules for staff and volunteers
- Use of Learn My Way, or providing learner data on other training approaches
- Participation in recent national/local marketing campaigns

12.8.3 Centers Creating and Sharing Their Own Online Courses

The Learn My Way Course Creator tool allows local partners to create and share their own online courses, not just consume them. It is an online program that enables any partner in the U.K. online centers network to make their own local course on the Learn My Way platform. A tutor, volunteer, or a learner can use the Learn My Way Course Creator to either create a new version of an existing course (e.g., translating the existing Learn My Way email course into Spanish) or it can be used to create a brand new course (e.g., "What is an App?" or "Coping with Cancer" or something very local or bespoke). In essence, Course Creator will become a sharing platform as all new online courses that are made will be shared with centers across the network.

As the course creator is fully integrated with Learn My Way, centers can combine the newly built courses with existing Learn My Way courses, in order to tailor the learning pathways to the needs of the learner. All learners' progress is captured on the Learn My Way platform in the same way as for all courses, so tutors can bookmark progress and monitor learning progress.

12.8.4 More and Better Dialogue with New and Existing U.K. Online Centers

Dialogue is essential if the U.K. online center network is to remain a functioning and successful ecosystem; there is more that can be done using online tools to replace expensive personal contact and face-to-face meetings. There are plans to introduce monthly online live chats for centers to talk to the Tinder Foundation senior team, which will replace less frequent face-to-face events. Other plans include a weekly online poll to ask centers simple questions about, for example, marketing themes, new courses, or volunteer training programs. Centers like meeting face-to-face. While this is expensive for Tinder Foundation to convene, Community Capacity Builders/Hubs may be asked to lead subregional events and meetings.

The use of online tools can increase the frequency of dialogue and feedback, while not increasing the cost of achieving higher levels of contact.

12.8.5 Diverse Income Streams Helps Survival

As a not-for-profit social enterprise, Tinder Foundation is now starting to generate commercial and corporate income. In 2014, this will be excess of £220,000, which will help the organization to be sustainable longer term.

Diversification of both sources of income, as well as diversifying the use of the digital expertise and the reach of the network will be important for the evolution of this mass movement. This is beginning with new online products and national partnerships, for instance, to deliver English language courses. Conversations also are beginning with overseas governments interested in replicating the success of the Tinder Foundation mass movement.

Over the past two years, the funding available through Tinder Foundation to local centers has reduced and the delivery model has gradually moved away from being exclusively driven by grants to centers. This has meant that Tinder Foundation is supporting local partners to bid for grants from other foundations and grant schemes, and is constructing products that centers can sell on to learners. One example is the Online Basics Qualification, where Tinder Foundation has built an online assessment engine and arranged the formal qualification status with an awarding body, city, and guilds, and encourages centers to sell the qualification to the learners. In this way, Tinder Foundation is supporting the local partners to think of income ideas and helping them to move away from grant dependency.

12.8.6 Starting with Social Issues and Building Digital into It

With the impact of the Tinder Foundation model on the social outcomes of individuals, one model in the future is to focus on the social outcomes and to build digital inclusion into the delivery of the solution. One example could be the integration of migrants into communities. The program would be designed to create activities of interest and relevance to both migrants and nonmigrants to achieve community cohesion, and digital skills may be one of those activities. Other social outcomes where U.K. online centers are already delivering include reducing offending, moving homeless people into hostels and then on to accommodation, improving the lives of people with mental health issues, and helping long-term unemployed people find work.

12.9 Conclusion and Blueprint for Success

A mass movement for digital inclusion is, by necessity, both simple in its design and complex in its delivery. There are some significant aspects to this mass movement that may be useful as a blueprint for others who would like to learn from this success:

1. **You can target the hard to reach and deliver at scale**
   This is achieved through a blend of clear focus, exceptional products, and collective vision. Tinder Foundation has a small team, but delivers at scale. Through its 5,000 local partners, thousands of outreach locations, 25,000 volunteers, and hundreds of national partners, Tinder Foundation has unparalleled reach into the most disadvantaged communities and the hardest to reach learners. It is a very cost-effective model at £30 per person supported, and this cost is reducing; however, to help millions of people, millions of pounds need to be invested.

2. **Use technology to help you to deliver**
   It's not just about teaching people to use the Internet, it's also about using the efficiencies and reach digital brings to you. Some examples in the Tinder Foundation model include online funding applications and management, learning content that is optimized for mobile, online dashboard to display targets transparently and publicly, and use of social networks to bring specialist groups together.

3. **A single learning platform**
   Learn My Way is very important to the success of this model; a single platform that binds the independent and diverse network. The new Learn My Way Course Creator now provides the added advantage of being able to create learning content as well as consume what is provided, empowering tutors and volunteers to make made-to-order courses to focus on local learners' needs.

4. **Use data to help evidence your impact**
   Tinder Foundation has a proven reputation for taking large, complex ideas and working out clear, practical ways to translate these into well thought-out programs that create social impact. A focus on robust data collection means the impact of its work can be clearly demonstrated.

5. Listen and evolve

All Tinder staff are not only responsive to center needs but actively seek the views and opinions of local organizations operating at a grassroots level. The Tinder Foundation approach is distinctive and unique due to a culture of inclusivity, dialogue, openness, and respect. A similar model will need to have clear channels for listening and clear ways of improving and evolving. It's not what you do, but how you do it that makes big change happen.

This is a network that is coordinated and led, but not directly owned or managed. By combining the right integrated products and tools with the right support and approach, this independent collective has achieved remarkable scale together, which hopefully can serve as a blueprint for success for others as well. Local, plus digital, plus scale, really does add up to a mass movement for digital inclusion.

Endnotes

1. U.K. Online Centers (2014). Centre Feedback Survey. http://www.tinderfoundation.org/what-we-do/uk-online-centres
2. Ipsos Mori (2013). Media literacy: Understanding digital capabilities. BBC, September. Online at: http://www.bbc.co.uk/learning/overview/assets/bbcmedialiteracy_20130930.pdf
3. Housing Technology for Race Online 2012 (2012). Digital by default 2012. Online at: http://www.go-on.co.uk/wp-content/uploads/2013/12/HousingTechnology_DigitalbyDefault2012_FINAL.pdf
4. Digital Housing Hub. Online at: http://digitalhousinghub.ning.com/
5. Oxford Internet Surveys (OxIS) (2013). Cultures of the Internet: The Internet in Britain. Oxford, U.K., October.
6. Baroness Morris, E. (2009). Independent review of ICT user skills. June. Online at: http://www.dius.gov.uk/~/media/3f79a51589404cfdb62f3da0deba69a1.ashx
7. Ibid.
8. National Health Service. Online at: http://www.NHS.uk
9. OxIS, Cultures of the Internet.
10. All figures in this section taken from 2012–2013 Learner Survey summary report. Online at: http://www.tinderfoundation.org/our-thinking/research-publications/2012-2013-annual-report-uk-online-centres
11. Ibid.
12. Level 2 in the United Kingdom is the equivalent of 5 GCSEs at A* - C, or the expected level of success for a 16-year-old.
13. Based on saving to U.K. Treasury of £8,000 per unemployed person per year moving to employment. Bristol University (2009). Online at: http://www.bristol.ac.uk/efm/news/2009/32.html
14. Volunteering provides a value of £18 billion (€22.5 billion) to the economy each year, and with 17.1 million people volunteering formally, this means each volunteer provides a value of c£1100. (€1370). See Volunteering England and NCVO. Online at: http://www.ivr.org.uk/

15. Research from NIACE shows that for adults, participating in two part-time courses in a single year will lead to improvements in health and better social relationships with a value to the individual of £148 and £658 per year respectively. NIACE. Online at: http://shop.niace.org.uk/media/catalog/product/v/a/valuingimpact_web_1.pdf

16. According to the BIS study, a qualification gained while in work increases annual income by an average of £426. BIS (2013). The impact of further learning. Online at: https://www.gov.uk/government/uploads/system/uploads/attachment_data/file/69179/bis-13-597-impact-of-further-education-learning.pdf

17. Government Digital Strategy (2012, November). Online at: https://www.gov.uk/government/publications/government-digital-strategy

18. Ibid.

19. Ibid.

20. Office of National Statistics (2013). Internet access: Households & Individuals, August. http://www.ons.gov.uk/ons/rel/rdit2/internet-access---households-and-individuals/2013/stb-ia-2013.html

Chapter 13

Beyond Failure: Rethinking Research and Evaluation in ICT4D

Paula Uimonen

Contents

13.1 Introduction

Information and communication technology (ICT) for development (ICT4D) is still an emerging field, even though the concept has been around since it was popularized during the World Summit on the Information Society (WSIS) in Geneva in 2003 and Tunis in 2005. It was widely recognized that ICT offered a tool for development, not least for the achievement of the millennium development goals

(MDGs). However, shortly after the UN summit, interest dwindled among leading donor agencies, only to resurface with the rapid expansion of mobile technologies and the widespread use of social media.[1] Today, ICT4D is again of interest to a wide range of actors, such as researchers, practitioners, donors, policymakers, and philanthropists.

Yet ICT4D continues to be perceived as a risky endeavor with high failure rates, making it a problematic field. ICT, in general, has a history of great expectations and plummeting disappointments, as exemplified by the "dot com" boost and bust at the turn of the century. In the context of development, perceptions of ICT have been equally polarized, ranging from the utopian visions of a "global information society" to dystopian prophecies of a "digital divide." Indeed, the development discourses that have accompanied the global expansion of the Internet have been highly contentious, as is often the case with technological development.[2]

As ICT4D continues to expand, it becomes more important to understand this field. It has been suggested that the post-WSIS decline in donor interest could be related to limited impact and too many failed projects.[3] Yet, there is no doubt that ICT has a significant effect on world developments. If anything, ICT is inseparable from the broader process of globalization that influences societal development in the global north as well as the global south. This chapter aims to probe deeper into ICT4D research in order to appreciate its practical complexity.

13.2 The Fallacies of Failure in ICT4D

There is a growing recognition of—almost fascination with—failure in ICT4D. Scholars have published articles on the topic for more than a decade and it has even been suggested that a new journal should be published that focuses on failure.[4] In 2010, the first FailFare in ICT4D was organized to feature "projects using mobiles and ICTs in international development that have, to put it simply, been a #FAIL—busted, kaput."[5] At the Fifth International Conference on Information and Communication Technologies and Development (ICTD2012) in Atlanta, Georgia, in March 2012, FailFare attracted a large and eager audience. Researchers shared failures from their projects, at times reveling in their encounters with unanticipated challenges, but, surprisingly enough, rarely questioning or scrutinizing their own assumptions and limitations. It is important to record and analyze failure in a field that is still largely unchartered, both in terms of research as well as practice. However, one might ask if the concept of failure deepens our understanding of the complexity of ICT4D or if it conceals as much as it reveals?

The opening sentence of a well-known and widely distributed publication by one of the most frequently cited ICT4D researchers, Richard Heeks, at the University of Manchester, states, "Do most information systems (IS) projects in developing countries (DCs) succeed or fail?"[6] Heeks proceeds with a brief review of case studies of information system projects in developing countries, whereby he presents a categorization of success/failure: total failure, partial failure, success. "What proportion of DC IS projects fall into each of the three outcome categories" he asks, responding with "No one knows for certain."[7] He then offers an "estimate" of failure rates in industrialized countries (where only a minority of IS projects fall into the "success category"), and while noting the lack of "evidence" or "theoretical rationale" that failure rates in developing countries should be lower, he argues that "there is evidence and there are plenty of practical reasons—such as lack of technical and human infrastructure—to support the idea that failure rates in DCs might be higher, perhaps considerably higher."[8] Heeks recognizes that the evidence is insufficient, noting a lack of literature, lack of evaluation, and a focus on case studies. Even so, he argues that "despite these limitations, there are some glimpses of evidence." Based on a somewhat sketchy review and analysis of some literature reviews and a few multiple-case studies, Heeks concludes:

> In summary, the evidence base is not strong—and it urgently needs strengthening—but it all points in one direction: toward high rates of IS failure in developing countries. If this is so, we should seek to understand why. That is the intention of this article—to develop and then apply a new model that helps explain why so many information systems in developing countries fail.[9]

Although Heeks himself underlines that the intention of his article is to develop a new model to explain failures, it is not necessarily his "design-reality gap model" that has caught the attention of scholars, a model that calls for a closer fit between technical design and social reality, but rather the underlying assumption of high rates of failure. Indeed, in a field where it has been challenging to provide evidence of the positive impact of ICT4D projects, Heeks' suggestions have evolved into the assumption that failure is the rule rather than the exception.

A more recent example of academic analysis of failure is found in a review of 40 articles published in *Information Technologies & International Development.*[10] This interdisciplinary open access journal has been ranked as the top ICT4D journal, an influential publication in the field.[11] In their review of articles published between 2003 and 2010, the authors examine the extent to which projects "failed to meet some or all of their development objectives."[12] They focus on three dimensions of development: development objective (mainly MDGs), development perspective (top-down versus bottom-up in design/intervention), and development focus (technology versus community in focus). The authors note that many researchers have been candid about failures or unintended negative outcomes.[13] In analyzing the reasons for failure, the authors conclude that "top-down, technology-centric, goal-diffuse approaches to ICTD contribute to unsatisfactory development results."[14] Yet, the authors also note that the majority of the papers displayed a top-down, push approach to development, most of them followed a techno-centric approach, meaning that technology was the focus, and less than half of the papers related to any specific MDGs.

To understand the high failure rate, Heeks elaborates on the design-reality gap that inevitably plagues the transfer of information systems from industrialized countries to developing countries, where the local context is markedly different.[15] He notes that many donor agencies are driven by "models of rationality," whereby ICT forms part of a "technically rational and technologically determinist agenda that focuses on the digital divide."[16] This infrastructure-driven model tends to reinforce the gap between "hard rational design" and "soft political actualities," leaving little room for local improvisation or local capacities, which are critical to successful adaptation, not least hybrids that can bridge existing gaps between technical design and business uses.

Similarly, the review article calls for a more development-oriented approach, with greater attention to development objectives, perspectives, and focus.[17] The authors underline the importance of paying more attention to "the subtle interactions, both between culture and technology, and between user and technology," as well as "ICT integration processes with a more comprehensive understanding of how communities and individuals shape the use of—and are affected by—technologies."[18] Awareness of and attention to context is highlighted, not least gender issues, which are often ignored.[19]

This identification of failure due to lack of context or techno-centric approaches echoes earlier critiques. Long before ICT4D was established as a field of research and development, well renowned scholars questioned the technological and historical determinism of dominant discourses on the information society.[20] Many policymakers and scientists believed the information society was universally applicable. This notion originated in the Western/Northern centers of power, but spread quickly to the peripheries, forming what could be defined as an "informational development paradigm" that framed the early development of the Internet in developing countries.[21] Technocentrism and eurocentrism, thus, is not something new, but has framed ICT4D since its inception.

Seeing that analyses of failure in ICT4D employ an evaluative framework, it is worth pondering some of their underlying normative assumptions. The evaluation of failure is by definition associated with value; a process of careful examination and careful judgment of nonperformance of what is requested or expected, to reiterate common dictionary definitions. Heeks' tripartite categorization of failure distinguishes between: total failure (an initiative that is never implemented or in which a new system was implemented, but immediately abandoned); partial failure (major goals are unattained or there are significant undesirable outcomes); and success (most stakeholder groups attain their major goals and do not experience significant undesirable outcomes).[22] Dodson, Sterling, and Bennett define failure as "the outcome of a case in which an ICT4D initiative has failed to meet some or all of its objectives."[23] The outcomes of an initiative, thus, are measured according to planned goals and objectives (e.g., Heeks), or objectives that should have been considered within a given framework, e.g., development (e.g., Dodson et al.).

Consequentially, deviations from original plans are considered failures because the outcomes do not adequately correspond to what was expected or what should have been considered. In other words, nonperformance is established.

13.2.1 The Limitations of "Failure"

Current frameworks for evaluating ICT4D conceal as much as they reveal because they leave out a big chunk of reality. It is not suggested that evaluations should not be used to determine the outcomes of ICT4D interventions. They can clearly add to the evidence base that decision and policymakers increasingly insist upon. However, there are reasons to raise a note of caution. It is extremely difficult, if not impossible, to anticipate the outcomes of interventions that are as dynamic as those found under the label of ICT4D. Not only is ICT a very dynamic field in its own right, with rapidly evolving technologies that interact with society in unexpected ways, but when technology is introduced in the context of "development," the field becomes ever more dynamic, to the point of being quite unpredictable. No matter how elaborate a model one may use to design an ICT4D intervention, it can never fully capture the dynamic intricacies of social reality. For as much as "design is a representation of an intentional future," a "world-in-miniature," we must keep in mind that development is all about a "world-in-the-making," the outcome of which cannot be pinpointed in advance.[24] By locking ICT4D initiatives into a predetermined framework, based on which success or failure is ascertained, scholars run the risk of perpetuating assumptions that may or may not reflect reality.

Could it be that there are not so many "failures" in ICT4D? This is not to say that all ICT4D interventions have been successful. Rather, it is important to question the underlying assumptions of failure (and by extension its antonym *success*). If we cannot fully predetermine the outcomes of a given intervention, then how can we classify it as a failure? We can attempt to predefine anticipated outcomes, and in most cases an aid organization has to do just that in order to get funding for a given initiative, but, in so doing, we are already missing the whole point of ICT4D, namely its unpredictable dynamics. In other words, as long as we try to measure the outcome of ICT4D according to what we can plan and predict, we will fail miserably in understanding and appreciating what ICT4D is all about, for the social dynamics of technology demand a far more astute reading of technology-mediated development.

Regardless of its actual outcome, any ICT4D intervention will have an impact on development. This holds equally true for ICT4D projects in which stakeholder groups attain their major goals (successes) as well as information systems that never get implemented (total failures). If anything, the development impact often can be greater in ICT4D interventions that fall short of their predefined goals, because they are likely to address or encounter some of the more problematic dimensions of social change.

Meanwhile, "failure" deserves to be problematized and contextualized in its own right. Anthropological critiques have established that "failure" is the norm rather than exception in development in general.[25] In postdevelopment theory, this predominance of failure is in itself characteristic of the contradictory underpinnings of the notion of development, a eurocentric and universalist construct that reflects the hegemonic power of the developed world vis-à-vis the developing or underdeveloped world.[26] In trying to recast the rest of the world in its own image, the development paradigm will inevitably fail, because it fails to capture social, cultural, economic, and political diversity.

There is more to failure than meets the eye in the discourses and practices of development. Using the examples of rural development projects in Lesotho in Africa, Ferguson notes that while these projects may have failed to reach the goals of donors and other development actors, they nonetheless had important social and political consequences, as they have enabled the expansion of bureaucratic state power.[27] Ferguson concludes that "what is most important about a 'development' project is not so much what it fails to do, but what it does do; it may be that its real importance in the end lies in the side effects."[28] Building on Foucault, he argues that these side effects, in turn, can be interpreted as *instrument-effects*, with far-reaching consequences, not least in terms of depoliticizing poverty, thus forming what he calls "the antipolitics machine" of "development."[29]

This is why we need to look well beyond failure to appreciate what ICT4D is all about. In any given context, the development and use of ICT interacts with a wide range of historically shaped social forces, not least power relations. Not only is it impossible to fully grasp this complexity in advance, but, more importantly, it is critical to understand that this social reality cannot possibly be appreciated by simply categorizing ICT4D initiatives into the conceptual straitjacket of "success" or "failure."

13.3 Beyond Failure: A Tale of Two Research Cases

Scholarly research is well positioned to reach beyond the false dichotomy of failure/success in ICT4D. This can be achieved through a combination of research methods that enable a more holistic appraisal of ICT4D in a given socioeconomic and cultural context. Two recently published monographs exemplify how research can deepen our understanding of technology-mediated development, while taking into account how national and global policy making intersect with local ICT4D efforts. In both cases, the research is based on long-term fieldwork, thus combining detailed accounts of ICT at the community level with an appreciation of socioeconomic changes over time. The monographs were presented in the open session *Writing Books in ICT4D Research—Why and How?* at the International Conference on Information and Communication Technologies and Development (ICTD2013) in Cape Town on December 7, 2013 and are summarized here.

13.3.1 Chile

In what is bound to become a classic text in ICT4D research, *Technologies of Choice? ICTs, Development and the Capabilities Approach*, Dorothea Kleine introduces a conceptual framework—the choice framework—to map the complexity of ICT4D.[30] The study is based on fieldwork in Chile, where Kleine has combined ethnographic research at the local level with interviews with national policymakers in order to analyze Chile's ambitious ICT policies in relation to existing social and economic realities. Kleine's choice framework builds on Amyarta Sen's capabilities approach, which stresses people's freedom to choose the lives they have reason to value. Viewing development as a "systemic process," the choice framework follows an analytic approach that is "people-centered, focused on choice, holistic, and systemic," centering on development in terms of what people choose to value.[31] As Kleine argues, the choice framework offers an "open-ended, systemic tool for analysis" well-suited for ICT4D, not least to "map" how ICTs relate to structure and agency.[32]

Kleine's analysis of telecenters, a place in which people can access publicly available computers, exemplifies the extent to which a more holistic approach can deepen our understanding of ICT4D. In the early days of ICT4D, telecenters were heralded as an exemplary model for public access to ICT at the community level, especially in rural and underserved areas. Donor agencies and governments around the world invested substantial amounts in setting up what was often called *multipurpose community telecenters* (MPCT). The results were mixed, and a growing body of scholarly literature pinpointed the many challenges and weaknesses of telecenters. Unfortunately, just as easily as donors had been swayed by the allures of this access model, the "telecenter movement" lost its appeal, as reality proved more problematic than anticipated.

However, based on local research at a public library telecenter in a small town in Chile, Kleine is able to map the complexities of this public access model. The library is located in a small town, Algun, in one of Chile's poorest regions. The telecenter is part of a national network of infocentros, which form part of the government's Campaign for Digital Literacy, an important aspect of the national ICT strategy Agenda Digital. In its efforts to enhance ICT-enabled development, the government has implemented a strong infrastructure with state-funded public access to the Internet. Unlike many other countries where telecenters are supposed to generate some income, the telecentros or infocentros in Chile offer access free of charge. Out of the four different models for public access, the BiblioRedes model in public libraries has proved to be "the most institutionally sustainable model."[33] This is also the model that Kleine focuses on in her study, detailing various dimensions of access (availability, affordability, skills) as well as time and space. Her analysis of telecenter users is equally comprehensive, taking into consideration gender, ethnicity, education, occupation, age, and disability.

This approach enables Kleine to draw a far more nuanced picture of telecenters, going well beyond the common reading of failure in terms of financial sustainability.

Noting the dominance of instrumentalist and econocentric approaches in the literature on telecenters, which generally does not question the underlying paradigm of market-focused development, Kleine argues that practitioners are "put under pressure to reconcile conflicting goals of including the most disadvantaged groups and generating sufficient revenue through service charges."[34] By using the choice framework, Kleine is able to reach a conclusion that offers a far more holistic appraisal of telecenters and the role of ICT in development in general:

> From the perspectives of the capabilities approach, multipurpose telecenters can be celebrated as new institutions in the social structure that may allow more people to extend their existence, sense, use, and achievement of choice toward the outcomes they personally desire. *Only a subset of these outcomes will probably be of an economic nature,* while knowing that the people who one cares about are safe and happy, understanding more about one's history and identity, imagining travel to faraway places, talking to people from other cultures, knowing what is going on in the world as well as national and local politics, expressing a view online, or simply enjoying music or testing one's skill in games are all *elements of the lives people may value.*[35]

13.3.2 Tanzania

Another example of how research can generate a more empirically grounded and holistic understanding of ICT4D is found in my own research on digital media and intercultural interaction at an arts college in Tanzania.[36] In this research, I combined insights I had gained as a practitioner with data gathered during ethnographic fieldwork. In 2004 I helped the college formulate an ICT strategy. I also carried out an ICT user study to establish a baseline for ICT integration. The user study explored user patterns and capacity development through a questionnaire, the results of which were fed into a set of recommendations.[37]

Although the ICT user study posed rather standard questions on user patterns and skills acquisition, the question that generated the most interesting results was a more open-ended reflection on the meaning of access. At the time of the survey, the college only had Internet access for a year and most students had very limited skills. Even so, the study showed that the Internet had already become a "taken for granted" part of student life.[38] In response to the question: "What would happen if you could not access the Internet?" students made it clear that the Internet had become an important part of their lives and their futures, without which they would "suffer," or as one student put it, "I can't live without the Internet now." Despite their low levels of use and limited skills, students placed tremendous value on the Internet. Statements, such as "I would be out of date," "I couldn't develop," "My understanding will be down," "I would miss a lot about my arts," and "I will miss a lot of things, there are other things I can't get in class," exemplified the extent to which students had come to rely on the Internet as a learning resource. Students were also placing great value on Internet-mediated communication: "I would loose [sic] communication and news," "I could not have the friends I have now," and "I could have few material and lost my relatives."

Five years later, in 2009, the grand visions of the ICT strategy were far from realized. If the study had followed an evaluative framework, this could have been categorized as a failure. However, whether the ICT project was a success or failure was not the point. Rather, it was to understand the broader process of cultural digitalization, which led to a probe of historically shaped institutional transformations that framed the development and use of digital media at the college, especially the link between digitalization and public sector reform. It was not just the implementation of the ICT strategy that fell short of the envisaged plan; the transformation of the college into an executive agency had not brought about the effectiveness and efficiency of public service delivery envisaged by policy and decision makers. Instead, the college's attempts to be more business-oriented had led it astray from its mandate of delivering arts training and production. In this regard, the poorly equipped ICT building where students accessed digital media was emblematic of a general deterioration of academic standards and artistic performances.

Probing beyond the notion of digital divide, this study used the concept "partial inclusion" to deepen the scholarly appraisal of digital media in the peripheries of the global network society. While Castells' (2004) work on the network society is good to think with, his insistence on a binary appraisal of inclusion/exclusion leaves out the many instances of partial inclusion that can be found in so-called developing countries or emerging markets.[39] Communities and institutions are not necessarily excluded from the network society, but due to material and social constraints, they are not fully included. Based on a detailed analysis of digitalization at the arts college, this study could explain what the state of partial inclusion entails, not least the frustrated aspirations for global inclusion amidst material scarcity and continued dependencies on the dictates of global power.

13.3.3 Added Value of Research

What makes these studies relevant for ICT4D research is their ability to capture the interaction between technology and society through careful analysis of structure and agency. This processual and people-centered approach to ICT4D is not concerned with measuring outcomes in terms of success/failure, but uses open-ended research to grasp what ICT4D brings about in a given setting. As Kleine argues, "… exploratory analysis is especially appropriate for new, fast-moving, and transversal phenomena that effect the development process."[40] New ICTs are clearly a case in point.

This kind of research can also elaborate on the global interconnectedness that ICT4D epitomizes, offering valuable insights into conditions that affect all of us. ICT is not only inseparable from the process of globalization, it is very much an engine of development in the twenty-first century. ICT4D can thus shed light on human development in general, for "in terms of finding socially, environmentally, and economically balanced, sustainable forms of development, *all* countries are still developing."[41] If anything, the process of modernization constitutes a "world-in the-making" that we have yet to figure out. From the vantage point of ICT4D, we can begin to grasp some of the dialectics and complexities of this process, which is why "in the present moment, it is the global south that affords privileged insight into the workings of the world at large."[42] In other words, ICT4D research in the global south enables us to understand global processes that influence the global north as well.

13.4 An Alternative Model for ICT4D Research and Evaluation

ICT4D researchers are often keen to make a positive change in the lives of the people they study and their academic interests often coincide with a desire to make a real contribution to development. This is true for development studies, which are expected to be normative, but also and perhaps even more so for technical disciplines, as exemplified by the many proof-of-concept studies found in ICT4D research.[43] However, the interaction between research and practice is not without its own challenges, since the two perspectives tend to differ in their priorities. Practitioners often seek practical knowledge that can be applied to their context of project implementation while academics seek knowledge that can further their theoretical understanding. If anything, it has been noted that "the conflict between conducting ICTD research and achieving development goals remains an unresolved issue."[44]

The Swedish Program for ICT in Developing Regions (Spider) is a world leading ICT4D center that offers an interesting model for research that contributes to practice in innovative ways. Based at Stockholm University and established in 2004 with funding from the Swedish International Development Cooperation Agency (Sida), Spider serves as a node in a network of ICT4D actors in academia, civil society, government and business. Building on Sida's long-standing support to ICT and research capacity development in the global south, which dates back to the late 1990s, Spider has, since its inception, supported ICT4D research. For many years, researchers from Spider's partner universities in Sweden carried out research and development projects on a wide range of topics in a variety of countries, often in partnership with local universities.

When Sida insisted on a more development-oriented focus, Spider reconsidered its modus operandi. An external evaluation had noted that "concerns have been raised about the strategic coherence of Spider's activities and priorities; its internal capacity to monitor, evaluate, and learn from its various activities; and its alignment with Sida's broader development priorities."[45] A complementary evaluation of Spider's university projects found that: "As a first general and important observation it should be stressed that the supported projects have a high relevance, addressing well recognized and wide-spread problems in the partner countries. … However, a few of the projects have had issues to keep local commitment or transferring the results to a long-term owner."[46] Problems of local ownership and long-term sustainability also surfaced in the scholarly analysis conducted by one of Spider's senior researchers, using a system dynamic model.[47] In 2011, Spider launched a new strategy, *Spider 2.0*, which was more clearly aligned with Sweden's ICT4D priorities, while placing greater emphasis on Spider serving as a knowledge broker in ICT4D.

In the new strategy, a clear division was made between ICT4D projects and ICT4D research. In order to reach the strategic objective "to strengthen development and poverty reduction in partner countries through strategic integration of ICT," a new modality was developed for ICT4D projects.[48] In 2011, Spider initiated a funding mechanism offering catalytic seed funding to innovative projects of one to two years duration, with a view to generate long-term growth, upscaling, and lasting impact. The projects were initiated by organizations in partner countries, mostly nongovernment organizations (NGOs) and government agencies, many of whom were new to ICT4D, but with previous experience in development. To strengthen collaboration, most of the projects were organized into thematic and/or geographic networks, as exemplified by the ICT4Democracy in East Africa Network, which brought together seven partners in Kenya, Tanzania, and Uganda.[49] Subsequently, Spider initiated a new approach to ICT4D research, offering small grants for research related to Spider-supported projects. The grants are made available for researchers at Spider's partner universities in Sweden to carry out research related to ongoing projects. In order to strengthen research capacity, Sweden-based researchers have to collaborate with researchers and/or research assistants in partner countries. While researchers are free to determine what topic they wish to investigate, the research project is only accepted following the approval of the project partners concerned, thus avoiding a situation where research is forced upon practitioners.

This research model builds on the multidisciplinary character of ICT4D, allowing experts from a variety of disciplines to carry out research in the field. While it is up to Spider's project partners to accept a given research project, there are no limitations in disciplinary background. So far, Spider has supported research from a variety of disciplines, including communication for development, computer and systems sciences, gender and technology, informatics, media studies, and social anthropology.

It is, however, challenging to achieve truly multidisciplinary research, as exemplified by Spider's network of partner universities in Sweden. Most of the research nodes are found in the technological domain, and some of the universities are explicitly technological. For instance, at Stockholm University, the node is the Department of Computer and Systems Sciences and, at Linnaeus University, it is Learning and Knowledge Technologies. Several technological institutes are part of the network, including Blekinge Institute of Technology, Luleå University of Technology, and the Royal Institute of Technology. This technological orientation is somewhat broadened through Informatics and Media at Uppsala University, Communication for Development at Malmö University and School of Business/Informatics at Örebro University. Nonetheless, similarly to other parts of the world, the ICT4D research field in Sweden continues to be dominated by technological disciplines. This is clearly problematic. The disciplinary split between engineers and social scientists places limitations on the multidisciplinary aspirations of ICT4D research, since "discipline siloing restricts the creative thinking and diverse ideas that come from combinations across disciplines."[50]

Meanwhile, Spider's unique combination of research and practice enables cross-fertilization between researchers and practitioners, while respecting their differences. Practitioners get an opportunity to reflect upon their activities, while learning more about the dynamics of ICT4D, which can serve as an inspiring eye-opener. As reflected by a practitioner in Kenya on the experience of working with a researcher from Sweden: "Mathias [Swedish researcher] injected some new energy and dynamism into the approach to field work (and) his research questions forced us to be more objective about our work in the field."[51] Meanwhile, researchers get an opportunity to carry out empirical research in real-life environments. Instead of creating a development project that they can do research about, scholars are able to investigate ICT in the context of a development project that is put in place by practitioners. While minimizing the technocentric, top-down approach that characterizes much of ICT4D research, this project-driven research is bound to have a more lasting impact, not least by strengthening the knowledge and competencies of practitioners during implementation.[52] As noted by Sarajeva:[53]

> Closer collaboration between researchers and practitioners contributes to ICT4D research that is grounded in reality, while at the same time allowing practitioners to draw on expertise that surpasses a particular project. The combination of research and practice is thus fruitful not only for future implementation, but also to improve ongoing activities. Establishing and forging a connection between the two fields can create synergistic effects, where the mere shift of perspective or alternative experiences can deepen the understanding of both practitioners and researchers.

In this research model, both practitioners and researchers are able to contribute to the ICT4D knowledge base. Not only are they able to learn from one another in a project setting, but they also are pooling their knowledge into joint action, thus strengthening ongoing implementation efforts. Since Spider values ICT4D knowledge from both fields, the results are widely shared as well. The *Spider Stories* publication series gives voice to project partners to tell their stories with their own words and images. Researchers share the results of their research in the *Spider ICT4D Series* publication, which contains thematic anthologies as well as single-authored thematic issues. True to the ideals of open sharing in ICT4D, these publications are shared freely online, thus easily available to the ICT4D community at large.

Research is also used to strengthen monitoring and evaluation (M&E) of projects. Results from Spider-supported research are used by Spider program managers in their ongoing M&E, thus complementing reports submitted by project partners. To deepen the analysis, the program managers use scholarly rigor in their evaluation of results, contextualizing specific projects in related research from different fields. Regardless of their outcome, each project is treated as a learning opportunity, with broader ramifications than originally planned. Consequentially, more lessons can be drawn from each project, thus deepening the global knowledge base.

This open-ended approach to ICT4D evaluation builds on scholarly stringency and allows for a more holistic appraisal than the failure/success dichotomy. Of course, projects are evaluated based on the original objectives and planned activities, outputs, and outcomes. However, the evaluative framework is expanded through a scholarly appreciation of the context in which a given project has been carried out. In cases where a project performs differently from the original plan, an effort is made to understand why this is the case and what the outcome has been, rather than writing it off as a failure.

Meanwhile, it is noteworthy that Spider has not had any "failed projects" since its new strategy was put in place in 2011. This lack of failure is not a matter of hiding or concealing problematic projects, nor is it a matter of simply accepting whatever outcomes projects have. Rather, it can be attributed to many factors, all of which take context into account. First, projects are conceptualized by partner organizations in the global south, not by organizations in the global north, which strengthens local ownership. Secondly, a great deal of planning is required before a project is initiated, a process that is undertaken in close dialogue with Spider program managers who serve as advisers and facilitators. Thirdly, project partners are given considerable freedom in implementation to adjust their activities according to the situation at hand. Lastly, ongoing monitoring and evaluation is carried out in a collaborative spirit of partnership, with Spider program managers acting as facilitators rather than controllers, eagerly helping partners along, while learning from their experience. Throughout this process, awareness of context is combined with an open-minded appreciation of the dynamics of ICT4D.

13.5 Conclusion

It is important to understand what ICT4D is about. Scholarly analyses of failure are problematic because they tend to leave out more than they clarify. ICT4D is a very complex field, which requires a more holistic and empirically grounded approach. This chapter used two recent examples based on fieldwork in Latin America and East Africa to exemplify the extent to which research can clarify some of the complexities of ICT4D, including the intricate interaction between global policymaking and social change at the local level.

The alternative research model developed by Spider allows for collaboration and cross-fertilization between researchers and practitioners while contributing to the global ICT4D knowledge base. Spider's research model is driven by a conviction that research can make a contribution to practice as well as policymaking in ICT4D:

> Since ICT4D still is an emerging field of development cooperation, it is critical to build a solid knowledge base, for decision makers, practitioners, and other stakeholders. By offering evidence-based, empirically grounded knowledge on what works and what doesn't, research can strengthen ongoing and future ICT4D efforts. Research can also reinforce monitoring and evaluation (M&E) of ongoing activities, by providing more complete analyses of outcomes and impacts.[54]

ICT4D research is particularly valuable for policymakers, guiding their efforts to formulate holistic and comprehensive frameworks for ICT4D, thus building on the impetus of WSIS. While the WSIS process facilitated a broad understanding of and commitment to the critical role of ICT in development, following a people-centered approach that sits well with ICT4D, more effort is required to translate these grand visions into reality. If anything, the post-WSIS decline in ICT4D support among leading donors indicate a persistent gap between rhetoric and action that has yet to be fully rectified.

It is unfortunate that policymakers still seem unaware of the growing body of scholarly work that could and should inform policymaking. At the WSIS Forum, an annual event for WSIS implementation and "the world's largest annual gathering of the 'ICT for development' community," according to the organizer, the International Telecommunication Union (ITU),[55] policymakers lament the lack of evidence about ICT4D while referring to "anecdotal evidence" as an alternative source of knowledge.[56] Not only do these policymakers ignore the existence of ICT4D research, but also the scientifically grounded appraisals of what ICT4D is all about. By now, it can hardly be said that the only evidence available on ICT4D is anecdotal.

Hopefully, we will see more fruitful triangulation of research, practice, and policy in the coming years. ICT4D is such a complex field that no single perspective can possibly capture its essence, let alone influence it in a progressive direction. However, if key actors, such as policymakers, practitioners, and researchers, join forces, we do stand a better chance of building the global information society that was envisaged at WSIS Geneva in 2003:

> We, the representatives of the peoples of the world, assembled in Geneva from 10–12 December 2003 for the first phase of the World Summit on the Information Society, declare our common desire and commitment to build a people-centred, inclusive and development-oriented Information Society, where everyone can create, access, utilize and share information and knowledge, enabling individuals, communities and peoples to achieve their full potential in promoting their sustainable development and improving their quality of life, premised on the purposes and principles of the Charter of the United Nations and respecting fully and upholding the Universal Declaration of Human Rights. (WSIS Declaration of Principles, Geneva 2013).[57]

Failure to achieve these commitments will undoubtedly have significant consequences around the world, as envisaged by the late President Nelson Mandela in his opening address at Telecom 95 in Geneva in October 1995:

> If we cannot ensure that this global revolution creates a worldwide information society in which everyone has a stake and can play a part, then it will not have been a revolution at all.[58]

ICT4D researchers are willing and able to contribute to the strategic use of ICT for global development. Practitioners and policymakers are well positioned to use this knowledge resource for the benefit of digital inclusion around the world.

Endnotes

1. Hellström, J., and P. Uimonen (forthcoming). ICT4D donor agencies and networks. *International Encyclopedia of Digital Communication & Society.*
2. Uimonen, P. (2001). *Transnational.dynamics@ development.net: Internet, modernization and globalization.* Stockholm: Almqvist & Wiksell International.
3. Hellström and Uimonen, ICT4D donor agencies and networks.
4. For an overview, see Dodson, L., S. R. Sterling, and J. K. Bennett (2013). Considering failure: Eight years of *ITID* research. *Information Technologies & International Development* 9 (2): 19–34; Best, M. (2010). Understanding our knowledge gaps: Or, do we have an ICT4D field? And do we want one? *Information Technologies & International Development* 6: 51.
5. Online at: http://failfaire.org/about/
6. Heeks, R. (2002). Information systems and developing countries: Failure, success, and local improvisations. *The Information Society* 18: 101.

7. Ibid., p. 102.
8. Ibid., pp. 101–112.
9. Ibid., p. 103.
10. Dodson, Sterling, and Bennett, Considering failure.
11. Heeks, R. (2010). ICT4D journal ranking table. Online at: http://ict4dblog.wordpress.com/2010/04/14/ict4d-journal-ranking-table/
12. Dodson, Sterling, and Bennett, Considering failure, p. 19.
13. Ibid., p. 23.
14. Ibid., p. 29.
15. Heeks, Information systems and developing countries, pp. 101–112.
16. Ibid., p. 106.
17. Dodson, Sterling, and Bennett, Considering failure, pp. 19–34.
18. Ibid., p. 28.
19. Wamala, C. (2012). *Empowering women through ICT*. Stockholm: Spider.
20. Lyon, D. (1988). The information society: Issues and illusions. Cambridge, U.K.: Polity Press; Webster, F. (1995). *Theories of the information society*. New York: Routledge.
21. Uimonen, P. (2001). Transnational.dynamics@ development.net.
22. Heeks, Information systems and developing countries, pp. 101–102.
23. Dodson, Sterling, and Bennett, Considering failure, p. 20.
24. Heeks, Information systems and developing countries, p. 105.
25. Escobar, A. (1995). *Encountering development: The making and unmaking of the third world*. Princeton, NJ: Princeton University Press; Ferguson, J. (1994). *The anti-politics machine: "Development," depoliticization, and bureaucratic power in Lesotho*. Minneapolis: University of Minnesota Press; Hobart, M. (ed.) (1993). *An anthropological critique of development. The growth of ignorance*. New York: Routledge.
26. Escobar, *Encountering development*.
27. Ferguson, *The anti-politics machine*.
28. Ibid., p. 254.
29. Ibid., p. 256.
30. Kleine, D. (2013). *Technologies of choice? ICTs, development and the capabilities approach*. Cambridge, MA: MIT University Press.
31. Ibid., p. 41.
32. Ibid., p. 51.
33. Ibid., p. 92.
34. Ibid., pp. 125–126.
35. Ibid., p. 125.
36. Uimonen, P. (2012). *Digital drama. Teaching and learning art and media in Tanzania*. New York: Routledge. Online at: http://www.innovativeethnographies.net/digitaldrama
37. Uimonen, P. (2006). ICT user study at Bagamoyo College of Arts. Bagamoyo College of Arts and Sida/Embassy of Sweden Dar es Salaam.
38. Uimonen, P. (2011). African art students and digital learning. In *Interactive media use and youth: Learning, knowledge exchange and behavior*, eds. E. Dunkels, G-M. Frånberg, and C. Hällgren (pp. 222–239). Hershey, PA: IGI Global. Information Science Reference.
39. Hannerz, U. (1992). *Cultural complexity: Studies in the social organization of meaning*. New York: Columbia University Press; Uimonen, *Digital drama*.
40. Kleine, D. (2013). "Technologies of Choice? ICTs, Development and the Capabilities Approach," MIT University Press, p 35.

41. Kleine, *Technologies of choice?*
42. Comaroff, J., and J. Comaroff (2012). *Theory from the South. Or, how Euro-America is evolving towards Africa*. Boulder, CO: Paradigm Publishers, p. 1.
43. Kleine, *Technologies of choice?*; Dodson, Sterling, and Bennett, Considering failure, pp. 19–34.
44. Ibid., p. 27.
45. McNamara, K. S. (2009). The Swedish program for ICT in developing regions (SPIDER). An independent evaluation. *Sida Review* 07: 4.
46. Bråsjö, U. (2010). *Evaluation of the SPIDER program. ICT project collaboration with Swedish partner universities 2007–2009*. Stockholm: Spider, p. 2.
47. Popova, I. (2012). *Modeling ICT4D: System dynamics model of Swedish University projects*. Stockholm: Spider ICT4D, Series no. 5.
48. Spider (2011). *Spider 2.0. Strategy and roadmap 2011–2015*. Stockholm: Spider, p. 7.
49. Online at: http://www.ict4democracy.org/
50. Best, Understanding our knowledge gaps, p. 51.
51. Obura, D. (2012). CORDEA. In *ICT for anti-corruption, democracy and education in East Africa*, ed. K. Sarajeva. Stockholm: Spider ICT4D Series no. 6, p. 7.
52. Dodson, Sterling, and Bennett, Considering failure, pp. 19–34.
53. Sarajeva, *ICT for anti-corruption, democracy and education in East Africa*.
54. Online at: http://www.spidercenter.org/research
55. Online at: http://www.itu.int/wsis/implementation/2013/forum/
56. I have participated in these since 2011.
57. Online at: http://www.itu.int/wsis/docs/geneva/official/dop.html
58. Online at: http://www.anc.org.za/show.php?id=3608

Chapter 14

In Conclusion: Tackling Future Digital Divides

Kim Andreasson

Contents

14.1 Introduction

The percentage of individuals using the Internet globally has increased from 16 percent in 2005 to 40 percent at the end of 2013, according to the International Telecommunication Union (ITU).[1] In the developed world, nearly 8 in 10 people are online. In emerging markets, mobile devices provide a new avenue for access as subscriptions grew from 23 to 88 percent between 2005 and 2013. However, equal participation in the information society (e-inclusion) remains elusive, in part due to existing barriers, but also because of emerging gaps in access and usage as digital divides evolve as the information society expands.

The first part of this chapter explores some of the challenges to the basic framework outlined in the introduction to this volume: access, usage, and useful usage. The second part introduces the cyber-dependency matrix, which illustrates the potential consequences of what happens as countries move toward an information society in terms of future digital divides, such as a global information divide due to cybersecurity and data localization strategies.

14.2 Part I: Challenges Ahead

This book has already outlined numerous current and emerging divides around the world. As such, this concluding chapter returns to the basic premise presented in the introduction, but with a view toward the future. Although the discussion is subject to development, which often creates new solutions while bringing new divides, the role of infrastructure, bandwidth, web accessibility, and what people do with their access appear to be certain near-term challenges.

14.2.1 Access and Infrastructure

Mobile connectivity offers perhaps the greatest opportunity for e-inclusion since the introduction of the Internet. In 2014, ITU data shows that mobile cellular subscriptions have reached 93 percent globally and growth in this segment has slowed to 2.6 percent, indicating that the market is approaching saturation levels.[2] Meanwhile, the ITU predicts mobile broadband penetration will reach 32 percent by the end of 2014, which is about twice the rate of three years earlier.

Despite the obvious potential of mobile connectivity, it also opens up new divides in which speed is one. For instance, in 2011, 90 percent of the world's population had access to 2G mobile networks, but the figure for higher speed 3G networks was only 45 percent, according to the ITU.[3] Similarly, mobile broadband penetration in developed countries is expected to reach 84 percent in 2014, but only 21 percent in developing ones.[4] By the time the latter markets catch up, the former are likely to have embarked on even greater speeds.

Mobile devices offer tremendous opportunities to bridge basic gaps in access. However, the importance of fixed-line infrastructure development should not be overlooked as it remains fundamental to improve quality, speed, and reliability, in particular in rural areas where mobile coverage is often insufficient. In Europe, 62 percent of the population has access to 30 Mbps broadband speeds, but only 18 percent of those in rural areas have the same level of connectivity.[5]

Fixed-line broadband has the added benefit that it can support greater bandwidth and create additional wireless access points. Hence, countries, such as India (widely known for its mobile adoption success), are also embarking on ambitious fixed-line development. In 2011, India announced the National Optical Fibre Network (NOFN), which aims to connect all 250,000 villages (Gram Panchayats) to broadband.[6] Many developed countries are undertaking similar efforts. Australia, for instance, views its National Broadband Network, which aims to connect 97 percent of the population in a sparsely populated country to the fixed-line network, as key to future economic growth and in providing equal opportunity for all.[7]

14.2.2 A Role for the Public Sector

Beyond improved infrastructure, governments also need to address underlying challenges toward access, such as regulations to promote competition and affordability.

In this regard, progress is being made around the world, although there remains room for improvement. According to the ITU, fixed-line broadband prices fell from US$70.1 to US$19.5 per Mbit/s globally between 2008 and 2012. However, there are great discrepancies. In the United States, on average, a plan would consume 0.4 percent of the gross national income (GNI) per capita, whereas in Cambodia, it reaches 34 percent.[8] The same pattern holds true for mobile broadband, although differences in pre- and postpaid services and the amount of data usage included makes it harder to compare.

In an interview for a report from The Economist Intelligence Unit (EIU), Torbjörn Fredriksson, head of the ICT Analysis Section at the Science, Technology, and ICT Branch of the Division on Technology and Logistics at the United Nations Conference on Trade and Development (UNCTAD), said that competition is fundamental in providing affordable access.[9] The Information Economy Reports from UNCTAD have also found a correlation between the cost of information and communication technology (ICT) and access, particularly among the poor.[10]

However, a competitive market (in terms of the numbers of operators) does not mean it is effective because affordable prices also rely on a strong and transparent regulatory environment. This is an area where there is an unusual amount of synergy between the public and private sectors. For instance, according to a survey by the EIU, telecommunications executives largely agree with government policymakers that strong regulations are beneficial as it levels the playing field in which they can compete for customers, particularly in rural areas.[11]

14.2.3 Usage and the Relevance of Content

The mere presence of fixed and mobile infrastructure is unimportant without usage. Surveys from Australia, the United Kingdom, and the United States all show that a key reason for low Internet adoption is a lack of interest or a lack of perceived benefits of access.[12] Providing local, relevant, and useful content in addition to raising awareness about them, therefore, requires far greater efforts. Another challenge is whether important information is actually used.

Many parents are initially delighted that their children use computers, although they have little knowledge of what they are actually doing with them. As it turns out, youth around the world often prefer entertainment to using ICTs for productive purposes, such as doing homework. At its extreme, gaming can become an addiction. In South Korea, the government found that about 2 percent of people aged 10 to 19 needed treatment for excessive online gaming, according to a report in *The Guardian*, a British newspaper.[13]

Few countries have done anything concrete to counter this growing challenge. However, to stem such trends, Vietnam opened a dedicated treatment center in Ho Chi Minh City and also ordered Internet service providers (ISPs) to block access to games between dusk and dawn, according to *The Economist*.[14] Though perfectly logical (one official informally told me that they prefer kids to go to school rather than to play games), the decision was controversial. Local gaming companies complained that they were put at a disadvantage as children found a way around the imposed barriers to access foreign games, hence, losing market share, whereas Western media decried the decision as limiting Internet freedom. Therefore, after four years, Vietnam is considering allowing full access to online games again, according to *Thanh Niên*, a local paper.[15]

In the West, meanwhile, research often shows that lower income families, people with less education, those with disabilities, minorities, and rural residents generally lag behind in both broadband adoption and computer usage.[16] When online, new challenges surface. Studies from the Kaiser Family Foundation and Mark Warschauer and Tina Matuchniak at the University of California, Irvine, show that black and Hispanic youth in the United States actually spend far more time using a computer than do white youth, yet do not achieve the same educational outcomes, raising further questions surrounding useful usage and how it can be stimulated.[17]

14.2.4 A Role for the Private Sector

From an economic perspective, the gap is wide between those who use ICTs to their advantage and those who appear to be wasting their time. In order to stimulate Internet adoption and use it for productive purposes, the public and private sectors—albeit for different reasons—must develop and promote relevant and useful content.

For instance, the private sector is interested in providing local content that meets local demand and such revenue-generating ventures can also result in greater inclusiveness. An oft-cited initiative is M-PESA, a mobile payments system designed and created for Safaricom, a telecommunications operator in Kenya, in March 2007. Launched to simply transfer funds, people soon found new ways of using the system, in particular, as an avenue for those without bank or credit card accounts to transmit money electronically for the first time. Supermarkets now accept payments through the system, as do other retail shops and various institutions, such as local schools.

In March 2007, M-PESA had 19,671 active mobile users; in June 2010, the number of subscribers surpassed 10 million, roughly one-third of the population of Kenya, and, in 2013, the service reached over 17 million active participants and is now being replicated in far-flung places such as Romania and India.[18]

14.2.5 Useful Usage and the Limits of Bandwidth and Web Accessibility

The desire to use ICTs for productive purposes, such as paying for tuition, can be hindered by the amount of available bandwidth and data capacity of networks, which can either make services completely inaccessible or so painfully slow that they are useless.

According to *PCWorld*, a trade publication, which cites Telegeography, a research company, Africa leads the world in demand for greater bandwidth, which is expected to grow by 51 percent annually until 2019.[19] The lack of existing infrastructure combined with rising demand is further complicated by the lack of local/regional content, in which Internet traffic in Africa—and many other developing countries—is often routed through other continents.

This is far from a developing country problem. Anyone who has visited an unusually crowded place has experienced the frustrations of limited network capacity, whether attempting to make a casual phone call in St. Tropez, France, at the height of the summer or browsing the Internet during a large event. The ITU also has called on more and improved statistics on data traffic and network capacity in order to help policymakers increase their understanding of the digital divide from a capacity point of view.[20]

A particular reason for limited data transmission is the rise of online entertainment. According to Sandvine, a consultancy, Netflix and YouTube usage account for half of all North American fixed-line data, which—in a crowded data environment—can negatively affect more productive usages.[21] Ericsson, the Swedish telecommunications company, says video is also the fastest growing category of mobile data traffic and predicts it will account for more than half of total data traffic on cellular networks by 2019.[22] Hence, greater international and domestic bandwidth and data capacity are a necessary (although not sufficient) long-term requirement toward improving future usage.

As a result, many telecommunications companies promote the notion of infrastructure sharing, in which they can lower their investment and compete on price. Some also charge by data usage while other actors have found innovative solutions to discourage high volume users. Swedish trains, for instance, offer 4G connectivity with the disclaimer that, because capacity in the mobile network is shared among all passengers, everyone receives an equal amount of data transmission (as of this writing, 200 MB) at full speed after which it decreases automatically, thereby limiting online entertainment.

14.2.6 Collaborative Efforts to Leave Nobody Behind

Efforts continue around the world to move private and public sector information and services online (e-government) and encouraging their use.[23] Yet, web accessibility remains a barrier toward useful usage and full participation in the information society. In Europe, for example, 41 percent of individuals used the Internet for interaction with public sector authorities in 2013, according to Eurostat, the European statistics office.[24] Yet, only one-third of Europe's government websites are fully accessible to people with disabilities, according to the European Commission (EC).[25]

In this context, the public sector is inadvertently creating new digital divides. However, in the United Kingdom, which aims to deliver information and services "digital by default," there is a recognition that nobody should be left behind. As such, the government has created "assisted digital" to support those who remain offline or who cannot complete online services themselves.[26] In theory, this enables improved efficiency for the government while maintaining inclusiveness. Yet, it should not come at the expense of improving website design.

There is often a lack of regulation in dealing with web accessibility and even in countries where there is a plan in place, implementation is often uneven at best. The web accessibility gap is primarily bridged by private sector entities looking for a competitive edge in attracting customers or through independent actors. For instance, the World Wide Web Consortium (W3C) is creating standards for web accessibility that, in turn, are promoted by interested parties.[27] One is the European Internet Inclusion Initiative (EIII), a consortium of private, public, and civil society actors that is building a website that combines existing web accessibility evaluation tools and also supports user testing of websites through crowdsourcing.[28]

Despite such efforts, questions linger whether they can be implemented at scale and be properly extended to all sorts of mobile devices from which many users now access information and services.

14.3 Part II: Cyber Dependency and Its Consequences

If sufficiently successful, strategies to tackle digital divides implicitly mean greater adoption of the information society and an increase in the dependency on ICTs. This may lead to unintended consequences and open up new digital divides in terms of cybersecurity and data policies.

To illustrate development toward an information society and cyber dependency, Figure 14.1 uses a combination of GNI per capita as a proxy for socioeconomic opportunities and Internet usage as the demand for ICTs.[29]

The cyber-dependency matrix allows an assessment of where a country currently stands in its development toward an information society and can also be used to predict where it is heading next. For instance, by evaluating the current digital divide challenges and their unintended consequences facing those further ahead, countries can learn from previous mistakes and better prepare for potential solutions. Low Internet adoption coupled with low GNI often indicates a lack of infrastructure and high mobile penetration, which could serve as a sign that more mobile services would be beneficial while building out fixed-line access. Similarly, higher Internet penetration and higher GNI means more people are online and taking advantage of connectivity, but also exposes their digital economies to new e-inclusion challenges in order not to leave people behind.

At the Stockholm Internet Forum 2014, Carl Bildt, the Swedish foreign minister, alluded to the fact that Sweden faces an "immigration divide" (in which some

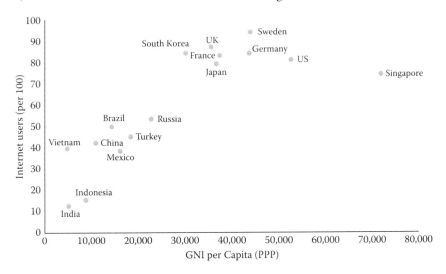

Figure 14.1 **Matrix of cyber dependency (select countries). Source: World Bank World Development Indicators 2012.**

migrants don't possess the same level of ICT skills as the local population) and an "age divide" (in which there are differences in ICT skill levels between older and younger generations).[30] To resolve the immigration divide, Bildt called on greater education for recent arrivals, while he joked that the country's age divide would resolve itself naturally.

Meanwhile, cybersecurity and the rise of new data policies in response to emerging technologies affect all countries in the cyber-dependency matrix, although to a different extent depending on where they are in their development toward an information society.

14.3.1 Cyber Security and Trust

As societies venture online, so do criminals and the cost of cybercrime is booming. According to a worldwide survey, Norton, a security company, estimates the global loss at about US$110 billion.[31] Cybercrime also can damage trust in online services, which is a particular concern for e-government, e-commerce, and financial institutions. In fact, only 12 percent of European users feel completely safe in making transactions online, according to Europe's Digital Agenda website.

Cybercriminals target users in developed countries further ahead in the cyber-dependency journey because of their perceived wealth, whereas those in less developed countries at the lower end of the matrix may face a proportionally greater risk, given a lack of awareness regarding the threats that come with connectivity. In Indonesia, for example, cybercriminals prey on the rapid rise in new Internet users.[32]

As a consequence, Indonesia has emerged as the country from which the largest numbers of cyber attacks emanate, not necessarily because of local crime groups, but rather because foreign entities have taken control of many computers there and use them for a variety of attacks elsewhere.[33] Sophos, a security company, found that 24 percent of Indonesian PCs experienced a malware attack, whether successful or failed, over a three-month period, which is the highest rate in the world, followed by China at 21 percent (this can be compared with Norway and Sweden at 2 percent and 3 percent, respectively), according to the threat exposure rate (TER) in the Security Threat Report 2013.[34]

The problem is confounded by emerging market dependency on mobile devices. Citing Nielsen, a research firm, *The Jakarta Post*, a local newspaper, reports that almost half of Indonesia's population browses the Internet via mobile phones, which is the highest mobile Internet dependency in Southeast Asia.[35]

Similarly, in 2012, China became the world's largest market in terms of mobile subscriptions, which surpassed 1 billion, according to the ITU.[36] In January 2013, a report also showed that 420 million Chinese accessed the Internet through their mobile devices during 2012, up by 18 percent from a year earlier.[37] Meanwhile, the 2012 Norton cybercrime report says the rise of mobile access is a particular problem as people don't use a security solution for their devices; in fact, almost half (44 percent) of those surveyed globally aren't even aware that they exist.[38]

This indicates that although all countries must improve awareness and education, those with lower cyber dependency often face greater challenges to bridge the "trust divide," which is necessary in order to avoid users falling prey to cybercrimes and thereby deterring them from using ICTs more generally.

14.3.2 New Data Frontiers

Largely unbeknownst to users, but where data are hosted, stored, and processed, is increasingly important and can lead to new "geographic information divides." Despite Western efforts to promote the free flow of information, it comes with the usual national security caveats.

The Edward Snowden revelations, which exposed extensive American surveillance using the Internet, highlights the tension between access to information and national security. In part, the U.S. National Security Agency (NSA) used legal—although controversial—ways to access information stored within American jurisdiction. For instance, foreign data hosted on U.S. servers are subject to monitoring without court order in case of national interest. Meanwhile, American cloud providers currently have an 85 percent global market share.[39]

The likely implications are that American cloud providers may see international business drop, while domestic providers in some countries are likely to thrive in this increasingly localized market.[40] For instance, the EC published an European Union (EU) strategy on cloud computing in September 2012, which could be the basis for moving data from American clouds and in the process generate new revenues and jobs for Europe.[41]

Countries and international service providers, therefore, must contemplate how to possibly counterbalance this trend to provide open and equal access to information regardless of where it is stored. To mitigate the Snowden revelations—and a perception of lost revenue attributed to them—a number of leading U.S. technology companies are pushing for government reform. In February 2014, Facebook, Microsoft, Google, and Yahoo, started publishing the small number of government requests they had actually received in order to increase transparency.[42]

Microsoft also announced that they would let their customers select where their data are stored in order to avoid potential regulations in certain countries.[43] Whether such technical and legal maneuvering will help restore trust remains to be seen as commercial initiatives are unlikely to overtake national security concerns, particularly as there is a lack of international agreements to deal with sensitive issues.

It is likely, therefore, that the rise of sovereign clouds, or data localization regulations, continue to be a growing global trend in which information is required to be stored in a certain geographic area, which also means that it could potentially be monitored or made inaccessible to outside jurisdictions.

14.3.3 A Global Geographic Information Divide

Limiting equal global access to information and cloud services creates a new digital divide in that local authorities are able to control data located within their jurisdictions and can impose censorships of various nature in the name of national security.

Emerging markets, such as China, are often highlighted in this area as it blocks access to information and websites that are readily available elsewhere in the world. However, digging deeper, Western countries often engage in the same practices. The United States is one of the biggest perpetrators of censorship, according to sources that track blocked websites or requests for removal, such as the Google transparency report.[44] For example, after the leaks of sensitive government information to WikiLeaks, the United States did not only attempt to block access to the website, but the White House Office of Management and Budget also sent a memorandum, on December 4, 2010, prohibiting unauthorized employees from visiting the website or to read the documents.[45]

The nature and extent of online censorship that is necessary due to national security reasons varies between countries and in accordance with local contexts. Yet, this is a point that is often misunderstood in the West, which promotes Internet freedom from a Western point of view. Hence, there is a need to understand Internet governance from a global perspective.[46] For example, an invitation to a recent event by the International Institute for Strategic Studies (IISS) underscored the point as follows:

> The Western discourse on cybersecurity and cybergovernance accepts as a given that arguments for Internet freedom and a multistakeholder approach to managing the Internet are beyond challenge. However, in many parts of the world, these arguments are the subject of vigorous debate, driven in large measure by perceptions that the United States and its allies are exploiting their dominant position in the cyberdomain for sinister geopolitical motives. Some of the challenges to Western approaches are driven by cynicism, but many reflect real fears and perceptions of vulnerability.

The situation is further complicated by the fact that all countries engage in online censorship to some extent and implies the difficulties in establishing any international norms in this area, leaving a global digital divide surrounding equal access to content. While acknowledging the importance of cybersecurity, countries should recognize local differences of opinion and realize the consequences of disguising it as national security, which can limit widespread uptake of ICTs by undermining trust and leading to geographic information divides.

14.3.4 International Objectives and National Context

Given the challenges ahead, there remains a need for the global community to work together to set international objectives while acknowledging the need for local contexts and regulations.

The Broadband Commission for Digital Development, established by the ITU and UNESCO in 2010, is an important actor in this regard.[47] It aims to highlight the importance of broadband on the international policy agenda under the assumption that expanding access is key to development and accelerating progress toward the millennium development goals (MDGs). As a UN High Level Panel report proposed that the post-2015 development goals, which are likely to be called the sustainable development goals (SDGs), should ensure that everyone has access to modern infrastructure, including ICTs, its work is also likely to continue beyond 2015.[48]

The geopolitical dimensions of the Internet, meanwhile, are primarily addressed by the Internet Governance Forum (IGF), a multistakeholder policy dialogue formally announced by the United Nations Secretary-General in July 2006. Given the increasing need for global consensus regarding Internet governance and the geopolitical issues that come with it, new initiatives have recently emerged, including the Stockholm Internet Forum, held annually since 2012, and Net Mundial in Brazil. Yet, the complexities of developing global objectives while recognizing the importance of all stakeholders within local contexts and regulations also means much work remains. However, the international community must address these challenges or else we face a certain future of global digital information divides.

14.4 Conclusion: A Part for All Actors and Their Measurement

To reap the digital dividends of the information society, countries around the world must tackle current—and emerging—digital divides. To do so, there is a role to play for all actors. The public sector needs to take the lead in certain areas, such as in setting education standards and in creating a strong regulatory environment. The private sector has economic incentives to participate in e-inclusion initiatives and thrives in providing innovative solutions. The international community and civil society remain fundamental supporting actors as a global information society necessitates a common understanding of the digital divide challenges ahead while implementing local solutions in a local context.

In this effort, progress must be measured in order to determine outcomes and such initiatives must be updated to reflect emerging digital divides. Indicative of this was the notion that the digital divide could be bridged by simply providing access to ICTs, which was reinforced by the simplicity in tracking progress as increasing numbers of people had access to a device or the Internet. Obviously, this did not explain the extent to which they were used or how. As indicated in several chapters in this volume, there remains a need for enhanced measurement in regards to digital divides, in particular surrounding useful usage and the link between progress and outcomes.

Digital divides are not going away, but that doesn't mean we shouldn't try and reduce them. Much is at stake as future economic development depends in large part on an inclusive information society. Core principles to tackle digital divides should include, but are not limited to, aligning national policies with international objectives, enhancing access and affordability, creating regulation and competition, and improving awareness and education to stimulate useful usage of local content creation and consumption while measuring our progress across all these areas. It's a tall order, but if we fall short, the potentials of the information society will be unfulfilled.

Endnotes

1. ITU (2013). Measuring the information society 2013. Online at: http://www.itu.int/en/ITU-D/Statistics/Documents/publications/mis2013/MIS2013_without_Annex_4.pdf
2. ITU (2014). ICT facts and figures 2014. Online at: http://www.itu.int/en/ITU-D/Statistics/Documents/facts/ICTFactsFigures2014-e.pdf
3. ITU (2011). ICT facts and figures 2011. Online at: http://www.itu.int/ITU-D/ict/facts/2011/
4. ITU, ICT facts and figures 2014.
5. European Commission. (2014). Digital Agenda Infographic. Online at: https://ec.europa.eu/digital-agenda/en/news/eu-digital-divide-infographic
6. India Bharat Broadband Network Limited (BBNL). Online at: http://www.bbnl.nic.in
7. Australia NBN Co. Online at: http://www.nbnco.com.au
8. ITU, Measuring the information society 2013.
9. The Economist Intelligence Unit (2012). Smart policies to close the digital divide: Best practices from around the world. Online at: http://www.economistinsights.com/analysis/smart-policies-close-digital-divide
10. UNCTAD. Information Economy Reports. Online at: http://unctad.org/en/Pages/Publications/InformationEconomyReportSeries.aspx
11. The Economist Intelligence Unit (2013). Redefining the digital divide. Online at: http://www.economistinsights.com/analysis/redefining-digital-divide
12. See, for example, National Telecommunications and Information Administration. Online at: http://www.ntia.doc.gov/report/2013/exploring-digital-nationamericas-emerging-onlineexperience; Ofcom (2013). Communications market report 2013. Online at: http://stakeholders.ofcom.org.uk/market-data-research/market-data/communications-market-reports/cmr13/

13. *The Guardian* (2013). South Korean MPs consider measures to tackle online gaming addiction, December 11. Online at: http://www.theguardian.com/world/2013/dec/11/south-korea-online-gaming-addiction

14. *The Economist* (2011). Online games in Vietnam: Game over? March 4. Online at: http://www.economist.com/blogs/babbage/2011/03/online_games_vietnam

15. *Thanh Niên* (2014). Vietnam mulls allowing online games again after four-year ban, May 8. Online at: http://thanhniennews.com/youth-science/vietnam-mulls-allowing-online-games-again-after-fouryear-ban-26098.html

16. See, for instance, National Telecommunications and Information Administration (2011). Exploring the digital nation: Computer and Internet use at home. Online at: http://www.ntia.doc.gov/report/2011/exploring-digital-nation-computer-and-internet-use-home

17. Kaiser Family Foundation (2010). Generation M², January. Online at: http://kaiserfamilyfoundation.files.wordpress.com/2013/01/8010.pdf; Warschauer, M. and T. Matuchniak (2010). New technology and digital worlds: Analyzing evidence of equity in access, use, and outcomes. *Review of Research in Education*, March (34): 179–225. Online at: http://rre.sagepub.com/cgi/content/full/34/1/179

18. Safaricom. Online at: http://www.safaricom.co.ke/mpesa_timeline/timeline.html; *The Economist* (2013). Why does Kenya lead the world in mobile money? May 27. Online at: http://www.economist.com/blogs/economist-explains/2013/05/economist-explains-18

19. *PCWorld* (2013). Africa to lead the world in international bandwidth demand, October 31. Online at: http://www.pcworld.com/article/2060120/africa-to-lead-the-world-in-international-bandwidth-demand.html

20. International Telecommunications Union (2012). Measuring the information society 2012. Online at: http://www.itu.int/ITU-D/ict/publications/idi/index.html

21. Sandvine, Inc. (2013). Netflix and YouTube account for 50 percent of all North American fixed network data, November 11. Online at: https://www.sandvine.com/pr/2013/11/11/sandvine-report-netflix-and-youtube-account-for-50-of-all-north-american-fixed-network-data.html

22. Ericsson (2014). Mobility report. Online at: http://hugin.info/1061/R/1790097/615436.pdf

23. The United Nations E-Government Survey, which has tracked development globally since 2003, confirms this progress around the world. See United Nations (2012). E-government survey 2012, e-government for the people. Online at: http://www.un.org/en/development/desa/publications/connecting-governments-to-citizens.html

24. Eurostat. Individuals using the Internet for interaction with public authorities. Online at: http://epp.eurostat.ec.europa.eu/tgm/table.do?tab=table&init=1&language=en&pcode=tin00012&plugin=1

25. European Commission (2012). Digital agenda: Commission proposes rules to make government websites accessible for all. Press release, December 3. Online at: http://europa.eu/rapid/press-release_IP-12-1305_en.doc

26. U.K. government. Online at: https://www.gov.uk/service-manual/assisted-digital

27. W3C. Online at: http://www.w3.org

28. The EIII is co-funded under the European Union Seventh Framework Programme (Grant agreement no. 609667). The consortium is coordinated by Tingtun AS and consists of a number of partners and associate partners, and for full disclosure, DAKA advisory AB, of which the editor is a managing director, is one of those partners.

29. This reasoning is based, in part, on McKinsey research that shows that the Internet's contribution to GDP growth is higher in developed countries than emerging markets. See McKinsey (2011). Internet matters: The Net's sweeping impact on growth, jobs, and prosperity. Online at: http://www.mckinsey.com/Insights/MGI/Research/Technology_and_Innovation/Internet_matters; for the argument that higher levels of cyber dependency leads to new security challenges, see Andreasson, K. (ed.) (2011). *Cybersecurity: Public sector threats and responses.* Boca Raton, FL: CRC Press.

30. Bildt, C. (2014). Keynote speech at the Stockholm Internet Forum 2014. Online at: http://www.stockholminternetforum.se/

31. Norton (2012). Cybercrime report. Online at: http://now-static.norton.com/now/en/pu/images/Promotions/2012/cybercrimeReport/2012_Norton_Cybercrime_Report_Master_FINAL_050912.pdf

32. DAKA advisory (2013). Meeting the cybersecurity challenge in Indonesia: An analysis of threats and responses. Online at: http://dakaadvisory.com/wp-content/uploads/DAKA-Indonesia-cyber-security-2013-web-version.pdf

33. *The Jakarta Globe* (2013). Hacker's paradise or host nation? Indonesian officials weigh cyber threat, October 25. Online at: http://www.thejakartaglobe.com/news/hackers-paradise-or-host-nation-indonesian-officials-weigh-cyber-threat

34. Sophos (2013). Security threat report 2013. Online at: http://www.sophos.com/medialibrary/PDFs/other/SophosSecurityThreatReport2013.pdf

35. *The Jakarta Post* (2011). RI highly dependent on mobile Internet, July 12. Online at: http://www.thejakartapost.com/news/2011/07/12/ri-highly-dependent-mobile-internet.html

36. ITU (2012). Measuring the information society 2012. Online at: http://www.itu.int/en/ITU-D/Statistics/Documents/publications/mis2012/MIS2012_without_Annex_4.pdf

37. China Internet Network Information Center. Internet statistics. Online at: http://www1.cnnic.cn/IDR/BasicData/

38. Norton, Cybercrime report.

39. EurActiv.com (2013). Europe pushes own digital 'cloud' in wake of US spying scandal, August 29. Online at: http://www.euractiv.com/infosociety/prism-cloud-european-silver-lini-news-530004

40. As an example of likely repercussions, see the debate in the United Kingdom, for example, *The Independent* (2013). MPs call for government to consider ending use of cloud amid concerns that U.S. authorities can access information, January 30. Online at: http://www.independent.co.uk/life-style/gadgets-and-tech/news/mps-call-for-government-to-consider-ending-use-of-cloud-amid-concerns-that-us-authorities-can-access-information-8473693.html

41. EurActiv.com, Europe pushes own digital 'cloud' in wake of U.S. spying scandal.

42. Reuters (2014). Web companies give first look at secret government data requests, February 4. Online at: http://www.reuters.com/article/2014/02/04/us-internet-nsa-idUSBREA121H920140204

43. Networkworld (2014). Microsoft lawyer: Let customers decide country where cloud data is stored, January 23. Online at: http://www.networkworld.com/news/2014/012314-microsoft-cloud-278034.html

44. See, for example, *Christian Science Monitor* (2013). Google transparency report curiously opaque, thanks to FBI gag order, November 14. Online at: http://www.csmonitor.com/USA/USA-Update/2013/1114/Google-transparency-report-curiously-opaque-thanks-to-FBI-gag-order

45. de Sola, D. (2010). U.S. agencies warn unauthorized employees not to look at WikiLeaks, CNN, December 3.

46. See, for example, IISS-U.S. discussion meeting (2014). How the U.S. is perceived in the cyber domain by other major actors, June 25.

47. ITU and UNESCO. Broadband Commission for Digital Development. Online at: http://www.broadbandcommission.org

48. United Nations (2013). Realizing the future we want for all. The UN Task Team Report. Online at: http://www.un.org/en/development/desa/policy/untaskteam_undf/report.shtml; United Nations (2013). Governance, public administration and information technology for post-2015 development. Discussion and findings of the Expert Group Meeting in Geneva, July. Online at: http://workspace.unpan.org/sites/Internet/Documents/Governance_PA_Report.pdf

Index